I0798552

Charlotte Rowe's Journal

This remarkable journal reveals the inner and outer life of Charlotte White Rowe, from the moment she began her 1816 voyage to India as the first American woman missionary to be appointed by the Baptist Board of Foreign Missions, to the life she had established four years later while living in Digah as a missionary, translator, teacher, wife, mother, and stepmother. In this short time, Charlotte's life changed immeasurably and the courage and determination with which she adapted to and faced these changes is extraordinary to behold. We witness Charlotte's spiritual struggle and her unassailable faith and belief in God. Charlotte Rowe survived against the many obstacles placed in her way, as an intelligent and resourceful woman of the nineteenth century—a woman of conviction, a woman who prevails.

—Emily Burgoyne, librarian, Angus Library and Archives,
Regent's Park College, University of Oxford

Charlotte White Rowe was deliberately erased from Christian history until Reid Trulson discovered her. For seven years he diligently searched for her diary and letters which had been known to exist seventy-five years earlier. Like Charlotte, the documents had disappeared until Trulson brought them to light. This diary is both a spiritual manual and a survival manual for a person called by God to minister, but who is opposed by religious authorities and by all nature. It is set in the early 1800s but is just as true today. This faithful transcription and annotation give us the workings of God within a gifted woman—a poet, a scholar, a convenient wife, a mother, a teacher, and a victor over disease. Christians in ministry owe Reid Trulson deep thanks for the resulting presentation—in this volume and in its companion biography.

—Catherine B. Allen, former president, Women's
Department of the Baptist World Alliance

The missionary undertakings of Charlotte White Rowe who arrived in Bengal and worked at Digah in Patna, Bihar, decades before previously known American Baptist missionaries in India are a new eye-opening for mission history. The passionate and scholarly work done by Reid Trulson in recognizing Charlotte Rowe's work is a fresh view of the contribution of women in mission and of American Baptist mission history in India. I had the privilege to remotely coordinate the 2019 field visit of Trulson and his team in their search for reminiscences of Charlotte Rowe in Kolkata (Calcutta), Serampore, and Digah, in Patna. I am extremely delighted to see his extensive work on her life and ministry. This is a wonderful contribution to Indian church history which will ignite further exploration of her ministry in India.

—Rev. Samaresh Nayak, executive director, India Mission Coordination Committee, Balasore, India

Charlotte White Rowe's journal is an important contribution to early Serampore Mission studies. It is very moving to read and fills in so many details about Serampore that were not known. Practical things, like the use of river water for drinking with lime added for purification, the meals, clothing, and sights, as well as details of different personalities, William Carey's work in the garden, his advice to her and his ideas about mixed race marriage. That besides the very moving story of Charlotte's acquaintance and marriage to Joshua Rowe. The journal is an absolute jewel in many respects. Trulson has done very well to transcribe this so accurately and provide so much background information about Charlotte's family and American relations. This excellent work has brought her journal to life.

—Peter de Vries, voluntary consultant, Carey Library and Research Centre, Serampore College, India

Charlotte Rowe's Journal

A Woman's Missionary Career in British India, 1815–1822

Edited by
REID S. TRULSON

Foreword and Appendix by
Cordelia Moyse

MERCER UNIVERSITY PRESS
Macon, Georgia

The James N. Griffith Series in Baptist Studies

This series on Baptist life and thought explores and investigates Baptist history, offers analyses of Baptist theologies, provides studies in hymnody, and examines the role of Baptists in societies and cultures around the world. The series also includes classics of Baptist literature, letters, diaries, and other writings. For a complete list of titles in the series, visit www.mupress.org and visit the series page.

—C. Douglas Weaver, Series Editor

MUP/ P728

Published by Mercer University Press
1501 Mercer University Drive
Macon, Georgia 31207

30 29 28 27 26 5 4 3 2 1

Books published by Mercer University Press are printed on acid-free paper that meets the requirements of the American National Standard for Information Sciences—Permanence of Paper for Printed Library Materials.

Printed and bound in the United States.

This book is set in Adobe Caslon.

Cover/jacket design by Burt&Burt.

ISBN 978-0-88146-991-2
Cataloging-in-Publication Data is available from the Library of Congress

To Cordelia Moyse, for her encouragement,
wise advice, and friendship.

CONTENTS

FOREWORD

Despite her dying in 1863, Charlotte Rowe first entered my life in 2018 when Dr. Reid Trulson enquired whether she was buried at Saint James Episcopal Church in Lancaster, Pennsylvania. As the archivist and historian of the parish, I was embarrassed to say I had no knowledge of this notable figure. But fortunately, parish records revealed she was buried in the churchyard surrounded by many generations of the Atlee family (her family of origin) and alongside her twin daughters. One of the reasons her name was unfamiliar, despite her baptism and burial at Saint James, was that only the twins had a gravestone. Dr. Trulson's scholarship, dedication, and enthusiasm for restoring Charlotte to her place in history has continued to be inspirational to me and to the parish of her youth.

As a church historian with a particular interest in women's and imperial history, I find it hard to overemphasize the importance of Charlotte Rowe's Indian journal. With his biography, *Charlotte Atlee White Rowe: The Story of America's First Appointed Woman Missionary* (Mercer University Press), Dr. Trulson performed a great service in rediscovering and re-presenting her pioneering role in church history. She was the first American woman recognized as having an individual missionary vocation when she was appointed as a single woman by the Baptist Board of Foreign Missions in 1815. Nevertheless, for over 200 years, her voice was largely lost to historians, theologians, and to those serving in mission fields today. The outline of her life could only be perceived in a few letters and missionary reports. However, with the publication of her journal covering the early years of her ministry in India, we now have the opportunity to gain a deeper sense of how a nineteenth-century American woman lived out her missionary vocation far from Pennsylvania. She served in India where the indigenous population was predominantly Hindu in faith and where the East India Company was the colonizing arm of the British state.

Writing under the pen name Honesta, her journal offers rich primary material for many academic fields. The most obvious is that of mission studies and particularly the contribution of women to evangelism. Alongside details of the physical and practical realities of mission life, the journal offers many insights into Charlotte's theology when she was engaged in cross-cultural mission. Throughout her journal Charlotte reflected on what her vocation meant to her and constantly wrote about her desire to be "useful." She found inspiration in Psalm 2:8: "*Ask of me, and I shall give thee the heathen for thine inheritance.*" Hinduism, Islam, and the caste system attracted her criticism, while idols and widow-burning attracted her rage. Sharing common missionary perspectives of her time in which Christianity and western civilization were seen as inextricably related, she believed one of the fruits of Christian spirituality to be material improvement. To her the education of her Indian students, most of them from wealthier families, was a means of rescuing them from superstitious mothers and opening up a world beyond simply eating, sleeping, bathing, and dressing. Her interpretation of Indian women's lives as indolent and her wish to make them industrious are steeped in western "orientalism."

Yet along with her anger and frustration, Charlotte's missional life involved compassion and joy for her family both near and far, her students, and other missionaries. She experienced vocational successes such as the publication of her Hindi spelling book, the acceptance of girls' education by local parents, as well as the provision of overseas funding for her schools. The result was the concomitant increase of native schools with Indian teachers. Due to her friendships with the first generation of British Baptist missionaries and marriage to the British missionary Joshua Rowe, she gives us a unique perspective on the work and families of the Serampore Trio: William Carey, often called the father of modern missions, Joshua Marshman, and William Ward.

Charlotte's journal and life story offer much material for reflection on the role of gender in religious life in her time. Her appointment as the first woman to be designated a missionary in her own right was a break with tradition which was not to be repeated for some time. By marrying a British missionary stationed in Digah with three motherless boys, she foreclosed an experiment in a new form of mission, namely that of single women. Yet their marriage does seem to have been a partnership. Charlotte clearly had a distinct ministry from her husband due to her linguistic ability. Becoming fluent in Hindi, she instructed native girls and boys, communicated with parents and native evangelists, and, unusually for her sex, led worship services. Joshua's mission field by contrast was largely the British expatriate population, educating their children or ministering to soldiers stationed at the Dinapore cantonment. Nevertheless, the familial and domestic sphere unquestionably was her primary responsibility around which she had to fit her educational vocation. However, on Joshua's death in 1823, her work was not considered "missionary." Tragically, she could only be seen by the Baptist Missionary Society as a widow who needed support, not a worker who needed resourcing to continue to grow her ministry. Even her self-advocacy before the BMS board in London could not change their gendered mindset, leading her to return to America to support her family by teaching.

Charlotte's journal is important not only for its capturing of missionary history but also because it is a spiritual autobiography. In it her interior struggles were recorded alongside exterior ones. Charlotte was rigorous in self-examination and often found herself wanting. She felt that on occasion she lacked meekness and a sense of gratitude in the light of the crucified Christ. She also had to work through her sense of being thwarted in her mission by her own health and family life (including miscarriages and the births of three children), as well as Indian cultural resistance to girls' education, before she found spiritual acceptance. Her deep faith was expressed not only in her prose but also in her poetry.

The effect of her journal is not only to give an insight into the everyday life and struggle of one of the first missionaries in India, but also to create a level of personal intimacy with her readers as we absorb the details and struggles of her domestic, spiritual, and missional life. The result is that when the text ends in 1822, in the middle of a life story, I felt bereft, wanting to hear more from this remarkable woman whom I could well imagine being my inspirational friend.

Dr. Cordelia Moyse
Visiting Scholar, Franklin
and Marshall College
September 2023

PREFACE

> *Life, he realized, was much like a song. In the beginning there is mystery, in the end there is confirmation, but it's in the middle where all the emotion resides to make the whole thing worthwhile.*
>
> —Nicholas Sparks in *The Last Song*

Charlotte Rowe's journal finds its place between beginning and ending—mystery and confirmation. I was searching for that middle.

Mercer University Press had published my book, *Charlotte Atlee White Rowe: The Story of America's First Appointed Woman Missionary*.[1] The book had been prompted by mystery: given Charlotte's significance, why was she almost completely unknown? Who was she? When, where, and how did she serve? Where was she buried? Why was she surprisingly absent from women's studies, mission research, and Baptist histories?

My pursuit of that mystery led me to previously unexamined letters, magazines, newspaper articles, missionary memoirs, church archives, and East India Company records in India, England, and the United States. Those sources produced abundant confirming details enabling me to compose a biography to reclaim Charlotte's life and ministry from obscurity.

During subsequent book talks across the U.S., I noticed two recurring reactions from listeners learning about this remarkable woman. The first was admiration for Charlotte's courage in braving multiple dangers, her strength in coping with successive traumas, and her tenacity in facing persistent gender bias. The second reaction was a desire to know more about her—her motivation,

---

[1] Trulson, Reid S., *Charlotte Atlee White Rowe: The Story of America's First Appointed Woman Missionary* (Macon, GA: Mercer University Press, 2021).

spirituality, and inner life as she navigated the unfamiliar social terrain of British-controlled India. My listeners' questions matched my own. We were seeking something more. *The middle where all the emotion resides to make the whole thing worthwhile.*

I had found a clue to orient my search. In August 1822 an extract from one of Charlotte's letters to her Quaker brother, Edwin Augustus Atlee, appeared in the controversial Philadelphia newspaper, *The Reformer*. The extract contained the clue: Charlotte had kept a journal and had sent it to Edwin. Later however, she forcefully directed Edwin to burn her letters and journal. Edwin refused to do so, saying, "They are too valuable…."[2]

Did Edwin preserve the journal, or did he eventually accede to his sister's wish and burn it? Two hundred years later, I began a search for the journal, hoping it would reveal a deeper picture of Charlotte as an early female agent at the start of the modern missionary movement—if it had not been destroyed or lost.

In 2022 a circuitous series of conversations by friends in Lancaster, PA, Jerusalem, and Washington, D.C. revealed that a painting of Charlotte, unknown when her biography was published, had been lovingly preserved in the home of one of her great-great-great-great nieces! The niece also shared three letters expanding the clue about the journal. Two letters dated 1958 showed that Charlotte's journal and a letterbox were then in the possession of William J. and Maxine Woolston of Philadelphia. Woolston was a great-great-grandson of Edwin Augustus Atlee and thus Charlotte's great-great-great nephew. Two historians had examined the material. One was Dr. Lee Norcross Allen, Professor of History at Eastern Baptist College in St. Davids, PA, who was effusive about seeing the "marvelous journal and letter box." He wrote, "This is the sort of thing that historians dream of happening, but which seldom materialize." The second was the late American Baptist historian Dr. Robert G. Torbet, author of *Venture of Faith: The story of the*

---

[2] Edwin Atlee, "Serampore Missionaries," *Reformer*, April 1, 1823, 73–78.

American Baptist Foreign Mission Society and the Woman's American Baptist Foreign Mission Society, 1814–1954. Torbet assessed the journal as "one of the most interesting documents of its kind he had ever seen."[3] Dr. Allen wrote, "Dr. Torbet assured me that he had not read any accounts that were more graphic than hers. And to make it more significant, she was...a pioneer among missionaries."[4]

The third letter indicated that Maxine (Yaple) Sweezy Woolston was transcribing the journal in 1960.[5] But had Charlotte's journal survived the remaining half-century? If so, where could it be found?

I discovered that ninety-six-year-old Dr. Allen had retired in Birmingham, AL after a long teaching career at Samford University. Encouraging communications with his wife, historian Catherine B. Allen, confirmed that Dr. Allen did not know the journal's location. Genealogical research and inquiries to extended members of the Atlee family finally connected me with Charlotte's great-great-great-great nephew, Dr. Joseph Woolston, son of Maxine Woolston who had transcribed the journal. Cleaning out his mother's house following her death, Dr. Woolston had rescued the journal and his mother's typewritten transcript from oblivion. After holding them safely for two decades, he generously donated them to the Special Collections of the Yale Divinity School Library in New Haven, CT for preservation and accessibility to researchers. Having found the journal, I was able to produce this new and annotated transcription of Charlotte's hand-written, 255+ page journal.

Edwin Augustus Atlee, Lee Norcross Allen, and Robert G. Torbet had rightly judged the journal's value. It is an early nineteenth-century treasure.

---

[3] Lee N. Allen to Wm. J. Woolston, January 30, 1958.

[4] Lee N. Allen to James Dallett, January 30, 1958.

[5] James Dallett to Maxine Woolston, May 17, 1960.

ACKNOWLEDGMENTS

This book exists in the first instance because succeeding generations of the Atlee family believed that Charlotte Atlee White Rowe should be remembered. Even after the details of her life and ministry in India and subsequent career in the United States were long forgotten, they had the foresight to safeguard her letters, journal, and portrait.

I am deeply grateful that Anne Ayers carefully preserved her distant aunt's portrait in her home. I remain amazed by how David Peck, Cordelia Moyse, and Linford Ranck formed a great chain of conversations leading to Anne Ayers, the portrait, and to letters documenting the journal's existence as late as 1960.

Historian Catherine Ballein Allen confirmed that her husband, Lee Norcross Allen, had seen the journal between 1958 and 1960 and was aware that Maxine Woolston was transcribing it. Thank you, Catherine, for your helpful suggestions as I searched for the journal, for enriching my knowledge of the social environment of Lowndesboro, Alabama, where Charlotte taught after returning from India, and for reading and commenting on the annotated journal manuscript.

No librarian or archivist is obliged to continue communicating with a researcher whose work does not involve a document in their collection. My exchanges with Emily Burgoyne at the Angus Library and Archive at Regent's Park College in Oxford, UK began as I researched Charlotte and Joshua Rowe's letters in their archives that were essential to Charlotte's biography. Thank you, Emily, for graciously continuing our conversation, for reading and commenting on the manuscript, for inviting me to deliver an online lecture for the Friends of the Angus, and for sharing about Charlotte Rowe among those in the UK who have either personal or professional interest in mission, women's studies, and Baptist history.

In 2019 while researching places where Charlotte had lived and worked in India, I met Peter de Vries, voluntary consultant at the Carey Library and Research Centre, Serampore College, Serampore, India. Peter later read this annotated journal and offered helpful details based on his extensive knowledge of the collections at Serampore. I was delighted when he identified Selemah Linderman and Arthur Johnson, two persons whose identities had otherwise eluded me. Thank you, Peter, for your interest in this project.

I am profoundly grateful to Joseph Woolston for preserving his distant aunt's journal, directing me to its location at Yale, and discussing the circumstances of its preservation with me. Thank you to the staff of the Special Collections at Yale Divinity School Library in New Haven, CT for providing access to the journal and assisting my research. The late Maxine Woolston's type-written copy of the journal is archived with the hand-written original at Yale. Though incomplete and at times inaccurate, her document served as a helpful cross-reference to my full transcription of Charlotte Rowe's journal.

I am grateful to Mercer University Press for publishing Charlotte Rowe's journal as a companion volume to her biography.

My sincere appreciation to Joseph Woolston for granting permission to publish the annotated journal and to Anne Ayers for bringing Charlotte's portrait to Pennsylvania, allowing it to be professionally photographed and granting permission for the image to be reproduced in this publication.

No project like this takes place in a social vacuum. I am ever grateful to my wife, Janelle, who has encouraged my continued research and writing, though it has kept me occupied for many hours in front of the computer screen. I love you and appreciate that gift.

I am grateful to Charlotte Atlee White Rowe for committing so much of her thought, perseverance, agony, joy, and spiritual conviction to the many pages that were carried over the Indian and Atlantic oceans to finally be bound together in this journal. Her willingness to reveal herself as both limited and overcoming gives honor to God to whom she sought to be useful.

And finally, I dedicate this book to Cordelia Moyse who has journeyed with me throughout this project. Thank you for reading the annotated manuscript from your perspective as an archivist and historian. I value your encouragement, wise advice, and friendship.

INTRODUCTION

Charlotte Rowe kept a journal. Like Charlotte herself, some of her words would spur controversy.

Charlotte began her journal in 1815 after boarding the *Benjamin Rush* to sail from America to India. For the next seven years she sent packets of journal pages to her brother, Edwin Augustus Atlee, a physician and Quaker preacher in Philadelphia. The journal, written by America's first-appointed woman missionary, survived. Because her brother refused to burn it.

EARLY LIFE

"The train of events which brought me here"

Charlotte Hazen Atlee was born in Lancaster, Pennsylvania in 1782 at the close of the American Revolution. She was the youngest of eleven children born to William Augustus and Esther Bowes Atlee. She and her siblings experienced the advantages of having an educated mother and a father who was a distinguished lawyer and Pennsylvania Supreme Court judge. The Atlees were prominent members of Lancaster's St. James Episcopal Church.

One week before Charlotte's eighth birthday her mother died. Three years later her father died. Eleven-year-old Charlotte was now an orphan. She was sent to live with her oldest sister, Elizabeth Amelia (Atlee) White, who with her husband, Maj. Moses White, already had a family of four children in Rutland, Massachusetts. Thus began what Charlotte identified as "the train of events which brought me here."[6]

In November 1803 Charlotte married Nathaniel Hazen White, a half-brother of Maj. Moses White and a merchant in Rutland. In

---

[6] Journal, January 8, 1816. Journal and Diary of Charlotte Atlee (later White) (later Rowe) 1815-1822. Yale Divinity School Library, New Haven, CT, Special Collections.

August 1804 Charlotte and Nathaniel welcomed the birth of a son. They named the baby Nathaniel Hazen White after his father. On Christmas Day, 1804, Charlotte's husband died. Five months later, nine-month-old baby Nathaniel died. Amidst that dual trauma, Charlotte moved to Haverhill, Massachusetts to live with her husband's relatives.

In Haverhill Charlotte experienced spiritual renewal. She called it her conversion and was baptized on June 29, 1806. Some who gathered on the banks of the Merrimac River to witness her baptism, however, considered her behavior to be improper. As Charlotte waded into the water she began to sing. In the words of a local lawyer, her spontaneous singing of a hymn on such an occasion was unusual, unnecessary, and "very like ostentation."[7]

Charlotte joined the Haverhill Baptist Church. Both the church and its pastor, Rev. William Batchelder, were very active in foreign mission. They formed the India and Foreign Missionary Society of Haverhill and Vicinity, which later became an auxiliary society to the Baptist Board of Foreign Missions. The church sent funds to support the Bible translation work of the British Baptist missionaries William Carey and Joshua Marshman in Serampore, India. And when the Massachusetts Baptist Missionary Society was incorporated in 1808, William Batchelder became one of its trustees. In Haverhill Charlotte discerned her own call to missionary service.

From Haverhill Charlotte moved to Philadelphia where she lived with her brother, Edwin Augustus Atlee, and his wife, Margaret (Snyder) Atlee, whose family would increase to eleven children. In September 1813 Charlotte transferred her membership from Haverhill to Philadelphia's Sansom Street Baptist Church. The pastor, the Rev. Dr. William Staughton, and his wife, Maria, were both from England and avidly promoted mission. In 1792, while still a seminarian in England, William Staughton had helped to organize the Baptist Missionary Society. He then helped select

---

[7] Saltonstall, 147–48.

and appoint William Carey and Dr. John Thomas as the society's first missionaries and was on the wharf in March 1793 to pray with Carey and Thomas when they departed for India.

Nine years passed since Charlotte White had first sensed God calling her to missionary service. Events in Philadelphia now heightened her thoughts of "missionary exertions."

William Staughton had been recommending that Baptists in America follow the British Baptist example by forming a national foreign mission society. When news reached the United States that Adoniram and Ann Judson, along with their missionary colleague Luther Rice, had become Baptists in India, it added urgency to Staughton's appeal. Luther Rice returned to America from India and worked tirelessly to organize Baptists for mission. In May 1814 delegates from Baptist churches in eleven states and the District of Columbia met in Philadelphia and formed the General Missionary Convention of the Baptist Denomination in the United States of America for Foreign Mission. Its first recorded contribution was fifty dollars given by a woman. Historian H. Leon McBeth identified that donor as Charlotte H. White.[8]

Because the convention would meet every three years, it was soon dubbed the Triennial Convention. Managers were elected to the Baptist Board of Foreign Missions to conduct the ongoing work of missionary appointment, instruction, and oversight. Charlotte's pastor, William Staughton, became its founding corresponding secretary. The board knew about Adoniram and Ann Judson already serving in Burma and immediately appointed Adoniram as its first missionary. Like the Congregationalist board before it, the Baptist board did not appoint Ann.

In June 1814, five weeks after the General Missionary Convention was formed, Charlotte and other women from her church met

---

[8] In 1979 McBeth noted that the first donor was "a woman." McBeth, *Women in Baptist Life*, 82. In 1987 he identified her as Charlotte H. White. McBeth, *Baptist Heritage*, 351. In neither book did he cite his source.

at Maria and William Staughton's home and organized the Sansom Street Baptist Female Society for Promoting Evangelical Missions. The women elected Maria Staughton as "First Directress" and Charlotte White as one of four "vice-directresses."

Meanwhile news of Harriet Newell's death had reached the United States. Harriet (Atwood) Newell from Haverhill, Massachusetts had sailed to India in 1812 with her husband, Samuel Newell, and Adoniram and Ann Judson as Congregationalist missionaries. When the East India Company ordered the couples to leave India, the Judsons (now Baptists) went to Burma and the Newells sailed to the Isle of France (Mauritius). Weakened after the birth of a daughter who died on board ship, Harriet died seventeen days later on November 30, 1812 at Mauritius. By December 1814 the first Newell memoir had been published and was being sold by W. W. Woodward in Philadelphia. Charlotte read Harriet Newell's memoir and was further roused toward mission.

The Judsons, who had been translating Scripture and writing religious tracts in Burma, now asked the board to send a printer to prepare their writings for distribution to the Burmese people. George Hough from Windsor, Vermont had trained as a printer before he was ordained. He and his wife, Phebe, came to Philadelphia where he applied and was appointed for missionary service in Burma. Charlotte met with the Houghs and discussed the possibility of sailing with them to Burma. She then followed George Hough's advice and sent a letter of application to the board. In it she wrote, "On the coming of Mr. and Mrs. Hough to this city, and my being made acquainted with them and their missionary views, my ardour has been revived, and a desire produced to accompany them to India...."[9]

The Baptist Board of Foreign Missions reviewed her application and voted on June 14, 1815 to appoint her. Mrs. Charlotte H. White had become the first American woman appointed by any

[9] Charlotte H. White, "To the Baptist Board of Foreign Missions," 112.

sending body to serve in international, cross-cultural mission. Her appointment roused controversy.

Previous appointments by the board's seven-man quorum had been unanimous, but not Charlotte's appointment. Henry Holcombe, pastor of First Baptist Church in Philadelphia, strenuously objected and sought to have her appointment revoked. The controversy continued for almost five months. Holcombe leveled accusations against William and Maria Staughton. He publicly charged Charlotte with ulterior motives, questionable ethics, lack of qualifications, a delicate constitution, and the audacity of being a woman seeking equality with male missionaries. Several members resigned for a period to deprive the board of a quorum.[10]

Finally, all the board members were polled. They confirmed that Charlotte's appointment was legal inasmuch as the board's constitution did not define the word "missionary" to mean an ordained male. When several members questioned whether the board had sufficient funds to send her, Charlotte quelled the objection. She had a modest estate from her deceased parents and husband. From this she made a donation to the board on the condition that it would be used to pay her expenses. Throughout her entire service as an educator in India, Charlotte would fund her own ministry.

STRUCTURE
"To write freely"

While still in the harbor on board the ship *Benjamin Rush*, Charlotte wrote to her brother, Edwin Augustus Atlee, pledging "to write freely"[11] of her thoughts and experiences. That also characterized her style. The pages she sent included journal entries, copies of letters, poems, and private diary confidences.

---

[10] For details of Henry Holcombe's views on the role women in the church and his maneuvers to "out-general" his opponents and revoke Charlotte's appointment see Trulson, *Charlotte Atlee White Rowe*, chs. 5 and 6.

[11] Journal, December 13, 1815. [Location: lying off Reedy Island.]

Edwin Augustus Atlee and his descendants preserved Charlotte Rowe's journal for two centuries. Maxine Woolston's 1960 typewritten transcript provides quick access to Charlotte's journal, however it has several drawbacks. Because she was unfamiliar with Charlotte's life story and handwriting, Woolston erred in transcribing some words and names. In preparing a transcript that she hoped could be published, Woolston occasionally corrected Charlotte's syntax, smoothed the language flow, and inserted new phrases. Most significantly, she removed prayers and religious passages that she likely felt would have little appeal to publishers or readers.

This new transcription reproduces the 255+ page, hand-written journal as Charlotte wrote it, preserving her original spelling, punctuation, grammar, and syntax. Words and phrases that were underlined to show emphasis in the original are italicized in this transcription. Charlotte used British rather than American English and sometimes employed vocabulary and spelling that are now obsolete. This transcription includes annotations that define obscure or archaic vocabulary, identify people, places, and events, and supply details about British India that provide context for Charlotte's thoughts and actions. The annotations retain the place names and spellings then in use, such as Calcutta (Kolkata), Dinapore (Danapur), Monghyr (Munger), etc.

If mentioned at all in public records of the time, women were customarily identified by their relationship to a husband, father, or brother and without their first names. William Moore, the Rowes' fellow missionary at Digah, had three wives, so "Mrs. Moore" tends to obscure three unnamed women and erase their ministries. The annotations seek to identify women by first name and, when married, with their maiden name in parentheses, e.g., Eleanor Moore, Hannah (Biss) Moore, and Anne (Clarke) Moore. The author has chosen to identify Charlotte by her first name in the annotated and contextual materials. This seeks to reflect the personal nature of her journal, avoid potential confusion related to her three last names (Atlee, White, Rowe), and give preference to her individual identity rather than her spousal status.

Although Charlotte sent her journal to America as separate sheets in serial installments, the pages were later bound as a single volume. Several first pages are currently missing from the handwritten journal but are found in the Woolston transcript. They are retained here and identified as [WT]. This new transcription identifies the page numbers from Charlotte's original document in brackets. For example, the sentence "Here I cannot lay by my pen without reflecting on the goodness of God towards me in all things: and especially in [98] preserving me alive, on this boisterous river, in a keelless boat..." indicates that page 98 starts with the words "preserving me alive...."

CONTENT:

"To throw my expressions into so public a channel"

Charlotte confided to her brother, "I cannot feel precise enough to throw my expressions into so public a channel."[12] Despite those misgivings, her journal provides an insightful window into her cross-cultural formation as an early female missionary. She wrote most of the 183 entries (84%) during her first three years in India:

Frequency	Location	Type
1815 – 2	4 On the *Benjamin Rush*	157 journal entries
1816 – 49	20 From Calcutta and Serampore	27 letters
1817 – 68	22 On the Hooghly and Ganges	
1818 – 36	137 From Digah	
1819 – 8		
1820 – 14		
1821 – 5		
1822 – 1		

The journal entries, letters, poetry, and diary reflections flow seamlessly from one to another. Her entries frequently erupt into prayer or spiritual reflection. Her effortless inclusion of Biblical

[12] Journal, March 8, 1818.

references and phrases reflects her familiarity with the Authorized Version, commonly called the "King James Bible." Modern readers will likely be disturbed by her references to "the heathen." The King James Bible used "heathen" more than 140 times to translate the words *goyim* (Hebrew) and *ethne* (Greek). Later translators would render the words as "the Gentiles" or "the nations." Charlotte's language reflects the King James Bible, the translation available to her. She was a woman of her time.

And yet, she also transcended her time, notably regarding gender roles. Charlotte repeatedly confronted gender bias in her life and ministry.[13] Her journal reveals a strong woman in a dialogue with herself while remaining confident in her call to public ministry. Her embrace of women's full participation in ministry is evident in her interpretation of scripture and in her matter-of-fact recognition of other women's ministries.

Adoniram Judson had felt himself called to be a missionary through the words of Jesus in Mark 16:15: "Go ye into all the world, and preach the gospel to every creature." Charlotte never cites that passage as decisive in her call. Nor does she quote Matthew 28:18–20, the New Testament text that several decades after her work in India was often quoted as the "Great Commission." Instead, her repetition of Psalm 2:7–8 reveals a motivation for missionary service rooted in Hebrew scripture

Charlotte's spirituality is intertwined with her record of her experiences in British India. It is grounded in her confidence in the providence of God. She acknowledges conflicted feelings, disappointments, and loneliness, yet her theology provides guidance and strength.

Her journal should be read with attention to euphemism, nuance, and things "in between the lines." With attention to details and silence. With openness to surprise.

---

[13] Trulson, *Charlotte Atlee White Rowe*, 54–61.

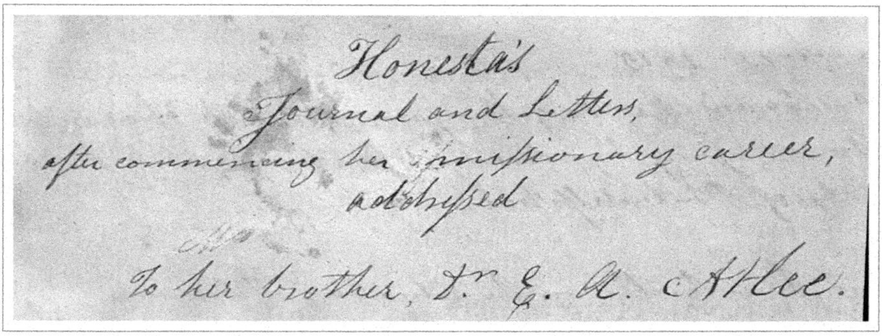

Honesta's
Journal and Letters,
after commencing her missionary career,
addressed
To her brother, Dr. E. A. Atlee.

Honesta.

Charlotte Rowe began her journal under the penname "Honesta" after boarding the *Benjamin Rush* in December 1815. Calling her work a "missionary career" was controversial since missionary appointment was restricted to men and a woman's expected "career" options were that of a wife, mother, and homemaker. "I give my thoughts as freely to thee, my dear Edwin, as the pen gives the thought-engraving-liquor, to the paper, the fair paper, which speaks me no guile." (May 15, 1816)

Courtesy Joseph L. Woolston

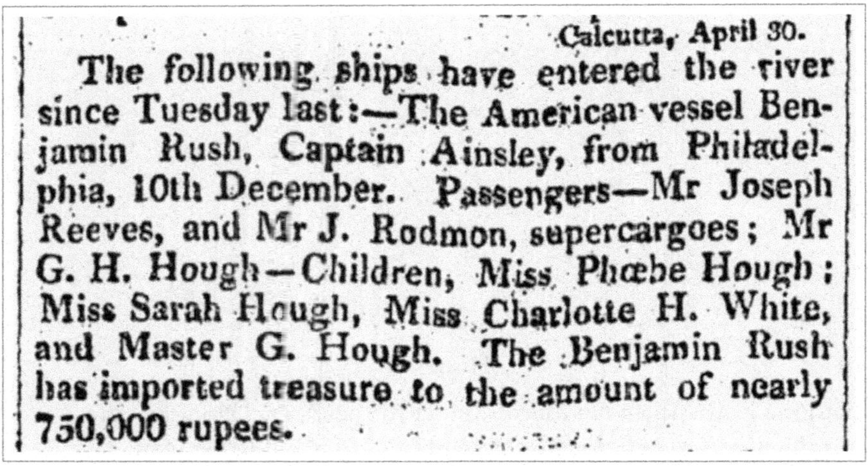

Calcutta, April 30.

The following ships have entered the river since Tuesday last:—The American vessel Benjamin Rush, Captain Ainsley, from Philadelphia, 10th December. Passengers—Mr Joseph Reeves, and Mr J. Rodmon, supercargoes; Mr G. H. Hough—Children, Miss Phœbe Hough; Miss Sarah Hough, Miss Charlotte H. White, and Master G. Hough. The Benjamin Rush has imported treasure to the amount of nearly 750,000 rupees.

Newspaper arrival announcement.

Charlotte H. White's arrival in Calcutta on the *Benjamin Rush* after 129 days at sea was noted in European newspapers. As she was a widow, "Mrs." was her correct title. *The Caledonian Mercury* (Edinburgh, Scotland). (October 19, 1816)

Public domain

John Ansley [Ainsley]
portrait by James Peal, 1801.

"Captn. A. [John Ansley] has been very attentive to us all and as a kind father to me." (April 24, 1816)

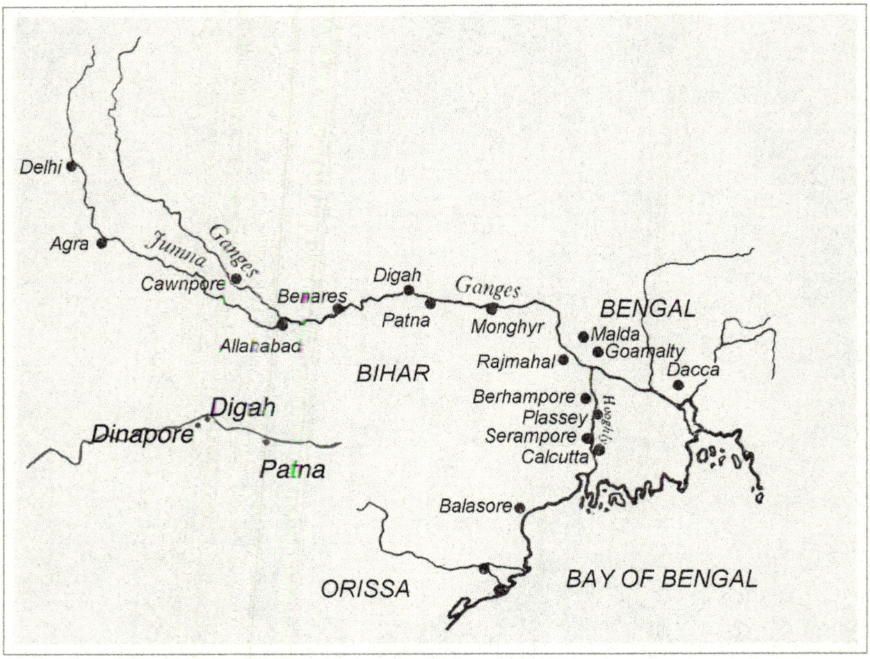

Map of Charlotte's journey
Calcutta to Digah, India.

The Rowes traveled up the Hooghly and Ganges rivers to Digah. "It is four years since the Digah mission was formed, situated on the great and famous river Ganges, 300 miles from Calcutta by the post-path, but reckoned 450 by water, the River being winding." (June 11, 1816)

Courtesy Peter de Vries

A budgerow.

Charlotte Rowe traveled between Calcutta and Digah four times by budgerow which ". . . is made like all the boats used on these rivers, *without a keel*, and therefore not very safe in a storm . . ." (July 13, 1816)

Budgerow being pulled
by Sita Ram, 1814.

"When the wind does not serve to propel [the budgerow] along against the stream, the men draw it, by means of a rope, walking on the shore." (July 13, 1816)

Temple at Nadia on Hooghly River
by Sita Ram, 1820–1821.

"Today we have passed *Nuddeah* [Nadia] where stands a temple famous both for its magnificence and its gross idolatry." (July 17, 1816)

A View of the Rajmahal Hills
by Sir Charles D'Oyly, 1820.

"Today, we have entered and crossed the *Ganges*. It is very wide here, where it gives part of its waters to the Hoogly. A long range of mountains, called the *Rajmhal* hills, appear veiled in the blueness of distance." (August 2, 1816)

Fakeers Rock in the River Ganges
by Thomas and William Daniell, 1800.

"I forgot to mention the two piles of rocks which we passed near Mongire, in the midst of the Ganges called the Faquers Rocks. Faquere [Fakir] means Religious beggar. Two of them live on these rocks, very romantically." (August 19, 1816)

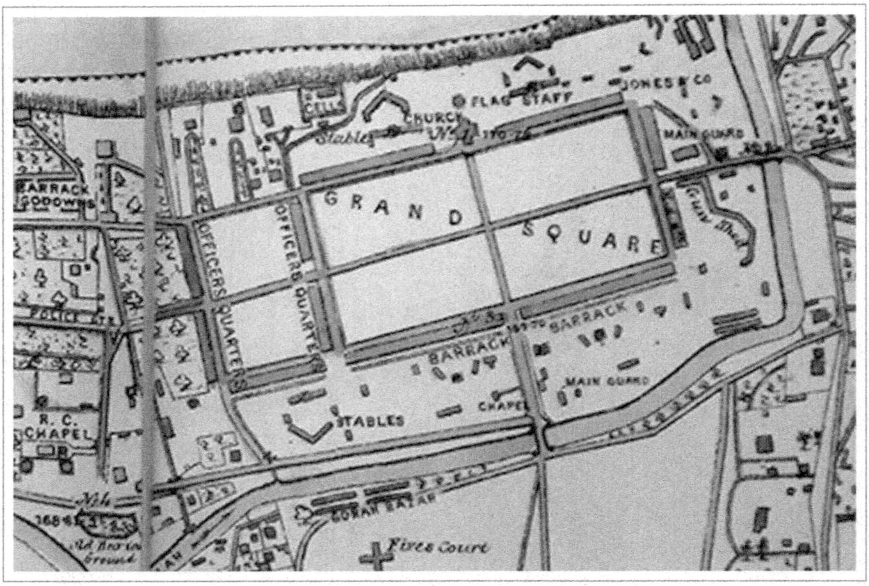

Map of Dinapore cantonment.

"Dinapore, within two English miles of us, the Cantonments enclose four large squares of grass, which is kept very clean and short, to afford parade ground for the Soldiers. The whole view round is very handsome. . . Beyond these Cantonments are barracks for *native* Soldiers." (September 13, 1816)

Birds-Eye View of Patna
by Sita Ram, 1814.

"Digah is between the ancient great city of Patna, and the modern military station of Danapore." (June 14, 1816)

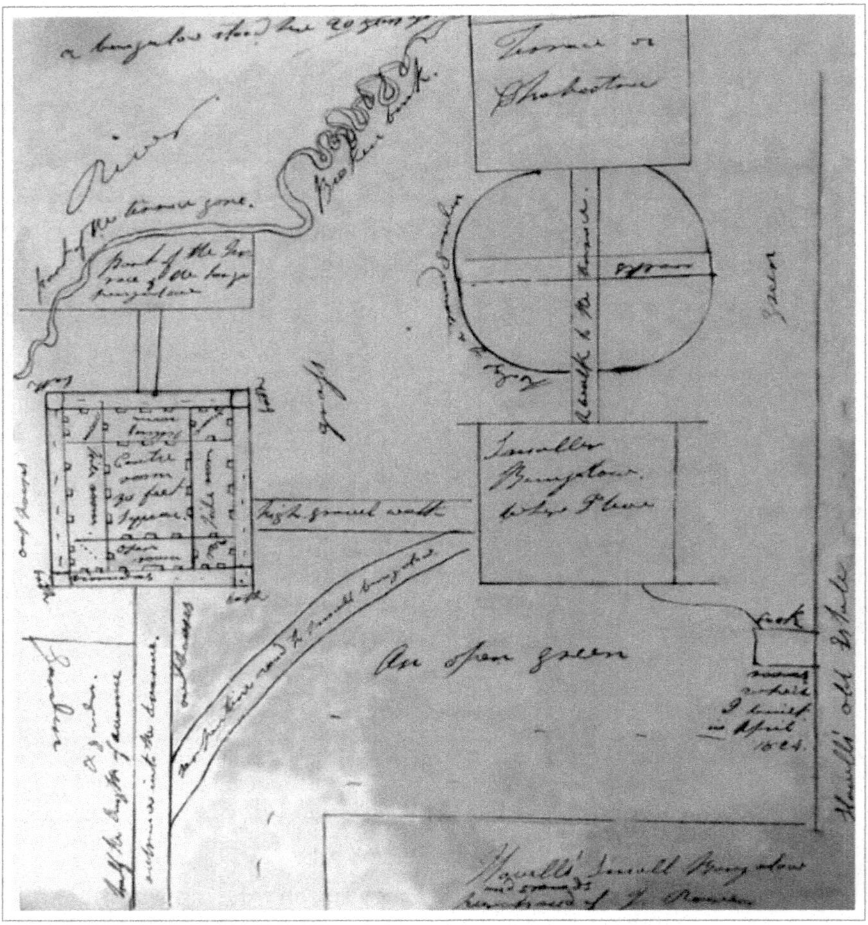

Digah Mission Station map
by Charlotte Rowe, 1824.

"At last arrived at that spot, which in providence I may consider my proper temporal home! . . . We put to, and Mr. Rowe led me up a steep path under the great Tamarind tree, from under which I first spied the two bungalows or houses, separated by a long Arbour." (September 10, 1816)

Courtesy Angus Library and Archive, Regents Park College, Oxford, UK

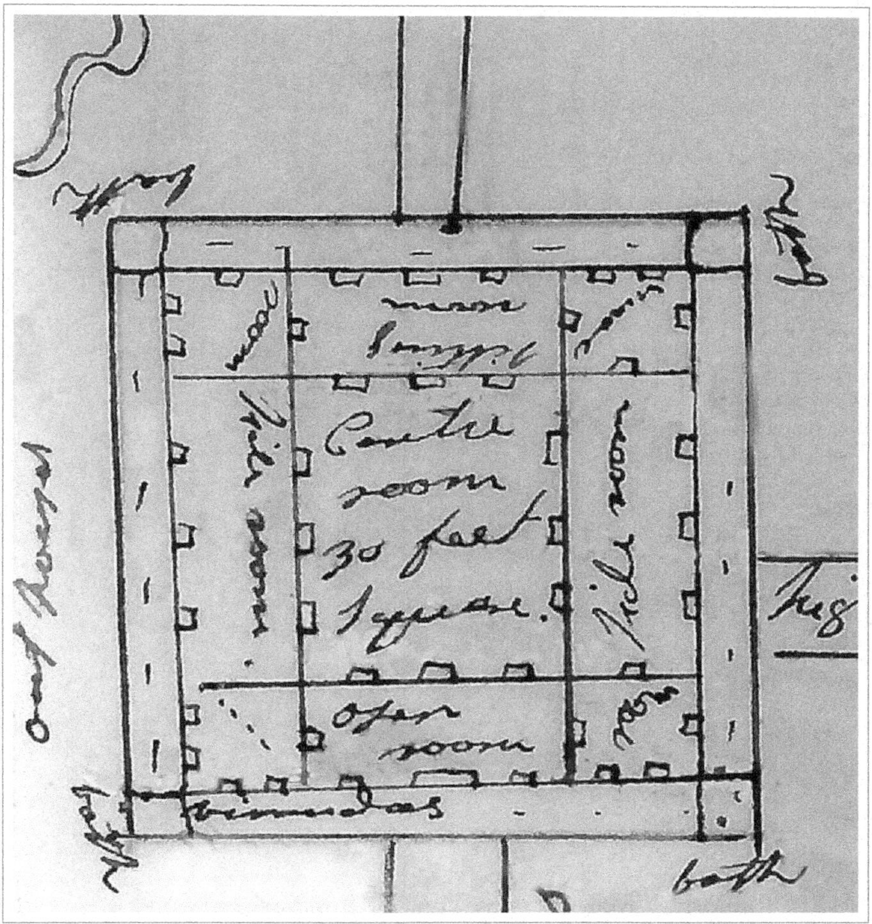

Detail of bungalow at Digah Mission Station
map by Charlotte Rowe, 1824.

"[A Bungalow] is a one story house, with a roof falling low from a great height, descending on four sides from a point at the top. It has three rows of rooms, which leaves one large hall in the centre; this is very high, shaded, and airy, having several large doors opening into the connecting rooms, through which it receives all the light it gets." (September 10, 1816)

Courtesy Angus Library and Archive, Regents Park College, Oxford, UK

Portrait from *Eustace Carey: A Missionary in India* by Mrs. Eustace Carey, 1857.

Charlotte White lived with Eustace and Mary (Fosbrook) Carey after arriving in Calcutta. The Careys lived with the Rowes when in Digah. "Our dear friends, Eustace Carey and wife, have been with us since the month of May, for their health, and that of their little William. They lost a fine little daughter, born after we left Calcutta." (August 23, 1817)

Public domain

Dawk walla mail carriers.

Dawk wallas carried Charlotte Rowe's letters and journal portions from Digah to Calcutta. ". . . [H]e runs five or ten miles, when another takes it from his shoulder, and runs his stage, and so on, there being only a foot path for men and beasts of burden." (June 11, 1816)

The Illustrated London News, February 20, 1858

Water carrier.
Steel engraving by W. D. Taylor after W. Daniell, 1834.

"Women are carrying from the river, great earthen things of water which answer for jugs, but are greatly swelled and without a handle." (June 4, 1816)

Washing clothes in river.

"The mode of washing here, ruins Irish *linen* clothes. They use lime and potash and slap their clothes on a slab at the river's brink, where they wash." (June 9, 1816)

Public domain

Captain Paul Cuffee, 1812.

"Let me know how Paul Cuffee does at Sierra Leon [sic]. I remember taking tea with him and you at Joseph Clark's." (April 9, 1817)

Public domain

A Samporea or Snake Catcher
by Charles D'Oyly, ca. 1830.

"I have also seen snake catchers play over the grass and catch two immensely large snakes which had been seen there by the children." (September 12, 1817)

Travel by dawk palanquin.

"I rejoice in the pleasing account of your son Edwin and hope he may reach India in safety if he should attempt the voyage. I hope he will take a Dawk palankeen and arrive here as soon as possible, which he may do in five days from Calcutta, for about 150 rupees." (October 21, 1820)

Detail from *"Modes of Travelling in India," The Illustrated London News,* 1863

A khidmatgar from *The Three Presidencies of India* by John Capper, 1853.

"I look[ed] up the Life of Mahomet, one evening after tea, and endeavored to read and explain some parts of it, to the servants, the Khidmustgar or waiter being a Mussulman." (September 1819)

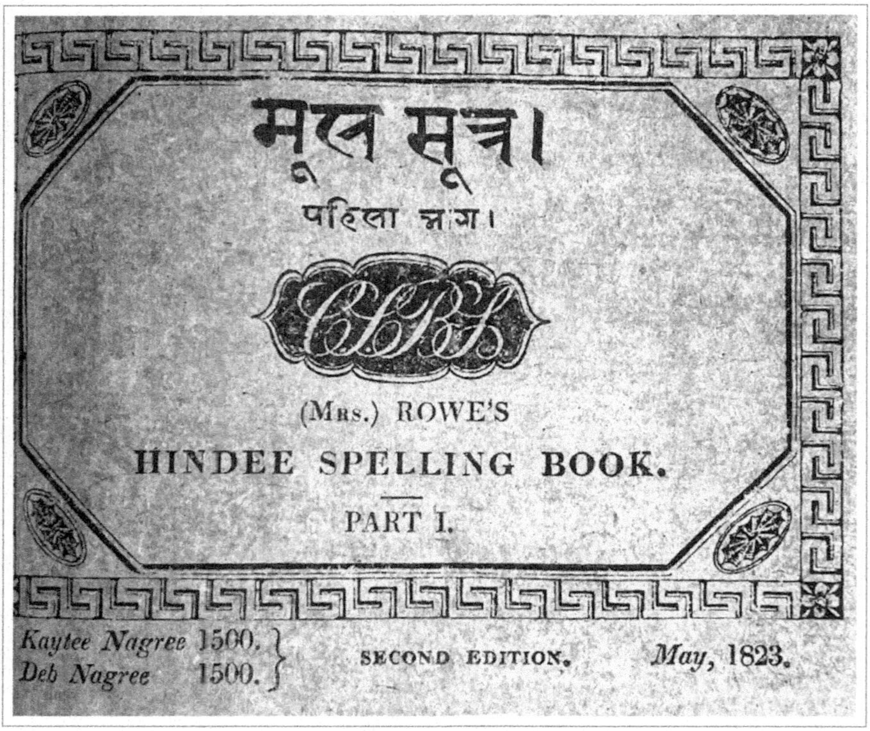

मूल सूत्र।

पहिला भाग।

CSBS

(Mrs.) ROWE'S

HINDEE SPELLING BOOK.

PART I.

Kaytee Nagree 1500.
Deb Nagree 1500.

SECOND EDITION. *May*, 1823.

(Mrs.) Rowe's Hindee Spelling Book.

"Sent my copy of the Hindee Spelling [Book] to Calcutta as a present to the *Calcutta Native School Book Society.* Mr. Rowe wrote the letter which accompanied it. I did not add the little Grammar, because he had not had time to examine it. It remains to be proved whether they will print it." (May 1, 1818)

Courtesy Angus Library and Archive, Regents Park College, Oxford, UK

Honesta's[1] Journal and Letters after commencing her missionary career, addressed to her brother, Dr. E. A. Atlee[2] by his Sister Charlotte

[WT][3] December 13, 1815. On Board the Brig. *Benj. Rush*[4] bound for Calcutta. Lying by Reedy Island, a few miles below the city of Philadelphia.

Now am I in truth in the situation I desired—on board a vessel destined to the East Indies, one of a few persons charged with an evangelical mission to the heathen. I am aware that I have embarked in a cause replete with trials and perils, but which I do not recoil at, knowing God's promises to such as leave all to follow his commands. His presence can vanquish fear and distrust. I regard nothing a trial, which his blessed presence sanctifies to my soul.

Now am I indeed separated, and probably for life, from all I hold dear by acquaintance. There are many whom I hold dear that I have never seen in a heathen land. Who may be deemed most dear of the two, let the world judge. Parting with the first has indeed wrung my heart and weakened my frame. My endeavors may prove

---

[1] Charlotte also used "Honesta" as her penname for articles she wrote about her experiences in India that were published in the *Columbian Star and Christian Index* newspaper in 1830.

[2] Dr. Edwin Augustus Atlee.

[3] Charlotte wrote two journal entries on December 13, 1815 from New Castle and Reedy Island respectively. This Reedy Island entry appears first in Maxine Woolston's transcript of Charlotte's journal but is currently missing from Charlotte's handwritten document. Reedy Island is about twenty miles down the Delaware River south of New Castle. Charlotte's New Castle entry describing her initial inner turmoil preceded this Reedy Island entry depicting her settled conviction that she was following God's will.

[4] The *Benjamin Rush* was a cargo ship owned by Philadelphia merchant Edward Thompson (also spelled Thomson).

as a drop into the ocean—yet the ocean would not really be so full without it. There is an ocean of need, where I go for the showers of grace. O! may the Lord qualify me for usefulness in his cause. Some may say: "His cause might have been as well served in her native land." Yes, but I never felt myself sufficiently refined to teach the refined and have therefore chosen to teach where instruction is more needed.[5]

The day is so cold and damp, that I can not remain out of my berth. Last evening, suffering greatly with the cold, I persuaded a servant to bring me a chafing dish of lighted coal. There being no chimney in my room, I soon became quite senseless. My companions also suffered in the same way. The servant happened to come to see after the fire just in time to save our lives. He excited an alarm and calling others to our assistance, we were all dragged on carriers upon deck where the ocean air soon restored us to animation.

Our vessel lying at anchor, affords me an opportunity for thinking quietly in my own little stateroom. My first thoughts are about the manner in which I ought to spend my time. Resolve: to rise as soon as a little light comes down through my bull's eye.[6] Attend to my private devotions as usual before breakfast. In agreement with

---

[5] It is unclear whether Charlotte's modest remark about refinement referred to social background, education, or both. No source materials have yet been located to describe her education as a child or adult. Charlotte's journal entries, letters, vocabulary, poetry, newspaper articles, and linguistic skills testify to substantial training, whether acquired in an academy or through more individualized instruction. She had been a teacher before sailing to India, see Journal, August 23, 1817. After returning to Philadelphia in 1829 she opened a girls' boarding school in her home. The curriculum included instruction in the rudiments of English, spelling, reading, grammar, writing, composition, parsing in prose and poetry, arithmetic, history, geography, use of maps, needle work, sewing, and knitting, French, piano, voice, deportment, drawing, and painting. Trulson, *Charlotte Atlee White Rowe*, 166.

[6] Bull's eye: a porthole window.

Dr. Staughton's instructions[7], I intend to leave the table as soon as I have completed every meal and take exercise on deck, or retire to my stateroom, as the weather permits. Resolve: never to contend in any argument for my own opinion, but having expressed it, direct from the argument on the first opposition, will appear piously cheerful but avoid being boisterous or profane. Resolve: not to make religion a topic myself, but join in the subject, if any of the ship's company broach it. Resolve: not to dishonor any Christian profession and to daily implore the Shepherd and Keeper of Israel to keep me from folly and sin.

[8][8] I have promised my brother E. to write freely to him. And as I shall have much time on my hand here, that might otherwise be misapplied, I think it best for me to keep retired and give my thoughts and my time to letter writing; and to making my own reflections on paper as probably I shall see many things, to me remarkable, on the grand, expansive deep.

Letter 1st. To Doct^r^. Edwin A. Atlee of Philadelphia, Pa.
Dec. 13th. 1815. On board the *Benjamin Rush*, bound
for Calcutta—Lying off New Castle.[9]

---

[7] William Staughton was Charlotte's pastor at the Sansom Street Baptist Church in Philadelphia. He was the founding corresponding secretary of the Baptist Board of Foreign Missions who issued instructions to new missionaries upon their departure. He urged them to keep a journal about their work and to also write about "the soil, production, customs, mythologies, animals, plants, literary works, &c. that prevail" where they would be serving. Staughton, "Instructions," *First Annual Report*, 115–116.

[8] Pages 1–7 of Charlotte's 255+ page handwritten journal are currently missing.

[9] Ships with cargo from Philadelphia moved with their pilot to take on poultry, pigs, and vegetables at New Castle "where the captains who remain at Philadelphia to settle their accounts at the custom-house join them by land, and from whence they sail with the first fair wind." La Rochefoucault-Liancourt, *Travels,* 539.

Dear brother

On the Car of a Sigh, I would send you my first letter, after parting with you. I now at last, after much suspense, about being on this voyage, address you as my ever dear brother. I must not say, ever distant, ever absent, for when I took leave of the tall trees as they sank behind the waves, on the shore, I said in my mind, "I shall see you again." The convulsing hour of grief is past—and I hope never to be repeated with me.

[9] I now feel a serenity, surprising, and a Peace in being on board this vessel. Yes, I believe it is all right. I have received such kind assurances of purposed attentions from all the Ship's company, that I really feel as if I had come amongst Friends and brothers. Even the sailors have met me, and saluted me most kindly, welcoming me on board the *Rush*, together with my missionary companions.[10]

Let me digress, and say, to Mr. Edward Thompson's Munificence and arrangements for our comfort I owe increasing thanks.[11] May Peace be his portion here, and heaven his home! *Your* friends, Mr. and Mrs. E. have both shewn themselves mine.

Since Dr. and Mrs. Staughton left me, [12] I have been tenderly

---

[10] George and Phebe (Mann) Hough and their two children. The Board appointed Rev. Hough on April 11, 1815. Missionary wives such as Phebe were not appointed. Sending a missionary was not equivalent to appointing one. Appointment established an official, mutual relationship that made missionaries agents of the sending body and made the sending body responsible for its agents. "Appointment also had spiritual significance. Through it, the body of Christ publicly affirmed that God had called a particular individual into the ministry of mission. In that regard, the appointment of a missionary was similar to the ordination of a pastor." Trulson, preface to *Charlotte Atlee White Rowe*.

[11] Edward Thompson provided free passage for the missionaries and built two cabins onboard the ship to accommodate Charlotte and the Hough family during their voyage.

[12] Maria and William Staughton accompanied Charlotte on a steamboat from Philadelphia down the Delaware River to the *Benjamin Rush* anchored at New Castle, Delaware.

fostered by the family of Judge Booth[13] at Newcastle. They accompanied us down to the wharf, the ship lying in the Stream. I passed such an afternoon yesterday, as I never before realized. When I found that the last Philadelphia friends were indeed gone out of my view, my poor heart felt the *fact* of its bodily separation from yourself and so many around you, whom I love. I believe it grieved as it never grieved before for separation from *living* objects. But kind heaven had provided an emolument in Miss Booth,[14] who remained to soothe me, as she well knew how, waiting to take me home with her. When I was able, I went. It was near night. I was introduced into a circle of bright minds. I endeavor'd to keep composed—a cup of tea refreshed me; and after tea, the organ roused my heavy heart, to taste the harmless pleasure of sensed thought on harmony's soft wing, wafted by Mrs. Rogers; and after my feelings were thus harmonized, I endeavor'd to shew my complacency with their amiable exertions to make me cheerful, by joining in pieces that I could sing. After their visitants left the circle, I was drawn into conversation on the subject of my *Expedition*, and endeavor'd to explain to them, the nature of it &cc. [10] Their attention increased, became sympathetic, and it seemed as if they wished the fire to be replenished, unwilling to be separate at 12 o'Clock. A regale[15] of pie and milk closed the social scene, and I retired to rest.

It only is necessary, I find, to inform the minds of those who are pious, to make them friends to my undertaking; as well as to the cause in which I have embarked. That heart must feel desolate indeed, which has no friendships. *I* cannot exist without them; and God kindly provides a some one everywhere, to share the spontaneous effusions of a humane heart. In Miss Elizabeth Booth, I found a sweet spirit, with which I felt a kindred interest. Prudence and

---

[13] James Booth, Sr. (1753–1828) and his wife Ann Clay Booth lived in New Castle, Delaware. He was Chief Justice of the Delaware Supreme Court which held sessions in New Castle before being located in Dover, Delaware.

[14] Elizabeth Booth was then nineteen years old.

[15] Regale: lavish supply.

modesty have nursed her, and piety and poetry are her handmaids. She gave me several pledges from her pen, but at my request, for which I must be content to fail in making a merited return.

We are all in confusion as yet, expecting to be at Reedy Island tonight.

You will have no objection to acquainting my next dearest friends, Dr. and Mrs. Staughton, with the substance of the above, as they introduced me to Mrs. Booth's family at the Inn, and gave me over to their care for the time previous to going on board the *Rush*.

I write to you with but little care, knowing that you have the telescope of the Christian to look through at my intentions; *and your keen eye can rouse the latent sense.*

Farewell! in love to Sister and
Children, and cousins,
Charlotte H. White
Dr. Edwin A. Atlee
Philadelphia

[11] Letter 2nd. At Sea. Latitude 21°. 20"—Jany. 6th. 1816. 4 o'Clock.

My dear Nephew, Edwin,

We left the Capes[16] on the Sunday after we left Philadelphia, since which time we have been favored with uncommonly fair winds; the sea sometimes pretty rough, which kept some of us sick. Mr. and Mrs. Hough and Mr. Rodman,[17] suffered several days from sea

---

[16] The *Benjamin Rush* passed between Cape May, New Jersey and Cape Henlopen, Delaware to enter the Atlantic. By water the capes were some eighty miles from Philadelphia and sixty miles from New Castle.

[17] John Rodman (also spelled Rodmon) and Joseph Reeves were the supercargoes on the *Benjamin Rush* as it sailed from Philadelphia to Calcutta with passengers Charlotte White, George and Phebe Hough, and their two children, Sarah and George Hough. "East Indies," *Caledonian Mercury*,

sickness, but I recovered in a few hours. Having passed the Tropic of Cancer two degrees, we find the air soft, and the weather much like that you have in the month of April.

The sea weed in view, supposed to come from the Gulf of Florida, presents a singular appearance, on the surface of the water in a warm Sun. It seems to be of a sensitive nature, susceptible of heat and cold, as in a cold morning or closing day, it does not rise within some inches of the Surface, but like the snake, bursts partly above it when the Sun shines clear. It runs in Streaks with the wind, at the distance of a rod, and the whole Surface of the Ocean, as far as the eye can discern the weed, resembles a field of newly cut hay, lying in windrows. It is of a yellowish light brown, and looks very pretty. It looks something like cedar boughs when in bud.

A tropical bird was taken on deck the other day, which bit our dry Doctor's finger badly.[18] His medical & surgical talents have been often called into exercise by pigs and poultry. With regard to poultry, Mr. E. takes all the care of these, making new discoveries daily as to their natural dispositions, diseases, requirements in aliment and medicine, accommodations &cc.

The striking of the bell, informs me that it is half past six. Here

---

October 19, 1816, 2. A supercargo represented the cargo owner on board a merchant ship to oversee the cargo and its sale.

[18] Most early merchant ships did not have a surgeon on board as ship owners considered that an added expense. On July 20, 1790, the first U.S. Congress passed legislation requiring all American-flagged ships of 150 tons or more with a crew of ten or more sailors to be equipped with "a chest of medicines, put up by some apothecary of known reputation, and accompanied by directions for administering the same." The *Benjamin Rush* was a 390-ton ship. Charlotte identified Mr. E. as a "dry doctor," likely a person without formal medical training who was apparently a sailor or ship's officer in charge of the ship's medicine chest and assigned to manage health issues of the passengers, crew, and animals. Gordon, "Sailors' Physicians," 139–140; Peters, ed., *Public Statues*, 134; "For Philadelphia," *Liverpool Mercury*, June 16, 1815, 4.

I am, lounging in my birth,[19] fatigued with a long walk on deck, at the setting of the Sun. The clouds afforded me a novel amusement, by their imitative capacity, in presenting the aspect of villages, and steeples, and light-houses; all which, if we had not been conscious of our distance from such dear objects, might have deceived us, for a reality. The mutability of [12] the substances which composed this perspective city prevented me from calling it the *New* Jerusalem.

The objects at Sea, both in day and night, are striking to the sight. In a dull day the clouds are more august; in a clear day they form a bright scalloped fencing all round the horizon: and at the setting sun, they lift themselves a little above their apparent foundations, leaving a space for the Sun to emit his crimson light forming a bright girth about the whole hemisphere.

The water has not given up any of its animal wonders to our view, as yet, except some Dolphins which at times keep close to the side of the vessel, keeping pace with it. At several feet depth in the water, their bodies appear of a deep blue, their fins pale blue, and their tail, an emerald green. When dying out of water, their scales emulate the colours of the rainbow, until death spreads a paleness over the then breathless victim, and it looks like any other dead fish.

Previous to our advancing so far into a tropical clime there was an unusual salubrity in the breeze, favorable to elevation of spirits and activity of body. I think I never experienced the sense of both in a greater degree, perhaps it was owing to being relieved from that cheerless coldness which had deprived us of comfort day and night, for my feet were quite benumbed, and to get warm, we at last, that is, Mrs. Hough and I, persuaded the steward to bring us a pan of live charcoals. We sat some time in our state rooms by them, feeling cheered, untill [sic] we unconsciously lost all animation, and had we not have been discovered and dragged up on deck, should have died away without pain, or sense of our condition.

We now begin to realize a quite different atmosphere, the heat becoming rather troublesome. We passed about three degrees from

---

[19] Birth: archaic for berth, a room in a ship.

Bermuda, have spoke one sail bound to St. Christophers, and saw three other vessels. The Captain does not intend to touch any where on the voyage, if he has good luck. He is quite a father to me in his behaviour.

[13] There are two cats on board, one of which has attached itself to me, and comes to take a nap sometimes on my birth; she used to keep my feet warm at night,

On Saturdays, it has become my province, to make up pastry and puddings, mince-pies, apple-pies, potatoe-puddings [sic], &cc.—and the agreement is, that such as have not done something towards these, shall have none. Mr. R's prepared cream, having become a little acid, served to supply the place of milk. My two barrels of fine pippins,[20] decayed all at once. I looked them over and gave them to the Sailors, before they were past eating.

I regret not having thought to send word to Miss Whitehead, of our sudden departure, as she had a parcel to send to Mrs. Newel [sic].[21] Please apologize for it, and give my love to her and Miss Moulder.[22]

I need say little about love to your folks—you know I do not

---

[20] Pippin: apple grown from seedling apple tree.

[21] Harriet (Atwood) Newell (1793–1812) from Haverhill, Massachusetts and her husband, Samuel Newell, sailed to India in 1812 with Adoniram and Ann Judson as Congregationalist missionaries. After the East India Company ordered them to leave India, the Judsons (who had become Baptists) went to Burma and the Newells sailed to the Isle of France (Mauritius). Harriet died on November 30, 1812 at Mauritius seventeen days after giving birth to a daughter, who had died on board. Miss Whitehead seems to have been unaware of Harriet's death when the *Benjamin Rush* departed on December 17, 1815,even though news of Newell's death had reached North America by August 1813 and a memoir of Newell had been published and was being sold by W. W. Woodward in Philadelphia. Woods, *A sermon, preached at Haverhill,* 245. Charlotte noted that reading Newell's *Memoirs* had renewed the call to mission she had discerned nine years earlier. See Journal, June 12, 1818.

[22] Sarah Moulder (1789–1832) was a daughter of William Henry and Mary (Miller) Moulder.

lack it; and your father does not like *professions*. Don't forget to write to me, just as you feel and think.

Your affect. Aunt
Charlotte.

Letter 3rd. January 8th. 1816. About 20° N. Lat. having passed the Tropic of Cancer.

My dear Brother,

When I scratched a few lines to you from Reedy Island, my fingers and toes ached with cold. Now, the sweet mild breezes are those of your May; and the warm beams of the Sun mock at the cold gleam he casts upon you, which a winter fire strives to make amends for. I envy not your frigid atmosphere, although I often ask myself the question, why am I here? I hope I am where God the great Controuler [sic] of Events designed I should be. I have nothing to answer to me this question satisfactorily [14] but my belief in His Omniscience, his Providence, and his promise, that he will never leave those who feel and own him. Yes, the subject of *why I am here* often weighs my heart, and I dare not think too much upon it. The train of events which brought me here,[23] and which God could have overruled to baffle my views, serve to quiet my mind, when I closely investigate. I hope it will not result in my shame. Thus far, I have been upheld in good spirits; and have realized none of those unpleasant things which I had foreboded, but experience an uniform behaviour of polite and delicate attention from all around me: and I hope by God's grace, enabling me to exercise uniformly, a prudent course of conduct myself, that I shall reach the end of the voyage, having nothing of a less pleasant nature to recount, than I have as yet realized. Dr. Staughton committed me to the particular charge of the Captain, who promised him to deliver me safe into the care of Dr.

[23] The "train of events" is documented in Trulson, *Charlotte Atlee White Rowe*, chs. 1–6.

Carey,[24] if all be living.

Our beautiful brig, left the capes of Delaware on the Sabbath morning after leaving your city. Before the day closed, we lost sight of our *native land*! After looking till I could see it *no more*, I took my seat on the top of the booby-hatch, and leaning my back against the capstan gave way to my feelings at the point of my pencil, thus, am I indeed cradling the ocean! Have I indeed taken the last look on my native land; and are my thoughts at right, that my heart should not break? When I looked on the leafless tree-tops sinking behind the waves, did a tear fall? No. I sighed, "well, well" (I trusted it was well). "True, I am apart from all my relatives, but I am not 'out of humanity's reach.' Sympathy already shown, tells me, a Stranger's breast is not void. What though no softly soothing arm encircle me, as sea-sickness steals away my energy! what tho' no hand of love stand ready to adjust my pillow—no sigh at seeing me ill, burst from an allied bosom,—that feelingly would take to itself my pains, if possible; What though no nightly companion, (as once it was) [15] press me to his side, when the ship rocks, and if he could do no more, lift his heart in prayer to Him who rules the deep, to shield both him and me! Sorrow not felt needs no Sympathy—health but momentarily impaired needs no physician—no gently adjusting hand. The bosom that feels no need of sympathizing love, needs not its ministrations. When the hand that conducts, afflicts *feeling*, it will provide an antidote. When He withdraws all outward comforts, and inward support, he will supply *Himself*. O may I rest beneath his wing, and I shall go or stay securely. Lord let me possess *thee* in my thoughts, nor be content without thy felt influence on my Soul!

The clouds hover blackly—The sea grows rough—his angry surges throw their white fringe—hollow sounds the wind upon the dark bosom of the extending deep—Lowering eve comes on with frowns. If now a wreck await us, how shall my warmly nurtured form resist the chill wave! If cast upon a solitary rock, how shall I look

[24] William Carey and Dr. John Thomas were the first English Baptist missionaries to arrive in India in 1793.

back with regret, or, reconciled to my fate, smile at the solitude of my misery—no tender cord snapp'd by my loss—Here is satisfaction. These conjectured horrors are possible: a night may not elapse e'er I may have tasted them. But 'God is at the helm.' On that thundrous cloud He rides; on yon gleaming ray that darts between the western towers of mist as the Sun sinks beneath the wave, He looks on us; Night will not shut *his eye*—Be thou my Stay!"

My heart holds many a Soliloquy on paper, and then I seem to be talking with you, dear Edwin. I went below, and retired to my birth, where I laid me down under the feeling of God's all-pervading cognizance, and trusting in it, fell asleep, rocked by the vessel. The morning woke me, and with it, brought these thoughts, which I copy from my slate, that hanging near my pillow, received them as I give them thee.[25]

When Nature's all her duty done,
And God's decree puts out the Sun,
When Stars forget their mystic course
And Chaos roars from darkness, hoarse,
[16] Creation, trembling, frighted, falls
Before that God whose word recalls
To non-existence, what she bore
And swears that "Time shall be no more"!
When, 'mong the chang'd, redeem'd and pure
Lovers of Holiness appear,
And waiting calm at Christ's right hand,
Prepared for Judgment, trusting, stand,
(Honour and Justice dire to tell)
And hear the wicked doom'd *to Hell*!
Then, then shall kindred souls that darted
From light at first, rejoice, ne'er parted—

---

[25] Charlotte's brother Edwin had become a Quaker, and Charlotte sometimes used the Quaker plain-speech pronouns thee/thou/thy when addressing him.

And range those fields forever green
Where sorrow, sin, nor death are seen.
Fields where no other Sun need shine
Than Jesus' Count'nence, all divine.
Then shall th' elated spirit know
All she believ'd or hoped below,
Where imperfections held her goal
But fruit triumphant swell'd her Soul.

Then father, mother, husband, child
Sister, brother, and friends that smil'd
Shall meet in Christ the *Resurrection*
In him arrived to sought perfection!
None there possess distinguish'd *union*:
Allied by intellectual communion
Each meets the other; loves at sight,
Rejoicing in their large delight –
Delectable! Unutterable Joys!
For *Christ* th' extatic [sic] soul employs!

With love to each of your dear family,
I subscribe myself thine,
Charlotte H. White
Dr. E. A. Atlee.

[17] Letter 4th. Calcutta Harbour. Apl. 24th. 1816.
Choicest Friend and brother,

I snatch the privilege of five minutes allowed by the kind delay of a Supercargo of the *Herald*[27] of Salem, now dropped down the

[27] Captain Graves and the American ship *Herald* (not His Majesty's Ship *Herald* from England) returned to Salem, Massachusetts on October 3, 1816, bringing a packet of letters from Charlotte. It included her letter to William Staughton informing him of her safe arrival in India. "Salem," *Charleston Daily Courier*, October 16, 1816, 2.

Hoogly[28] to inform you of our safe arrival at this Port, yesterday at 5 o'Clock P. M. All well.

Dr. Carey not being at his office in Calcutta, but at this residence at Serampore, the Captain could not see him when he called at his transient abode in the city. His youngest son, Jonathan, called last evening to see me on board; he will inform his father of our arrival. Captn. A.[1] has been very attentive to us all and as a kind father to me. I can say no more now—shall write much by the *Scattergood*.[2]

God bless you and all friends
Adieu
Your Sister
Ch. H. White

PS. Please inform friends—Dr. Staughton's letter incloses [sic] one for you of a former date. The *Dryade*[3] dislodged the Missionaries at Ceylon; welcomed by Government. C.H.W.

---

[28] The Hooghly is a distributary of the River Ganges flowing into the Bay of Bengal and on which Serampore and Calcutta are located.

[1] Captain John Ansley (also spelled Annsley, Annesly, or Ainsley).

[2] Edward Thompson owned both the *Benjamin Rush* and the *Thomas Scatterwood*. The *Rush* arrived back in New Castle, Delaware in late November, 1816, and the *Scatterwood* arrived back on December 10, 1816. "Philadelphia," *New York Evening Post*, November 28, 1816, 2; "New-Castle," *New York Evening Post*, December 12, 1816, 2.

[3] The Congregationalist missionaries sent from Newburyport, Massachusetts on the *Dryade* by the American Board of Commissioners for Foreign Missions were James and Sarah (Bardwell) Richards, Daniel and Susan (Bulfinch) Poor, Horatio and Rachel (Furbush) Bardwell, Benjamin C. and Sarah (Peet) Meigs, and Rev. Edward Warren.

[Journal continued. April 23rd. 1816. 8 o'Clock A. M.]

The prospects on each side of the River Hoogly are merely rural at the distance that we here behold them. I am told the trees in sight are Banana, Cocoa, mango and others in set groves like orchards. The dwellings of the native inhabitants are of a conical form and covered with thatch—they are mere wigwams.

The natives are seen fishing on the Banks which are very little above the water—and the cattle, some standing at the brink and some grazing about, are so lean, that their ribs [18] may be almost counted by the help of the Spy-glass. Mostly white cattle, very small; and a black herd resembling cows but larger, are mixed among them, which are a species of buffaloes with long horns, tamed for the use of their milk, which produces an oil, much in demand amongst both natives and Europeans, for culinary purposes, instead of Lard, butter &cc.

It is said that the Hindoos do not eat the flesh of any animals, and these in particular, holding the cow as sacred, and *her lord* as their God!!

The natives appear to move slowly, and look thin and slender. A boat load of them came to our vessel this morning from Diamond harbour[4] post office, for Letters of dispatch. They chattered like ducks, and beat a childish little drum, to take attention.

I feel more pleasantly this morning than I have done as yet, in prospect of Landing.

Nine o'Clock. Were called up on deck to see a publick house as they termed it, at Fulta:[5] it appears to be quite a palace—but from

---

[4] Diamond Harbour was located on the east side of the Hooghly some thirty miles south of Calcutta. Here a harbormaster and customs officers boarded ships proceeding north to Calcutta, and the East India Company's ships loaded most of their cargo bound for England. Partington, ed., *British Cyclopedia*, 600–601.

[5] Fulta (also Falta) was a small village and a former Dutch fort about nine miles north of Diamond Harbour on the east side of the Hooghly.

what I can discern, it is not an abode of the feminine *virtues*. Very fanciful out houses and gardens spread to view on each side of it. The pillars on each side of the entrance gate, are so formed and so white, that I at first sight took them to be two persons dressed in white muslin.

On the opposite side, stands a block of native huts shaded by trees. The Khajure tree[6] looks like bunch of long ostrich plumes. The Cocoa is something like it, but stiffer and coarser, in its foliage. These and the palm or *Tarry*[7] resemble each other for having *all* their foliage in a bunch at the top, but the palm *leaf* is its only branch, and is formed precisely like a large green fan when spread open, the edges of the largest leaves are fringed or split just as an old fan does, at the folds. The lower trees are very various and beautiful, presenting different shades of green, others discoloured like our trees in the fall. These humble scenes please me much: at this distance, contentment seems to reign among [19] them. The people evidently know but little and are satisfied with little. Their force of character, must be chiefly in their religious observances, of which I shall know more by & by.

Eleven o'Clock—There is something new continually. The Captain called us up to see the Bazar [sic]. It is a native market, on the very brink of the river, where the people have erected huts and stalls of thatch; and even cloth held up by four poles, to screen them from the Sun. We can see earthen vessels placed as they are in Phil[a] market. Poles in heaps, clusters of fruit on the stalls and many things—and the glass enabled us to discern the fruit upon the trees. Seeing our vessel coming up they came out to us with a boat full of fruit, consisting of pumpkins, water-melons, potatoes, cocoanuts, Bananas or plantains, and some eggs.

The banana or plantain, looks something like a cucumber or pawpaw—a thick, flexible skin is pulled off, and exposes a pulp

---

[6] Khajure: a date tree.

[7] Possibly the toddy palm, *borassus flabellifer*, a South Asian palm with large fan-shaped leaves.

entire, more like butter in a cold day, but sweetish and mucilaginous, it is eaten from stem to stearn [sic], with no interruptions. I was delighted to see pumpkins & watermelons, as they seemed like home—but the latter is so only in name, it is so vapid.

The poor natives make my heart ache. They appear in so very deprived a state. They tell us no fixed price for their articles, hoping to get a great price. It is said that a man can subsist on a rupee per month and that four dollars, which is about eight rupees will support him a year, in the way they can live.

Two o'Clock P.M. We were called again on deck to hear the birds sing—the sun is too hot, to allow of our being many minutes on deck. The river being narrow brought us up to the Shore. A thicket fill'd with chirping birds, afforded to our Senses more delight than any thing yet witnessed after hailing the land of human beings.

As we advanced up the river, other objects quite novel varied the scene. The next, which presented [20] itself, stood in horrible contrast with the last mentioned, five gallows, on which hung as many Skeletons of men, in Iron cages; they had been executed there some years ago for crimes. The carnivorous birds had flay'd their flesh, and now their bones are ready to drop through the wires.

The next object distinguished from the train of native villages, is a Salt factory, The Salt lying in heaps, roofed over. After this, the most picturesque scenery opened to view. Elegant seats owned by rich men, either native or European, rows of trees crossing each other, but no images about them, as I have seen else-where in rich men's yards and gardens. The houses are very airy, having very large and numerous venetian windows & doors. Piazza above and below, flat on the roof, and a palisade on the top of the walls. They appear to be stucco on the outside.

After this, Fort William came in view,[8] for grandeur in appearance and extent, exceeding any front of a city, I ever saw. We are near Calcutta!

---

[8] Calcutta and Fort William were both located on the east side of the Hooghly River with the fort on the southern side of the city.

Having now dined, I have retired to my stateroom (according to Instructions given us by Dr. Staughton's written rules for our conduct while on board) and I have the Cabin filled with police officers, and natives who have brought goods to sell to the Ship's company. A peep or two from the crack of my door shews me several Bengallees, clad in flowing white muslin having great parcels of country goods open, on the floor.

These men look very differently from the poor creatures we first saw come to our vessel. They were naked, all but a breadth of dirty looking cloth, wound round the top of their thighs and round their waists: But these men have the whitest muslin wound round their thighs down to their calves, & an end of it hanging very full, from the belt, or that part of the same breadth which winds many times round them, and this end hangs quite down to their insteps. A tight muslin Jacket, and a great sheet slung about their shoulders finishes their dress, except that some of them have turkish turbands [sic] of muslin, while others have their hair cut [21] close about their forehead and ears, having a long tuft behind, which they wind up in a knot—Their hair is very black, straight, and glossy. They wear shoes that turn up in front like skates, but are turned down at heel, to render them easy to slip off at the door or entrance of any place where people are met, but especially, in presence of their superiors. So they were all barefoot who were in the cabin. Is not this custom of taking off the Shoes, founded in scripture? Genesis.

In an hour we shall be at the strand in Calcutta. Here let me pause, and ask myself—how can I, an unmarried female (for a widow is truly, unmarried) feel courage to land on this strange, luxurious shore? I feel prepared for it, and *now*, no disagreeable sensations about it, expecting the guidance of those who understand the customs. This period was preparing for in my own mind, by means of frequent prayer.

7 o'Clock. The good Captain took a boat and went ashore and called at Dr. Carey's house or office in the city, but was informed at the door, that the Dr. had just left the city to go home to Serampore. Captn A. then desired to see any of his family who might be there.

Young Mr. Carey[9] came to the door, whom the Captn informed, that he had a lady, a missionary in charge, whom he was pledged to introduce to Dr. Carey and deliver over to his care. Mr. Carey promised to write to his father immediately, and to call himself in the morning at the vessel. The confusion and pressure of business on their arrival, prevented the Captain from recollecting to ask for our letters of introduction, finding he had gone ashore without them, threw me into some agitation; and I sat down in the dark stateroom, to meditate and pray. While in this situation, I was called to meet a gentleman who had come on board to see the missionaries. I felt rejoiced, and hastened into the Cabin, and being introduced to Mr. Jonathan Carey, had a few moments chat before the others came out of their stateroom. He seemed cold and rather distant, until I handed him my letters of introduction. He came he said, to shew us to lodgings, if we desired it that evening, but Mrs. Hough's children being in bed and asleep, we thought best to defer going on shore until [22] the morning. He promised to call at Nine.

April 24th. [1816].

Still on board the *Rush*, though past the time that we thought to have gone on shore. The state of the air in the stream, is not too warm. Mr. Carey has not yet made his appearance.

Three palanquins have just arrived, said to be sent by Mr. Carey for conveying us to lodgings—The wretched appearance of the men who bore them on their shoulders, and the idea of our being unattended into this great and strange place, deterred me from going there, preferring to wait until a fourth vehicle came by which the Captn could attend us, or until Mr., Carey came—as a palanquin takes in but one at a time, being much like a hearse.

[9] Twenty-year-old Jonathan Carey (1796–1874) was the youngest of William and Dorothy Carey's seven children. His two sisters Ann (1782–1784) and Lucy (1791–1793) died in infancy in England. His four brothers were Felix (1785–1822), William (c. 1788–1853), Peter (1789–1794), and Jabez (1793–1879).

While waiting, I ventured to enter into conversation with a few of the native merchants who were on board still. They could of course speak a little English. I asked them of what Cast[10] they were? "Of the Gentoo cast.[11]" They gave me to understand that their occupation was to keep accounts. I observed, that their dress was very graceful, but not calculated to exercise in. They said that their business was selling goods only. There was something very pleasing in their countenances and behaviour perfectly at ease—and extremely courteous—often bowing very gracefully. The chief speaker amongst them had his thumb nails an inch long from the finger—I enquired why he wore them so, and if they were not inconvenient? He replied, that "once a year he cut them and offered them together with some sweetmeats, to his god, which Sacrifice preserved him from all misfortune."

I was interrupted in this novel *tete a tete*, by the introduction of Mr. Eustace Carey, who came to take me on shore. He is nephew to Dr. Carey, and is a missionary, settled in Calcutta. His manner was so conciliating, that I felt perfectly at ease, and much rejoiced at my good fortune. As Mr. and Mrs. Hough had been taken to his Uncle's *official house* in the city, he ordered the [23] bearers of the palanquins waiting, to carry me there (and in this case I was carried in the proper sense of the word. It is very common in the Eastern states of America, to say "I *carried* such a person to such a place, when he only drove the horse that drew them along.)

Mr. Carey came to the strand in a gig, but the Sun being vertical, he thought I should not be able to withstand the heat in the open air. We all met at Dr. Carey's house, but Eustace took us immediately to his own house. The Captain felt exhonerated [sic] from any further care over me, when Mr. Carey received me from under his charge. It was not without feeling grateful to Captn A. for his

---

10 Charlotte's spelling of "cast" (vs. "caste") accords with William Carey, Joshua Marshman, and William Ward's spelling of the word.

11 Gentoo: a Portuguese word for Hindus distinguishing them from Muslims in India.

kind and polite attentions to me during all the voyage, that I took leave of the vessel; wherein bounty almost to luxury, had prevailed throughout the voyage.

I can ill describe my feelings while bourn [sic] on my way thro' winding, dirty, narrow streets of mud huts, and open circular ways, where many carriages might pass, and houses that exhibited both ease and beauty. The stateliness of some of the buildings, compared with the meanness of the native huts intermixed with them, was conspicuous—although I could behold nothing as I passed, but as I peeped through the doors of the palanquin, pushed an inch open; and then the glare of the sun, and the heat and dust came in enough to suffocate me. That vehicle is so low too, that one can see nothing high. Not being accustomed to sitting like a tailor, I unconsciously shook the *paalkee*[12] as they call it, and made the poor fellows call out, "*halo mat* beebee Sahab," "Shake not, Lady." I did not understand what they said, but I conjectured that I had put them to inconvenience, for I made the paalkee swing on their shoulders, like an unsteady squirrel cage for it is held on one pole from the centre at each end, which goes over the shoulder of two men, before and two behind taking a right and a left shoulder, each end. I then tried to recline, as there was a leather cushion serving for that purpose behind me, but the trotting of eight feet, shook my brain beyond enduring, and I was obliged to sit holding on my ancles[13] crossed to support myself erect, until I was in pain all over. When the men set the [24] paalkee down, I found it very awkward and most difficult to scramble out of it, having become stiff with the position I had sat in during a run of 2 or 3 miles. The sweat streaming down their foreheads and naked backs made my heart misgive. What a barbarous country must this be, and how hardened must Europeans have

[12] Palanquin: also called a palki, was a box-like litter in which one person was carried. It had two horizontal side poles or one horizontal center pole borne on the shoulders of four or six bearers. Charlotte also spelled it paalkee and palankeen.

[13] Ancles: archaic spelling of ankles.

become here, to see men do what belongs to four footed animals—fellow men—fellow Souls too! My arrival at the door was announced, and Mr. Carey came and gave me his hand to raise me up out of the palankeen. After some refreshment was partaken of, we all went to Mr. Eustace Carey's house where Mrs. C.[14] gave us a hearty welcome. Eustace said he "wished an hundred missionaries has come with us, as there was work enough for them all."

The news of our arrival, having reached Serampore, several of the younger missionaries came in that evening to see what sort of folk we were—and a more jocular party of pious people I had seldom met with. One in particular seemed very full of quiping, [sic] and kept the others in high good humour—He was a short little man, dressed in white vest and pantaloons and an indigo blue silk coat. They called him brother Rowe. Another tall and thin one whose Wig betrayed as much philosophy as significance they called brother Yates. And a third, rather older, of a mild, smooth aspect, and less to say, they called brother Ward.[15] I was much pleased to find so many people with whom we could exchange rational ideas, as well as to see good wheat bread on the tea table, and something like ice cream in a glass bowl with water round it, that they called butter; and some tea cakes. At about ten o'clock they had family worship, and then all the gentlemen went elsewhere to sleep—leaving Mr. and Mrs. Hough and myself at Mr. Careys.

The next morning our friends interested themselves in getting our baggage through the custom house—and succeeded with paying very little, as Gov[t]. are more favorable to the arrival of missionaries, than when Mrs. Newel [sic] was here. Towards evening these brethren took us up to Serampore in the mission barge—The time was spent agreeably, with singing hymns, at which I gave a good account of myself, having a good voice. [25] We were made welcome by Mr.

---

[14] Mary (Fossbrook) Carey (1791–1829) was Eustace Carey's first wife.

[15] Joshua Rowe, William Yates, and William Ward, respectively.

& Mrs. Marshman.[16] Mrs. Ward[17] is in England, for her health, with her daughter, Hannah.

We find the Establishment to exceed our expectations, in point of extent and style. The weather, though nearly arrived at the hottest, is not so oppressive in the house as I have every summer felt it in America, owing probably to the structure of the houses, which are spacious, having the ceilings *very* high, because one story high: and it is necessary to suspend from them a fanning machine like a long door; This hangs by strong ropes from five to eight feet from the ceiling, and having a rope fastened to one side of it by a hook, a man pulls it, which sends the fan from one wall to the other, fanning a whole room full of people at once. It is most delightful to sit under it.

The kind, and manners of attendants employed in this country, strike me singularly. The female servants are wrapped up head and all, in a white sheet—and the men who are *Hindoo by cast*, that is Braminists, wear their legs and thighs wrapped up, and a great turban. Those servants among them who are Mahometans by cast, esteem themselves more, as being the descendants of the former conquerors of the native Hindoos; and they wear a long white cotton coat like a surtout,[18] having one breast bare, where the garment ties together with tapes. The number of these creatures seen about a table makes a stranger imagine that they must be employed for self-aggrandizement—The case is quite otherwise with all who are not connected with the Army—It is involuntarily obligatory on housekeepers of *any* respectability, because, (to give the reason in few words) their priests order it so, and there is no remedy whatever, against it—The customs are fixed and bound by *priestcraft*—here the

---

[16] Joshua and Hannah (Sheppard) Marshman.

[17] Miss Mary Tidd sailed from England to India in 1799 where she married British Baptist missionary John Fountain. He died August 20, 1800 before the birth of their only son, John Fountain. In 1802 she married William Ward who had been single.

[18] Surtout: a coat worn over another coat, like a waistcoat.

word applies truly; and Government defends their religious schemes.[19] Now, charge not missionaries with growing pompous after they get to India—to be obliged to keep so many persons to do what two or three would cheerfully effect in America, is their bitter plague.

I must now mention the School—Mrs. Marshman [26] who has been at the head of it from the very first, is an astonishing woman. She now has the charge of 60 young Ladies, if they must be called so, who board with her, and whose every garment is taken account of when they go to the wash, She is both the teacher and preacher in her School, moralizing on everything that presents itself for enlargement.

She also has charge of house-keeping, as Mrs. Ward who formerly held that department, is absent. All this weight of care gives her a serious, determined, manner; yet combined with affability. She possesses a strong, vigorous frame, and an energetic mind. Her daughters however, born and brought up on this country, are tall and very slender and pale. She has taken seven orphans of the missionaries who have died here, to bring up. One of these was lately

[19] An 1810 guide for persons entering the civil, military, or naval service of the East India Company stated that the need to employ many servants was based on Indian custom and religion: "The multiplicity of menials employed in the houses of European gentlemen in Bengal…is founded on the tenets of religion, especially among the Hindus; and is by no means likely to be abrogated within our time.… [O]wing to the division of the latter into sects, called by us *casts*, which render the occupations of all perfectly distinct, a necessity exists for hiring such of each *cast* as may attend to those duties they undertake, without becoming subjected to the animadversions of their priesthood, or to those penalties attendant upon even the most trifling deviation from the marked path. Add to this, that the climate arbitrarily imposes the necessity for retaining some classes of servants, unknown in England.…When all matters are considered, it will be found, that that host of domestics appertaining to the establishment of a gentleman in Bengal, proves, in the aggregate, little, if at all, more expensive than the ordinary number retained by families of respectability in most parts of England. Williamson, *East India Vade-Mecum*, 1:181–183.

married to Mr. Yates, and lives on the premises belonging to the mission houses.[20]

The English ladies here who are *fair skinned*, are very fair and pale, never exposing themselves to the Sun. The ancient customs of the primeval inhabitants are still in vogue; and Europeans are obliged to submit to them from the nature of the climate, so far as never to put her head out of doors without an umbrella at midday—a stroke of the Sun might lay her senseless. But I think there might be no impropriety in a lady *walking* with a gentleman to guard her, after the Sun has gone down, even in Calcutta. The reason perhaps that they do not, is that the streets are not paved for walking, and the dust is many inches deep everywhere. I should be tempted at first view of things, to style this a land of luxury and refinement—It is so, contradictorily. But the best of things of other lands, are inferior here—and a variety of lesser comforts have to make up for them. As to refinement—so far as a strict observance of etiquette constitutes refinement, it is here—but refinement as I have been accustomed to consider it, is from some causes which may become apparent [sic] forgotten here. The Apostles taught religion, and refinement as its voucher, growing out of religion. There is refinement then amongst all such as make the religion of Jesus Christ their

---

[20] Catherine Grant had sailed from England to India on the American ship *Criterion* with her parents William and Ann Grant and their fellow Baptist missionaries Joshua and Hannah Marshman, Daniel and Ann Brunsdon, their unmarried colleague, William Ward, and Miss Mary Tidd who was sailing to India to marry John Fountain. Hoby, *Memoir of William Yates,* 78–79. They arrived in October 1799. Eighteen days later William Grant died. Mrs. Ann Grant then married John Chamberlain on December 28, 1805, the Baptist missionary whose first wife, Hannah (Smith) Chamberlain, had died a year and a half earlier. *Guide to Microfilm.* Ann Grant Chamberlain died September 18, 1806 after giving birth to a son, William, who died soon thereafter. Chamberlain, *Memoirs of John Chamberlain,* 201, 204, 208. Her daughter Catherine was taken into the care of Mary Ward in Serampore. William Yates married Catherine Grant at St. John's Cathedral in Calcutta on January 3, 1816. India Office Records.

model.

[27] I have seen some temples, and some wells, and some seats under trees, erected by *devout* Hindoos, who thought to merit eternal felicity by thus accommodating wayfaring persons, and from a snug dwelling in view of them sit and wrap themselves up in self-complacency, as in thin sheet, and smoke at ease, and sleep, and eat alternately. The natives say that the English make themselves *wants*—on the contrary, I should be mortified to see the English do some things which they do at large, and to avoid which, creates other customs or wants. As to a love of luxury, a day spent in Calcutta, will convince one that the natives adore it; while the English enjoy every day those needful mercies, which a Hindoo denies himself all the year, that he may make a great show once in the year. The low and servile casts, filch from their employers' provisions before they are cooked, to support themselves, and lay up their earnings to give a feast at some expected exigency. They are so numerous, that to employ them at low wages is doing service. Men make *all* the clothes worn by Europeans, whether males or females. They work muslin beautifully—they do the washing and ironing, even for their fellow natives. They cook, and wait on guests and serve the table. Women, nurse and wait on children, and attend in bed-rooms as dressing maids to Ladies; men do this for gentlemen, in other apartments. Dressing maids and children's attendants, dress something like Dutch women, only that their petticoat is so long and so full as to hide their bare feet when they walk, and they wear a sheet about all their person and over the head.

April 27th. [1816]. At Serampore. Lord's day.

As the dawn of day is the only time of enjoyment, I soon learned to prize that moment, and rising early, went to the garden gate, doubting whether I should find it unlocked—but Dr. Carey was there, busy with his plants. After some chat concerning the plants, he entered upon more general topics respecting concerning [sic] the Missions. He said that the field for missionary labours was not confined to the natives only. That an immense population [28] of Europeans consisting of English, Irish, Scotch, and Dutch, were spread over the country; also a race of natives calling themselves Christians, who are of Portuguese descent, and are as far from the truth as the heathen, but without their horid [sic] rites. Add to these, a mixed race who are tainted with heathenism from their mothers. That the field for missionary labours amongst all these was beyond calculation; and that it was the duty of missionaries, to preach the pure gospel to those who would received [sic] it, be whom they may.

As it was Sunday morning, he said, that Mr. Ward and Mr. Rowe had gone into Serampore to preach at the Danish chapel—the hour was at seven o'Clock—the Danish Governour[21] generally attended. Serampore is under the care and government of the King of Denmark: on which account the Serampore missionaries have enjoyed so much tranquility. He said that the Hon.ble Company, governing the rest of Bengal, had dropped their prejudices against the missionaries:[22] and he hoped that er'e long they would abolish the cruel sacrifices practiced by the natives. When they took the country, they were stimulated by no such motives as actuated Mahomet or the crusades—but resolved to let every man enjoy what religion his conscience dictated, and had promised to protect them in the enjoyment of their rites—this does very well when human life is not made to fall a sacrifice to idolatrous superstitions.

The Governour of India, Lord Moira, resides just opposite Serampore, on the bank of the Hoogly, which flows between the

---

[21] Col. Jacob Krefting governed the Danish colonial city-state of Frederiksnagore (Serampore) on the western bank of the Hooghly from 1805–1828.

[22] Parliament's Charter Act of 1813 renewed the East India Company's rule in India for twenty years and ended its commercial monopoly over Indian trade except for tea and opium. The company retained its monopoly over all trade with China. The Act stipulated that the Company should take a greater role in educating Indian people and included so-called "pious clauses" allowing missionaries to arrive and work in India. That provision enabled Charlotte to freely enter India in 1816 whereas the Judsons and Newells had faced expulsion upon their 1812 arrival in Calcutta.

two Governments.[23] It is fourteen miles from Calcutta, which is also on the other side of the river from Serampore. The Governor's Lady, the Countess of Lowden,[24] is a very pious woman, and has done much toward promoting true religion in the East. She is a friend to schools, for both the natives and half-natives. Their little daughter, now eleven years of age[25] is, the Dr. says, a prodigy in Piety and talent. She is particularly fond of St. John's Gospel, and one day told her father that she intended to versify it; stating the blessed advantages of the Christian faith, and how it is to be obtained. She is now gone to England with her mother. Before she went, she expressed a wish to [29] leave her father a Remembrance, and to that effect composed a Poem on the Beatitudes, and presented it to him. The Dr. expressed much joy for so promising an Instrument of grace. He says also, that he is much pleased with the domestic habits of the Governor and the Gentlemen who compose his family. Dr. Carey promises us the pleasure of going over to view the Governor's grounds, which contain a great variety of animals and birds.

The Doctor touched on the subject of his son Felix. When Felix lost his family in the river he felt keenly for him.[26] He closed the

---

[23] I.e., between the British and Danish colonial governments. Lord Moira was Francis Rawdon (1754–1826), the Earl of Moira who would become the First Marquess of Hastings and hence Lord Hastings in 1817. He fought for the Crown in the American Revolutionary War and in France before serving as Governor General of India from 1813–1823.

[24] Flora Mure-Campbell (1780–1840), Marchioness of Hastings and 6th Countess of Loudoun.

[25] Flora Elizabeth Rawdon-Hastings (1806–1839).

[26] Burma's King Bodawpaya had summoned Felix Carey to move from Rangoon to the capital city, Amarapura, and to relocate the mission's two printing presses there. In August 1814 Felix, his second wife N. (Blackwell) Carey, and their two young children, William and Eliza Frances Carey, proceeded up the Irrawaddy River. During the journey a sudden squall capsized their boat. Only Felix escaped. His wife and children drowned, and his household goods and the two printing presses were lost. Charlotte and the Houghs had sailed to Calcutta en route to Burma to get another printing press and type that William Carey was donating to replace the lost presses.

subject by saying, that when afflictions come by the hand of God, he could bow to them with happy submission; but when they occur from man's own wickedness, they are more difficult to reconcile.

Dr. Carey's present wife, a Danish lady of high rank,[27] adopted the infant of the first wife, which was left motherless; and his other daughter lives with Mrs. Marshman.[28] Mrs. Carey is eminent for fine sense and warm piety. She is much afflicted in her own person, with ill health, but has been fortunate in obtaining in Dr. C. a man of feeling and regard to her infirmities. He takes her in his arms and brings her down stairs to place her in her little bath chair drawn by a bearer—and when she returns from her ride, he is ready to take her up and carry her up stairs again, and lay her gently on her couch. She lies there, reads or knits thread stockings; and is allways [sic] ready to sympathize in the most endearing manner with all who go to her to tell their sorrows. When her husband has finished his day's work, and comes to take his cup of tea beside her, she entertains him in the most intelligent manner. Indeed, he has said that he married her for the refinement [of] her understanding. They were married, I was told, as she lay on the sofa, unable at that time to sit up, on account of Rheumatism or some bodily weakness which often makes her lame.[29]

---

[27] William Carey's first wife Dorothy (Plackett) Carey died December 8, 1807. On May 9, 1808, he married Charlotte Emilia Rumohr, a Danish woman who lived at Serampore and was a friend of the mission.

[28] Charlotte is referring to the daughters of Felix Carey and his first wife, Margaret "Peggy" (Kinsey) Carey. Dorothea "Dolly" Carey was one month old and Lucy Carey was three years old when their mother Margaret died on December 22, 1808. Dorothea was adopted by Charlotte (Rumohr) Carey. Lucy went to live with Hannah and Joshua Marshman. Hunt, *Prisoner of Hope*, xiv.

[29] Charlotte Emilia Rumohr (1761–1821) was born in the Danish Duchy of Schleswig. Illness starting in her childhood forced her to seek a warmer climate in Italy after which she moved to India. She met William Carey in Serampore where she had built a house. "Memoir of Mrs. Carey," October 1822, 361–365.

Mr. Ward and Mr. Yates go out among the natives to talk and reason with them concerning the Truth. They seat themselves under a tree, where the natives come to them, for they are accustomed to do reverence [30] to *their* gods, "under every green tree" and there they hear, in their own language, strange things, and hard to be believed by them, because they enforce the doctrine of "truth in the inward parts" and purity of life.

I was much delighted with what I heard in Calcutta. Accounts had recently been received from the Island of Java, of the very favorable reception given to Mr. Spratt by the Governor of that Island; whose term of office being nearly expired, and expecting to be shortly succeeded by another, freely essayed to do all the good he could to the missionary cause, before he left his station. He gave a parcel of ground on which to erect an Establishment for missions, and with it gave materials for building, and set men to work at it; allowing several thousand Rupees to carry it on!

The Government of the Island of Amboyna[30] sent to Calcutta, soliciting for a missionary, which was the reason Jabez Carey went thither. He was in a Lawyer's office at the time the request came, but offered himself for the missionary service, having for some time endeavored himself to be a hopeful Christian.

Our Ship's Gentlemen called to see us last evening, on their way up the river to some factories, where they expect to get articles of trade. Mr. Marshman was very interrogative on political subjects relative to America.

½ past 12 o'Clock. Attended public worship at the Mission Chapel on the Mission premises. It is a long building, one high storey, containing a large hall for public worship, and many rooms for other purposes. Mr. Hough preached. Shook hands with, and spoke in English to five native females, who are converted from idolatry & have married soldiers. They said in English, "God bless you." I felt and uttered a reciprocal ejaculation. Several old gentlemen in Military attire, and a stranger, were present, beside the mission family.

---

[30] Ambon Island, part of the Maluku Islands of Indonesia.

This day have I beheld the desire of my Eyes, a Congregation of Hindoos listening to the gospel, preached to them in their own language.

[31] How devoutly (and it was a blessed feast to my Soul) did my heart go up in prayer to God, for the illuminations of his grace, on their benighted Souls! while they heard the venerable Dr. Carey. Oh, how my spirit pleaded with the Father to hearken and reward the prayers and exhortations of that beloved labourer for Souls. "Bless the Lord O *my* Soul, for this day, and the comforts of it! It is the first spent in a gospel manner, since I left my native shore—how precious do the privileges of religion feel to us, after so long a privation of all but secret prayer. Grace in the heart, produces a visible distinction in the countenances of men: it is nowhere more conspicuous than amongst these natives; any of them on becoming converts to the religion of Christ, may be distinguished from the others. They cast away either the hard look, or sneaking disguise, which they wore in their countenances before. The Christian religion seems to lower the proud and raise the low to a level, at least in decency and modest frankness. These sit quietly (but on the floor as is their custom) with their attention called within them—while those who still retain their cast, but come also to hear, sit looking eagerly all around them.

Ram Rattan,[31] a native convert, is a princely looking man. He had a little child with him, and was very fatherly. He with *Sissoo Ram*, met Dr. Carey while I was walking with him in the garden, the first morning after I arrived here, and as the latter had some particular business with the Doctor, they walked on before, while the former walked with me; and as he could hold no other conversation with me, he gathered fragrant flowers and put them into my hands. They make free to shake hands with me. In this man's former

---

[31] Ram Ratan (Rattan) was of the Kyast (Kayastha) or "writer's caste." William Carey baptized him in April 1808 along with Carey's son William. William Ward took Ram Ratan and Krishna Prasad, the first Brahmin whom Carey baptized early in 1808, on an itinerant preaching tour as far as Mudnabati and Dinajpur. Carey, *William Carey*, 235, 236, 238.

state of belief, he would have esteemed it an indignity to be asked to offer a flower to a *female*—nay, to any but his Goddess, as flowers bestrew the river's brink.

The wives of some of the native converts attended worship at an earlier hour, in the young Ladies' Room. [32] Thus the poor, injured, depressed females of the East, are beginning to emerge from their darkness and seclusion. They were all of them clad in unbleached coarse cotton, which gave them a dirty appearance. Several yards of this cast about their bodies, compose skirt, gown, mantle and veil. Some of them had their infants with them.

My mind was feasted tonight with a Sermon from Dr. Carey. O how pleasant it is, to be no longer restrained in a Ship. My thoughts can once more ascend on columns of vocal praise. My Eye can now unlock its fonts, at hearing the sacred word of prophecy. Tex. Isa. 51.

Dr. Carey's aviary is a space between two buildings wired like a cage on the open sides, and is as large as a room. It contains some hundreds of birds, of all colours and note, but of course no carnivorous ones among them. It is emblematical of the whole missionary family as it appears to me.

Serampore May 3rd. [1816].

This date I received a letter from Mr. Joshua Rowe, making proposal of marriage. This evening held my first interview with him on the subject. I was much surprised at receiving such a letter, on so short an acquaintance with him, for I had had very little conversation with him at any time, and never had received any pointed attentions from him. He informs me, that it is the desire of the brethren to detain me amongst them. That a field of usefulness is before me here, which I might not find at Rangoon, for a long time. I could only hear what he had to say—and resolved on making Dr. Carey my counselor in the affair. I thought I could rely on what *he* might advise, or dissuade from.

There seems to be something providential in it. There being no time to trifle away as Mr. & Mrs. Hough will go to Rangoon by the first vessel that will take passengers, and I must shortly determine whether of the two I shall choose, to go with them to the place where man has destined me, or to go with Mr. R. where God seems to have left a field waiting for me to cultivate.

[33] About ten o'Clock, this morning I went in a gig with Mr. John Marshman, to see Juggernaut in his temple.[32] O horrour! Stupidity! I saw the great, many-wheeled car, in which he is to ride to visit his brother!! "Come blest Religion, heavenly fair" and shew to man, otherwise rational, *thy* Reason, Truth, purity, and Symplicity [sic]—Come tarry thou not!

We walked round the car, and viewed as we passed, the paintings on it. They are all designed to excite lude [sic] ideas, in order to stimulate the people to perform such rites before their God! Serampore contains 22,000 inhabitants, most of whom are natives—how vast then, is the stream of iniquity amongst this people. And this is but a corner where the like exists.

Some of the wealthy natives have erected decent houses on the street in Serampore. The respectability which the Europeans maintain has a good effect on the native population. And the disgust which they uniformly express at Idolatry, has the effect of making the richer part of the native population ashamed of it.

While we were at Juggernaut's temple, hundreds came to pay their evening sacrifice to him. When they got near the middle of the yard, they went down on their knees, putting both hands together flat, and touching them to their forheads [sic], bowed themselves down quite to the dust. In the temple sat Juggernaut and his brother

---

[32] The main temple for Jagannath (meaning "Lord of the Universe" and anglicized as Juggernaut) was at Puri in Orissa. The second largest Jagannath temple was built in the fourteenth century at the village of Mahesh near Serampore. Large crowds came to Serampore to see Jagannath pulled through the streets atop a forty-five-foot-tall wooden car with sixteen wooden wheels.

and sister, in a row opposite the door, which we were not allowed to enter. On the pavement were dishes and servers of Fruit, such as watermelon, custard-apple, cocoa-nut, mangos, and fragrant flowers, which the *proprietors* of the temple had set in evening sacrifice.

These men grow rich, imposing just what taxes they please on those who arrive at festival times to worship. O how my heart saddened to see them. But to believe them to be objects of worship by beings called *men*, ah, I cannot express, my feelings. The Grand Juggernaut is at Orissa.

Serampore being under the Danish Gov^t^. the Governor general of *Serampore*, resides there. He is very polite to the missionaries, and sometimes goes to his Chapel to hear them preach in English. There is a Portuguese Catholic church at Serampore.

[34] A few evenings ago, as we walked, we met him, (the governor) in his Palanquin, borne by four half-naked bearers (a sight familiar to us now) four other bearers following behind, for the purpose of relieving the others, at about every quarter of a mile. Six grooms, clad in white, with white turbans, and long staves, silvered over, in their hands, ran before him, to clear the way. Every thing must give way, the populace jump on each side, as a matter of course.

A lady may *walk* at Serampore, without disgrace, when the sun has set; as then others go out to take the air, in various ways. This is the city of refuge for Malefactors on the other side of the River, under the Government of England.[33]

Yesterday we went over the River to see the park and grounds of "His Lordship," the governor of India. His residence stood full in view from the mission house. We [saw] birds of beautiful as well as of curious kinds; an ostrich as large as a pony; and all kinds of parrots, and a bird larger than a parrot which talks and screams like a

---

[33] When the East India Company objected to the unauthorized presence of British Baptist missionaries in India, they found refuge in the Danish enclave of Serampore. The Danish governor, Norwegian-born Col. Ole Bie, protected their right to live in Serampore against the demands of the British governor general.

parrot, some of which are white, other mixed with bright colours—this bird they call the Kuckatooah. There were the Hyena, Sloth-bear, Succatory [sic] Cow, Elephants, Royal tigers, Leopards, a porcupine, and a variety of monkeys—one of which was attended by a bearer like a child; he set it down and went some distance from it, and it opened its arms and walked up to him like a child, fearful of its steps, making a most hidious [sic] screaming. Two Lyons also, a male and female, but not of the largest size. They were kept in buildings having bars in front; a tyger [sic] put his paw through once and caught hold of a man's arm, and tore it badly,

While we were walking about the grounds, "His Lordship" rode by—he looked very affably and bowed. His style was similar to "his Danish Lordship's" but more gaudy, and having attendants behind in his train.

May 4th. [1816].

Rose early and met Dr. Carey in the garden while at his plants, which he watches with parental care and fondness. Took an opportunity of broaching the subject of Mr. Rowe's letter to me. He gave me the most satisfactory character of Mr. Rowe, saying that both himself and the brethren would be pleased to have a union take place. He said he had felt much on my account, being destined to Rangoon. [35] That there I should not be useful in the way I wished, for a long time. That though his heart was much fixed on the Burman Mission, affairs relative to it at present were not such as would render me happy. That he hoped I would not keep Mr. Rowe long in suspense, but use the candor befitting christians. He said, he wished me to consider him as desiring my real welfare, and that I would consult him on all subjects wherein I felt any difficulty or required advice. That he should always feel it a pleasure to inform me. Then resuming the subject of the proposed union, he said, I must not expect to find excellence without faults on earth. He considered it providential he said, that Mr. R. should have come down the river from Digah, 400 miles, just at this time, both on his account, and mine. And that he hoped a union between Mr. R. and myself, would prove a subject of joy to the latest period of our lives, which he had no doubt would be the case, if we both exercised the discretion and forbearance becoming married people.

Having thus satisfactorily discovered the sentiments of my newly adopted father & friend, I resolved to obey his advice, and confirm my willingness to accept the hand of Mr. Rowe in marriage. He is a widower with three little sons,[34] all of whom accompanied him on his visit here. The eldest of the three is nine years old. They are noiseless, and pallid—showing little of the energy of sprightliness common with little boys of this age. Docility appears to be the prominent feature in their character, at present. I have always felt an aversion to connecting myself with a family of children—but these little boys are so mild, and have passed their screaming age, that I feel very little repugnance on that score. A domestic field of usefulness is opened, in them; and according to what now lies before me, I have three distinct vineyards to cultivate: as a school of half-European and full-European together, are waiting the arrival of a Governess to supply the place of the Mrs. Rowe who deceased two years ago at Digah.[35]

May 10th. [1816].

I think God has had some more extended design in bringing me to India, than only to make an [36] individual happy. I hope it may result in His glory, who brings about events, at his pleasure.

My soul has cause to bless his name, for his goodness, in bringing me amongst christians of distinguished character—the Baptist Society for promoting foreign missions. I have *changed* nothing in my profession, but place of destination. Mr. Rowe was ordained in England by Dr. Ryland, and set apart for this foreign mission. He

---

[34] Joshua Rowe's sons were Joshua (age nine), William (age seven), and Josiah (age six).

[35] Elizabeth (Noyes) Rowe died at Digah on October 19, 1814 after giving birth to Elizabeth Maria Rowe. Joshua Rowe, "Extract," 294.

studied Divinity with Mr. Sutcliff. He married a pious orphan,[36] both being very young, and they embarked to India, in 1803 or four, in company with three other missionaries and their wives, Messrs. Moore, Mardon & Biss. The Embargo being on at that time, they were obliged to go by the way of America where thy passed one winter.[37] Mr. and Mrs. Rowe, were hospitably entertained at the houses of Mr. Caldwell[38] and others at New York, where they boarded and remained until they took passage again for India. It is a subject of some gratatation [sic] with us that I became acquainted with the same amiable family the summer before I left America while in New York, expecting to set sail from thence. We can talk of many persons whom we both knew while we were quite unknown to each other. We seem to unite in thinking that a particular providence has brought *us* together.

I have been much occupied with male manteau-makers, having greatly to encrease [sic] my stock of white gowns, as no one can wear anything else nine months of the year here, and a clean dress *must* go on every day in order go look clean and be sweet. I thought I had a sufficiency to serve me any where, when I left America—but though I may have *gowns* enough, they are such as cannot be worn, or cannot be borne, in this sultry clime. Everything colored that in America admits of washing, is so discoloured here by the use of lime water, in washing, that nothing but pure white will serve. Men & women, boys and girls, as well as the natives, all wear white. I am glad I had even as many as I brought, for had I not, I must have borrowed before I could either get clothes from the wash or have

---

[36] Elizabeth Noyes.

[37] The East India Company refused to grant licenses to Baptist missionaries to sail on their ships from England to India.

[38] The Biss family and their missionary colleagues (the Rowes, Moores, and Mardons) had circumvented the East India Company's travel embargo by sailing from England to India via the United States. Hannah Biss gave birth to Deborah Cauldwell Biss in New York at the Cauldwell home in 1804. John Cauldwell was serving as the first treasurer of the Baptist Board of Foreign Missions when Charlotte was appointed as a missionary in 1815.

new ones made us.

[37] Mr. Rowe demands my company of evenings, together with the mission family, consequently, I find little time to write. But without taking time to date, I may clap down a few sentences, at intervals of being alone.

This country contains the greatest variety of flowering *trees*, and flowering bushes, and sweet-leafed shrubs, that I ever before met with. The flowers which adorn the beds or borders of walks, are larger and gayer, but not so fragrant as ours—but some of the trees & shrubs send forth gales of odours. The birds chatter from morn till morn again. I could gladly dispense with the squeaking of the Vultures at midnight, and the cawing of the crows every hour like geese; but when the day begins to dawn when birds' eyes first discern it, there is a general awakening of these birds of prey, and then farewell sleep! Indeed, they may be thought kind messengers from Aurora to rouse the sleepers to enjoy the exhalations of morn, rising from the expiration of the dampness on the surrounding herbage. No perceptible dew falls during these hot months. Yet the absence of the Sun during the night refreshes parched nature, and gives coolness to the latter end of night.

The fruits are bewitching at this season. The mango especially, which affords food and delight to the thirsty palate. Strangers are cautioned against indulging in them to the degree that the older inhabitants may safely do. Some of the trees yield a fruit as large as a nutmeg melon, the same form, but of a smooth rind, and having brown stones through it. This they boil or roast like potatoes, and it eats much like them—They call it *bread*-fruit. Other trees yield drink, as the palm tree and some others, which is tapped at the top of the tree, not as our maple trees are, by cutting the bark anywhere. Scions[39] grow from the top, which they cut at the end, and tie to the mouth of an earthen pot. During one night, it exudes a quart—and if taken at four o'clock in the morning, is like soda water; but it soon

[39] Scions: young shoots or twigs.

becomes first sour, then intoxicating, and is the only [38] arrack used by tipplers and soldiers here. Thus has God provided for a country where animal provisions are scarce, and if indulged in as in Europe or America, would be injurious. There is a great variety of vegetables, of a description I never before saw—but I am told, that in the winter so called, European vegitables [sic] are plenty. Fish is obtainable, but no oysters. I opened my last barrel of oysters this morning and sent a plate full to each of the families of this happy compact, as a treat at breakfast. They are now very fine indeed, not tasting so salt and briny as at sea. Oysters put up like these; and Dr. Allison's Lemon Acid, should be highly recommended to voyagers.[40] I found them very refreshing as well as healthful, at sea.

Little Sally Hough has taken the summer complaint and is now very thin. This is a sad climate to *bring children* into. The heat on the sunny side of the house is oppressive; but there is generally a cool draft through some part of the house, let in by wet mats on the outside of some doors or windows. They supply the moisture to the air, which the heat destroys: and sometimes too much of it, gives colds to the inmates.

Through the negligence or sleepiness of the family Watchman, last night, the Jackals got into the poultry house, and killed 38 ducks 4 geese, and 2 rabbits. He will have to refund the market price for them out of his wages, to make him more careful.

It is very wrong to represent this nation as deficient of common capacity. They are capable of all the arts both good and bad, that most other nations are. As to the bad arts, we have to thank the Christian religion, inducing better conduct, that we are not as deeply practiced in them. Why then, may they not, by the same means,

[40] Dr. N. S. Allison's Pure Lemon Acid was a patent medicine available from New York to Mississippi. Philadelphia newspaper ads claimed the Lemon Acid retained its qualities for years and was "particularly advantageous to persons travelling or riding any distance from sea port towns." "N. S. Allison & Co.," *United States Gazette*, May 5, 1813, 8.

undergo as great a reverse? If education were as much esteemed by them as by us, there would soon be a visible reformation. I view them as a nation differing from my own only in point of complexion and Religious instruction.

[39] Dr. Carey is of [the] opinion, that marriages should take place between Coloured people and the White people. He does not mean the Africans, but the Asiatics, and the white. He does not think there is any in the Bengalees to forbid the marriage alliance taking place with the English. The latter come very near it, but escape the alliance Dr. Carey alludes to.[41] Dr. Carey and others abhor slavery—there is no such thing between Europeans and Asiatics; a few natives are held as slaves by their fellow natives, from being bought as a charity from indigent parents, who offered their children for a morsel of bread.[42] The Americans are reprobated here, for keeping up the slave trade. No one abjures it more sincerely than I do. And I am happy in being able to inform them, that a slave from

---

[41] Carey advocated that British men should marry Indian or Anglo-Indian women rather than keep mistresses or concubines. By the mid-1700s with encouragement from the East India Company, an estimated 80% of British men in India had such marriages. In the 1790s several governors general began reversing the Company's intermarriage policy in order to create social distance between rulers and the ruled. This fostered increasing British prejudice against Indian and Anglo-Indian people. Hyam, *Empire and Sexuality*, 115–117.

[42] Charlotte had been in India less than two months and could not have been fully knowledgeable about slavery in India. Governor General Charles Cornwallis (whose surrender to George Washington at Yorktown had ended the American Revolution) had prohibited the *export* of slaves from the Calcutta Presidency in 1789. The *importation* of slaves into the Presidency was banned in 1811. A correspondent to the *Bengal Chronicle* in 1831 wrote, "That slavery exists in Calcutta is a fact too notorious to be denied. Slaves of both sexes are generally purchased from indigent Hindoo and Hindoostani mothers. A young girl will bring according to her age and usefulness from 16 up to 100 rupees." Not until the India Slavery Act of 1843 (a.k.a. Act V) was slavery abolished *within* India. Richard Allen, "Suppressing a Nefarious Traffic," 873–894; Stark, *Hostages to India*, 130.

a Southern state, is a free man the moment he puts his foot on Pennsylvania ground. I would not have my native state cast under the *odium* of encouraging slavery.[43] I was happy to inform him also that the Africans enjoyed equal privileges with ourselves—and that there were congregations of them in our state, of every denomination; and that a Bishop resided at Philadelphia, a very venerable man.[44]

Lord's day evening, May 11th. [1816].

Pleasing prospects, and exemption from wrankling emotions, have not the effect upon me which I desire. My heart should bound with holy love, and thankfulness, and my religious fervour [sic] should increase. But altho' I am in a measure grateful, and ascribe all my blessings to God, beholding with wonder, the way he has led me, and his dealings with me; yet my love to *Him* is too cold. I remember the expanding desires which I felt when first I experienced religion—when I was convinced of renewing grace in my own Soul, to declare to all both near and afar off, the mercies which are treasured up in Christ—and I longed for the opportunity of making them known to those who had no opportunity of knowing them: and to rouse those who had read and heard of them but disregarded them. But *the woman*, prevented me. Now I find myself [40] in reality, in the circumstances I craved where *the woman* is herself; called on to

---

[43] Pennsylvania was the first state to pass a law to abolish slavery. The 1780 Act for the gradual Abolition of Slavery clearly stipulated that it was to be a *gradual* abolition. Children born to enslaved mothers were to be set free at age twenty-eight. Enslaved people remained so for life if their status was registered before November 1, 1780. Charlotte may not have known that in 1780, two years before her birth, her father William Augustus Atlee had registered two enslaved people: forty-year-old Peggy, to be enslaved for life and eight-year-old Moses, a servant "for about four years to come" who was a slave for life owned by George or Francis Sanderson. Register of Negroe & Mulatto Slaves & Servants, LancasterHistory Museum; Turner, "The Abolition of Slavery in Pennsylvania," 129–142.

[44] Bishop Richard Allen (1760–1831), founder and first bishop of the African Methodist Episcopal Church.

take a labouring part in the Lord's vineyard. I am happy, here to reflect on the birth of such feelings in my heart, nine years before the opportunity of gratifying them would be afforded me.

Arose early this morning, and with my Friend,[45] and several young Ladies of Mrs. Marshman's family, went to the Danish church to hear our dear Dr. Carey. I feel delight in hearing him pray and preach; he speaks with so much earnestness, and clearness of reasoning. He stands up and addresses the audience as if in conversation with friends. Mr. R. observed to me as we walked homeward, that he considered him the most eminently good and useful man now living, in the Christian world. He is very plain in his dress; and peculiarly so in his manners, not seeming to wish to form new acquaintances; but a little familiar conversation proves him to be a sincere man: and at times he is very jocose. The missionaries take turns on Lord's Day afternoon, to preach to the Bengallees, in their native language.

They have now assembled in the Mission Chapel or hall for evening family worship. While I write I hear the sound of sacred singing (I cannot call it music) from their lips; but to my Soul's ear, it is the sweetest music I ever heard. O that the Lord would excite the hearts of this benighted nation to seek Him; and send them "like doves to their windows" eager to find a shelter from the dangers of superstition, in the blessed Gospel of Jesus Christ!

The native women take my hand, such of them as have embraced Christ, and looking up to heaven, say, "God bless you." They are told my errand hither. Some of them have learned a few words of English, but no one of them could hold any conversation with me.

My expected change of destination, will preclude my going on with the Burman language. I shall have to acquire the Hindee or Hindoostanee. Dr. Carey says that the Hindee is the Dialect spoken

---

[45] Joshua Rowe.

by the Bramins, because it is the original language of the Hindoos [41] and partakes of the Sanscrit, which they deem the most holy language—The Hindoostani is the Hindee, mingled with Persian words, owing to the Mahometan's having introduced so much of the Persian and Arabic, from Arabia and Persia. This latter dialect is considered the most elegant, and is spoken throughout Bombay as well as Hindostan. The Bengalee partakes largely also of the Sanscrit or *Shungscrit.*

Dr. Carey has formed a grammar of the latter, but he says it can afford me no assistance in acquiring the Hindostani; and there is no grammar extant in that language, in the native character. Gilchrist has published some sort of a grammar of it, but in the English character, which may give me some idea of the language. He says that the Hindostani language is fit only for a horse—In fact, that it is no language. Well, it is the language spoken at Digah, which now appears to be my place of Destination, and I must learn it, be it what it may. If I should be so ingenious as to acquire such a knowledge of it, as to enable me to converse freely in it, and teach our pure religion to the heathen children, I shall be sufficed, and the language will be good enough, that can convey the knowledge of Jesus Christ to them. In this, I have an agreeable task before me.

How wonderful seem the leadings of providence! It seems, that I must needs have come hither. Mr. R. was standing on the bank of the river near the mission bungalow at Digah, one evening, when a boat for passengers came up close under the bank, to moor for the night. He called to the chief boatman, and enquired if the boat was now in service, he instantly resolved to engage it, to take him and his family to Calcutta. In two days he was ready to embark, and arrived at Serampore in two weeks. He was induced to take the trip, in expectation of meeting, about that time, a lady of his youthful acquaintance from England, to whom [42] he had, by means of writing to friends in England, made proposals of marriage, and solicited [her] to come to India to him. He reached Serampore a few days before we did, and I had been there nine days, when a letter arrived, informing him of the Lady's marriage some time since. He is pleased to say, that he felt much relieved by the intelligence, as he had felt himself in honour bound to marry her, should she have come. Being thus set at liberty, he lost no time in trying to secure the hand of one whom he had observed, but [to] whom [he] could shew no particular attention, on account of the dilemma he laboured under.

His three little boys have learned to regard me as their future mother, and follow me when I go to walk in the garden with their father.

Mrs. Marshman extols the Digah station, for its healthiness, and the abundance of every thing to be had there, as well as the fruits in the gardens, &cc. and tries to make me expect a pleasant retreat. She made a visit there when grapes were last in season.

Mr. R. and myself design going to Calcutta in a few days to prepare for our Nuptials. I am much engaged in various ways. Mr. R. has brought me a piece of glazed country muslin, of which the morning dress for that day is to be made; the evening dress is to be plain mul-mul muslin. I may not write much more for some days.

Calcutta, May 15. [1816].

I ought to style myself the happiest woman in the world. A mere exemption from the anxieties I used to feel at sea, would have been a felicity; but to be connected with so distinguished a brotherhood, as the English Baptist missionaries are, may be felt a positive happiness, since everyone of them male and female, smile satisfaction when they press my hand. These privileges were indeed totally unexpected when I was at Sea, yet they were earnestly prayed for. I think I find in my friend, a sweet congeniality of mind. Yet I am not such a novice in [43] a friendship of this kind, as to imagine the present seeming, perpetual congeniality, will always exist. When the courtier becomes the husband, he assumes a different character—I do not say, I would not infer, a character less promotive of the real happiness of a wife. He acknowledges that he esteems me as the gift of God to him, in answer to many prayers.

Well, I am telling secrets, but I should say the same were I holding a *personal* interview with my dear brother Edwin, whom I always have in my mind's view, whenever I take my pen to write in my Diary. If we meet no time else, it is when pen and paper commence chatting. I give my thoughts as freely to thee, my dear Edwin, as the pen gives the thought-engraving-liquor, to the paper, the fair paper, which speaks me no guile.

The road from Serampore down the river to Calcutta, is a turnpike or terrace of pounded brick. A row of trees on each side, convert[s] it to a pleasant avenue, all through. The river is crossed in a ferry boat. The country is a perfect level as far as the eye can reach; and at present rather barren, the crops being taken up. I discern no fences dividing fields here. The only obstacles to incursion, as a deep ditch on one side, with the earth thrown up, on the other, but mostly a foot-path a little raised. Nearer the houses, a green myrtle, or thorn hedge, keeps off intruders. There seem to be no trees but what are for domestic use. Their foliage partakes of different shades of green, and brown. In our ride we passed a native village, a bazaar for hay, another for cattle, small ones for fruit, &c. The drays and carts are poor little things with thick, wooden wheels, no iron in all the vehicle. They are drawn by lean white cattle or bullocks. Small cattle carry great stacks of straw. Native travellers ride in a little thing like a covered cart, driving a pony three feet high, lashing it along, with at least three adults [44] in the *hackney* so called. The poor little animal shows every rib, and looks so sorry as if it is was heart-broken. Indeed, it is enough to break the heart of both a *man* and such a beast, to see it—but they who ride, are neither man nor beast—they are void of the "tender mercy" which should distinguish a man from a four-footed animal, and also of the human instinct peculiar to beasts towards *their* fellow beasts.

Europeans are very careful of their horses, not allowing one horse to take them more than five or seven miles, before they change him. The heat overcomes them. Indeed, the case now seems reversed, for the groom who always follows his master, runs all the way, while the horse is relieved—he, however, can bear the heat better than a fine, full-fed horse.

We have never been left to go to a boarding house, the missionaries are so hospitable. Eustace Carey's house is my home when in Calcutta.

I shall now give a description of a morning spent in *the garden* at Serampore, or Dr. Carey's garden.— I had learned to improve the dawn of day in the open air, and used to take my ramble about the garden before I was intimately acquainted with Mr. R. And after that, the garden was the scene of our walks. He usually woke me by calling below my window: but *one* morning I got into the garden before him. I usually took a pocket volume with me, and being yet alone in that part of the garden near the gate, I stepped a few steps down into the tank descent, and sat on the dry stone reading, intending to be seen by Mr. R. should he come into the garden. I had not sat many minutes, when I heard him quite near, singing. He walked by not seeing me, and I rose and walked after him, but his steps being quicker and larger than mine, he got quite out of my view, as he turned the walks behind the bushes. He walked the whole garden through, and I in search of him, often like the hare turning a nearer path in order to meet him.

[45] Not finding me, he went to my room window and called, but had no answer. By this time I had reached the greenhouse in the garden where I found Dr. Carey busily engaged with his plants, setting some inside and some outside, both himself & a gardener examining each plant; and preparing pots for fresh seed. I began to think it might have been Dr. Carey whom I heard, and partly saw, and therefore inquired if he had been long in the garden! "O dear yes, an hour and a half." I then took another path, but he whom I sought was not to be found.

We did not meet until after morning family worship, when we had no little mirth in explaining the affair. This anecdote may give you the best idea of the extent and boweryness [sic] of our Eastern garden. Every morning the paths are strewed with flowers from the higher trees and shrubs. In the Serampore mission house garden are four *tanks* or reservoirs of water. They appear to be about forty feet square each. They are dug in the four quarters of the garden, for the purpose of supplying it with water for the benefit of the plants. The gardeners dip it up, and overflow the beds, which [are] so made as to lie below the level of the garden, for the purpose of retaining the water during the night. During the rainy season, these tanks get filled with water, and it continues sweet for months, the ground being saturated, replenishes the water as it is drawn out, until the moisture within that depth is expanded by evaporation. They are never quite dry, but become unfit for animal use. In many parts of the interior, water is not to be found, except in tanks, & wells.

May 22nd. [1816].

On Monday last, the Lord saw fit that I should be afflicted with a sudden and severe attack of Dysentary. I had been cautioned against indulging in too much fruit—but my passion for it in this sultry clime, was difficult to controll, [sic] so long as I felt no ill effects from it. I was fond of laving my palate with it, in the morning before I dressed: and thus receiving too much and on an empty stomach, disordered it. I receive this shock, as a warning to my future indulgence in mangoes [46] especially, as they contain an exuberance of sweet and acid juice. It is peculiar, that in a plateful, no two taste exactly alike, each partaking of various flavour. They are like nothing but green or yellow goose-eggs, as the children colour them at Easter time, pull off a thick skin, and a yellow, juicy pulp covers a large kernel. The natives plant orchards of this fruit, which are left open for the enjoyment of travellers, but the fruit is generally owned by proprietors, and is watched over when nearly ripe. The boughs of the trees meet throughout the grove, affording a delightful shelter from the Sun beams.

The prickly heat on my skin begins to irritate me. This is the only inconvenience I feel from the heat: it affects one more generally, and is more angry than what is common to delicate skins in summer in America.

Mrs. Eustace Carey, at whose abode I still am, has administered both medicine and aliment to me, herself; and I owe it to her experience and tenderness, that I have so soon recovered from an attack of disease, which often proves fatal in this climate. I hope that when I am settled at Digah with my Joshua, I shall be able to make her some return. With what satisfaction would I attend to her dear sinking husband, who looks like a walking spectre. Last evening I was able to sit in the hall or *centre room*, at a prayer meeting. 36 persons were present, and some of *all* complexions. I feel no repugnance at mingling with the native Christians. I respect them as beloved fellow heirs of grace, and the natural and primeval proprietors of the country.

I regret to learn that Mrs. L.[46] when in America, received so little attention from my country women. Her husband is a very respectable European, and she & he are held in sincere regard by everybody who know them; and they are generally known, as he is a merchant, and a very benevolent man. Mrs. L. is always welcomed into polite circles, and scenes of affliction. Her complexion is not noticed, when once you are acquainted with her. But I pardon them in [47] part; since I know they are not accustomed to *Asiatic* faces. We should remember, that the Jews and Jesus Christ were Asiatics.

[46] This was Selemah F. Lindeman, wife of Peter Lindeman, an undertaker in Calcutta, who became serious after hearing the Gospel and "publicly married the native woman with whom he had cohabited for years." (December 11, 1804, Ward's Journal Mss, 400) Linderman was a close friend of the mission and a trustee of the Lall Bazar Chapel. The Baptist missionaries conducted their first Calcutta meetings in the Linderman house. Mrs Lindeman participated in prayer meetings with the missionary wives at her house. Peter and Selemah Lindeman sailed in February 1811 to England via Boston (February 14, 1811, Ward's Journal Mss, 747). They returned to India few years later. Thank you to Peter de Vries (Serampore College) for identifying "Mrs. L."

It is the loss of the knowledge of Christ, that has reduced this nation to idolatry. May the same Christ arise over it "with healing under his wings!"

This country raises wheat, rice, and kinds of pulse, in abundance; and some Indian corn and oats. The bread is beautifully white and light, baked by men whose profession it is: but they raise the dough with the sap of the Tarr or palm tree, which causes so great a fermentation as to expand the flavour of the wheat before it can be baked. The natives call the sap Tarree from which the English call it Toddy; which in our country, signifies a beverage made with spirits & water with an apple roasted and soaked in it. Thus *I* define the Tarr tree to be literally the *Beverage tree*, as the word may be interpreted by an American, such as I am.

Ram Mohun Roy, a rich Native, has a seat like a Nabob's (Nawaub) on the road to Serampore from hence. He is said to disapprove of Idolatry. Tis so far reformed from the Hindoo or Braminical faith, as to become an Unitarian.[47] It is said that he confesses himself to be a worm and a sinner—but cannot as yet admit the New Testament doctrine. He is charmed with some of the passages in Isaiah, calling them sublime. He has translated into Bengallee and English, such of the books of the Hindoo Shastre, as treat of the unity of the Godhead in oppositions to idols. It is now only requisite, that his heart be touched with a ray of divine light. To enable him to discern Christ, the begotten of God the Spirit, atoning for sin by the sacrifice of himself upon the cross.

Were a few such men to come to this belief, idolatry would rapidly grow unpopular. There is not yet one rich and influential native, turned from the errour [sic] of his way, and made it known. The

[47] Ram Mohun Roy (1772–1833) would influence British Baptist missionary William Adam to become a Unitarian missionary. Adam arrived in Calcutta on March 19, 1818. By 1821 he would become a Unitarian. "Arrival of the Rev. Messrs. Sutton and Adam," *The Friend of India* 1, May 1818, 19; Adam, *Correspondence,* 131; Hill, "William Adam"; Collet, *Life and Letters of Raja Rammohun Roy*, 67ff.

Lord is using [48] the weak things of the world to confound the mighty. The poor peasantry have begun to preach the everlasting gospel to their idolatrous brethren!

June 2nd. [1816.] Serampore.

My time is so much occupied in preparing necessary things to take to Digah, I have very little time to write. I pass from Calcutta to Serampore, as circumstances require; and expect soon to return there on a business in which my welfare is deeply concerned—I do not fear to take the step.

Lord's Day—This morning the Banns of our intended union were ordered to be published, by Mr. Rowe.

The Rev^{d}. Mr. Parsons,[48] Chaplain to the East India Company, and settled at Calcutta, is to pronounce them, in the Episcopal Cathedral. This is the mode to which all denominations of dissenters have to submit. They may purchase a lisence [sic] at a considerable expense, but they dare not be united in marriage, but by an Episcopal clergyman. No Baptist minister is allowed to perform the ceremony, as yet.

Mr. Rowe preached this morning at the mission Chapel, from Romans 8. v 7. He set the hymn from the pulpit. There is a pathos in his delivery which is very pleasing. xxx[49]

Here I sit in one of the rooms attached to the Chapel, my beloved Dr. Staughton's, brother Edwin's, and brother John's likenesses, hanging, and seeming to be witnesses of all I write. I often wish they knew my condition, "with not a wave of trouble crossing my breast": and were aware of my prospects in the future usefulness if health permit; of which I feel no apprehension, as I have passed through my seasoning to the Indian air and Diet. I have become very fond of rice and curry, so much so, that I prefer it to any dish presented. There were on table today at the mission house, a loin of

[48] Joseph Parsons (1780–1835) was a chaplain in the East India Company.

[49] The marks "xxx" are in the original.

veal roasted; a joint of Mutton; a Kid's-head pie; a piece of smoked flitch of bacon; a piece of roasted pork; a boiled fowl; a hash, [49] and curry; pea soup, potatoes, and pickles. For the desert we had peach-pie, an almond pudding; ripe mangoes, plantains, and plums, with various kinds of preserves—and a glass of wine. A little brandy in water, is recommended by physicians here, to bilious persons, porter to mothers who nurse their own children. The water of the river, being generally settled with a lime, is not very healthful to newcomers, and if the water stand long enough to settle without the aid of alum, it becomes unpleasant. The rivers here always flow muddy, owing to the Sand beds in the stream.

You must take into consideration, that there are a great many to partake of the above described table, and that one good loin of American veal would comprehend almost all the number of pounds weight of meat upon the table, animals being small here. While dining a man servant pulled the punka,[50] which gave air to three long tables side by side. The young ladies of Mrs. Marshman's school occupy the side tables. The smaller children dine in the next room, attended by the school Iahs.[51] Several men servants attend on the family tables. I am very agreeably surprized at finding such a plenty of good things in India.

While Mr. R. and myself were walking in the garden last evening, Dr. Carey approached us very smilingly and [brought] a gentleman up to us, saying to me, "I will present you one of your countrymen, Mr. Titcomb of Newburyport."[52] We expressed our

[50] Punka: a large fan suspended from the ceiling with an attached rope pulled by a servant.

[51] Ayah: an Indian woman serving as a children's nurse-maid or a ladies maid.

[52] Capt. Paul Titcomb was the supercargo on the brig *Dryad* on which Congregationalist missionaries had sailed to India. They wrote of him: "We already begin to experience painful sensations, at the thought of being

satisfaction at seeing each other, more distinctly than we could while passing at sea, he having been on board the *Dryade*. [sic] He has tarried to join in this days privileges, which affords us frequent opportunities of chatting about my relatives and other persons of our acquaintance in that town. As Mr. Marshman is a man of very general information, and very inquisitive of strangers concerning the state of religion and politics in their part of the world, it gave me pleasure to find that Mr. T. could satisfy his inquiries, which were rather [50] to be confirmed than informed.

Serampore. June 4th 1816.

I have been in the habit of noting some incidents as they transpire since my arrival in India, with a view to amuse my beloved brother, for whose perusal these sheets are intended.

Just returned from my morning walk with Mr. R. who comes to my venetian early every morning and says, "Charlotte, will you walk?" We meet the birds and odorous zephers at five o'clock, wither

---

separated from Mr. Titcomb, the supercargo; for, by his Christian familiarity, personal activity in all our meetings for prayer and religious conversation, and the deep interest he takes in the prosperity of our undertaking, he has almost become one of our number." Two years later, Capt. Titcomb would be the supercargo on the ship *Independence* on which American Baptist missionaries, Edward and Eliza Harriet (Newman) Wheelock and James and Elizabeth Williams (Hubbard) Coleman, would sail to Calcutta en route to Burma. *The American Baptist Magazine* noted that Titcomb was a Congregationalist who "evinced a noble superiority over those sectarian feelings which have so often kept pious men asunder from each other.... His knowledge of a sea life, and of what was suitable for missionaries destined for India, qualified him to assist us in making preparation for their outfit. He used his influence to obtain a passage for them as cheap as possible; and after our brethren had commenced their voyage, the same influence was employed in promoting their comfort, respectability and usefulness." Titcomb became ill after arriving in Calcutta in April 1818. He died aboard the *Independence* on its return to America and was buried at sea on July 30, 1818. "American Missionaries," 554; "Mission in Ceylon," 381; "Obituary," 78.

on the road by the river brink, or in the garden, This morning we walked a half mile down the river to an old deserted temple of Juggernaut. There is a wild flower hedge growing round it. Near it, is a Banian[53] tree, which is peculiar for its having long shoots like thick ropes, growing down from the branches. They hang down quite straight, seeking the ground, and when they reach it, take root and afford strength to the branch from which they sprung, growing on in thickness, until they become trees. Thus, the Banian would become an impervious family of trees, were their shoots to be allowed to take root in every instance. When they are tastefully pruned away, the tree becomes a tabernacle of arches, ever green and ready to afford shade to multitudes of people. If there is anything perennial on earth it is this tree. Native merchants sit and sell goods there, from which it has taken its name *Bania*, or as the English pronounce it Banian, a merchant.[54]

Beneath this natural Archade [sic], is a monument erected to the memory of some famous heathen; and at a little distance, a white temple dedicated to Seib (here bring drawing of a temple by Sir C[s]. Doyly).[55]

As we returned, we went into the old dwelling of the good Mr. Brown,[56] who deceased some time since, highly beloved by all who

---

[53] Alternate spelling for banyan tree.

[54] Banian: an Indian merchant negotiating trade between foreign buyers and local suppliers.

[55] Sir Charles D'Oyly (1781–1845) was born in Bengal to English parents. From 1808–1817 he was the East India Company's Collector in Dacca. He would become the City Collector of Customs in Calcutta (1818) and the Company's opium agent and commercial resident or tax collector in Patna (1821). He became known for his numerous drawings of Indian subject matter.

[56] David Brown (1763–1812) had been a Company chaplain at Fort William, pastor of the Old Mission Church in Calcutta, and a founder of the Calcutta Bible Society. In 1803 he bought and moved to Aldeen House in Serampore. The house became a meeting place for missionaries and evangelical chaplains. Carey, *Oriental Christian Biography*, 1:351.

knew him. Mr. R. sighed and said, "Here have I enjoyed many a pleasant breakfast with Christian friends." We went on the top of the house, which is flat throughout, and very spacious, commanding a fine view of the River Hoogly, and of Barrakpore immediately opposite to us, where Lord Moira, the governor of India, resides. It exhibits a continued settlement of fine houses along the bank, interspersed with green trees.

[51] As we walked home, we were amused with the conduct of the half-naked inhabitants; whose appearance is truly pristine. Women are carrying from the river, great earthen things of water which answer for jugs, but are greatly swelled and without a handle. They call these koojas. They tilt them first on their hip, and from thence, mount them on their heads. (here bring in the picture) They have rings on their wrists and arms, and ankles, and toes, and a large slender ring in their noses, as large as those put into a swine's nose, in America, to keep it from grubbing. The women are covered, when the let down their arms, but when they raise either arm, the waist is exposed to view. They are, at the same time so shy and *modest* that they draw the sheet down over their forheads [sic] as they pass a stranger. Don't lead my American sisters to conclude, that they are the only females who mistake what is true modesty. I have the happiness of knowing many there who do both comprehend and observe the distinguishing trait of female excellence.

Other natives are standing in the river waist deep, saying their prayers, touching themselves on the breast and forhead [sic], much as the Roman Catholics do. They perform the ablution of immersing themselves, after they have prayed to their thousand gods. Some, more distinguished amongst them, and of a statelier mien, wear a string of large beads, each bead having attached to it, the name of some god: if they touch each one of these, and look stedfastly [sic] either at the clouds or at the water, they have performed their round of prayers to as many presiding deities or departed fellow beings, by them deified. This is but Roman Catholicism *out of doors*. Others who are desirous of "a name to live" are sitting on a mat, reading a book which is very formally spread open before them on a brace. All this scene is at the river's brink. They are a nation of Pharisees, and at the same time, the most adept thieves and deceivers; avaricious and mean. There is great need of the Gospel here. I am glad to see in any instance, the fabric of superstition crumbling to dust. This will be the case in proportion to the light spread by the Gospel amongst them. I sat down to commemorate the Sacrifice of our Lord, with 26 native female converts, last Sabbath, and 12 [52] native males, together with the mission family at Serampore. They live very correctly, it is said; I cannot feel reconciled to seeing them half clothed. They wrap themselves in their sheet when they sit at worship time, and they all choose to sit on the *floor*, as you speak. These people vary in their complexions—all are darker than the American Indians, and some a blue-black. Their features are quite different from those, having large eyes, and an aquiline nose with variations from that, but the expression is different. All the women wear their hair long, and put up in a knot behind. Some of the men wear it so too, but they cut it short on the forhead [sic], to distinguish them from the women, who wear their's regularly parted. Some of the men, shave half the head quite naked, having parts or patches of hair above their ears, but kept short. Others shave all the head except a lock on the crown, whereat the departing soul will escape when they die, as they believe. *These* last, resemble the aborigines for the tuft on the head, but there is no resemblance of features in them, to either the Africans or Copper-colored men of our backwoods. The features of the native Bengallees are softer than those of the Hindoos from the upper provinces, & the Mussulmauns.

Very few corpulent persons are seen among the natives. Their forms are in general, slender and of a good height. When those who have any knowledge of us pass us, they make their "*Salam*" audibly, in doing which, they bow their body very low, touching the palm of the hand right to their forhead [sic]—it is a most graceful salutation.

Their different cast [sic] or *jant*,[57] subjects them to distinct occupations. If it confined them to certain trades, there would seem

[57] Jant (also spelled Jhund): a Hindi word denoting a social group.

nothing extraordinary in it; but it regards every domestic avocation. In wealthy or opulent families everywhere, there are a variety of servants—such as house-keeper, cook, chambermaid, laundress, waiter, scullion &cc. but these may all eat together, or assist each other by mutual consent. It is not so with the *casts*,—they may walk or talk together, but they *must not* eat together, nor one cast cook for another cast, nor do the work of another cast, on pain of being turned [53] out of Society. And this is it, which causes the necessity for so many servants. The custom is unchangeable, because ordained by their Bramins and Moollas, whose rights and religious observances, the Government have pledged themselves to protect, and not to interfere with. To be broken in Cast, is to be excommunicated from *every* social and religious privilege: than which, nothing is a greater grievance to a Hindoo believer; but he has the consolation of knowing, that it can be *purchased* back from his priest, if he can but scrape pice[58] enough to take him a fee—This is only buying absolution. Under this severe shackle, it is an act of magnanimous self-denial in a native to turn Christian, for in becoming one, he is proscribed all intercourse with his family and friends, and all legal right to his portion of property. The cross to be taken up by them, is therefore very great, but meritorious. Those who turn Christians, are obliged to take refuge from the fury of their friends, under the entire protection of Europeans.

Religion seems to thrive most amongst the White Soldiery. When I first made my private observations on the labours of the missionaries here, I thought it a deviation from their peculiar office, to preach in English, and go among the European Soldiers to preach; as also, to keep Schools for English children. But further observation, and consequent reflections, have induced me to view the subject differently.

The more general religious example becomes, and the further the knowledge of truth and falsehood extends, the greater will be the

[58] A pice coin was worth one sixty-fourth of a rupee. A rupee was worth about fifty cents.

facilities for civilization. From the ancient maxim that "example is better than precept" I infer, that the natives beholding the happy effects of Christianity upon the white population, will ere long, quietly become willing subjects themselves. Yet I should deem it circumscribing the usefulness as well as the proper deportment of a missionary who could preach the Gospel in the native languages, to hold him from that sole engagement, by any other.

The French language is not spoken here; However, a knowledge of French or Latin, would enable a learner of either of the Asiatic languages, to get on with more ease, than without. The chief essential requirements in a female teacher, in these [54] schools, are, a good deal of profitable reading, especially the Scriptures, Geography, Grammar, Arithmetic, Drawing and ornamental needlework. The piano, is a great luxury, but the extremes of drowth [sic] and moisture, and scorching wind with dust, disorganize it, past control, for any length of time, and skilled tuners are seldom to be met with.

It seems, withal, that the highest, brightest, and most essential accomplishment, is a good stock of *Patience*. And nothing but a holy zeal will supply the streams to this ever essential flood—for less than a flood will not do.

All missionaries say, that a great change for the better has taken place in Society at large, within 20 years. And their confidence is great, that a still more perceptible change will in 20 years more, be effected. There are many native schools in operation, and many more on the point of being opened. Those in Calcutta, Mr. Eustace Carey superintends. He is considered as possessing superior colloquial talents. His health is very bad.

June 5th. [1816].

Today is excessively *hot*, as is the case before the annual *rains* set in. The thermometer stands at 109 in sunshine. Yesterday it was 91 in the centre room. The air out of doors is just like the heat from an oven. Today the thermometer has ranged from 93 to 98, within doors. Mr. Marshman says, it is the warmest day he ever felt in India.

This evening a prayer meeting was held in the Chapel hall, on account of Mr. Hough having to set sail for Rangoon tomorrow. I feel pity for them, in going to a Gov[t]. so arbitrary. They become the *property* of the King, the moment they land on his soil, and cannot leave it, but by his permission, or even without purchasing the privilege. If the King demand a man's wife or daughter, she must be resigned or resign her head or her father's. I am told that the King of Ava, has for his mere amusement, ordered a boatload of men and women, even his own subjects, to be sunk, that he might have the sport of seeing them struggle and die, or swim for their life. I confess I thank God, for turning my course to a different part of the world, where every thing seems peaceful, and every wish practicable, under the Gov[t]. of the Company.

[55] Mrs. Judson has recently buried her little son.

There are, they say, 30 converted natives at Chittagong, bordering on the Burman Empire.

June 8th. [1816].

Last evening I walked with Mr. R. to the Mission burying ground. Close beside it, is a lot of ground sold to the native converts at Serampore, whereon they have erected a little village. We went thither also. Several of the males were lying on the hard cool bricks in the little piazza of the hut. I looked into the hut, and saw a little lamp burning in a niche in the wall, and a person covered with a sheet lying on the earthen floor asleep. Just before the door, was spread a rug and a bolster, for the master to sleep on, when ready to retire. Mr. R. remarked, that from seeing that, it was not hard to conceive of the propriety of the man mentioned in Scripture "taking up his bed, and walking." There appeared to be no furniture except a few brass koojahs in one corner, in which they cook and bring water. Iah invited me to sit down, so that I conclude they could have exhibited a stool.

June 9th. [1816].

Well may *I* give praise unto the most high. I will unite with the joyful, and shout with songs in the assembly of the upright, for the Lord is exceeding good to me, he hath led me unto the still waters, he hath restored my Soul!

Have taken the air of the garden—found more air stirring than usual. The ground is parched for want of rain, yet everything looks green and gay, and fresh blossoms appear as the faded ones fall off, daily.

Of late, the sudden blasts of wind, though terrible, and disagreeable for the dust they raise, cool the air a little. When they are accompanied with rain, they are very acceptable. It is four weeks since a small shower fell.

From the close economy of the Americans, or the habits of such as have come hither, they have acquired the character of *Selfish*. People here say, that they betray this trait, in transactions of business also. I think this is chiefly because they forget that they themselves ever were in England before they came here—where I do not suppose 18 suits of clothes essential for a gentleman from week to [56] week, any more than it is needful in America. I have laid out a great deal for necessary changes of raiment since I arrived. I have not been accustomed to locking up my clothes, consequently, have had some stolen. The natives can sell what they steal, as soon as stolen. Mr. Lawson had to put his servants in prison a few days since. They had fleeced the house of almost everything, before they were detected. They acknowledged their fault at last, on their knees, imploring pardon: and were liberated, being fined something.

The mode of washing here, ruins Irish *linen* clothes. They use lime and potash, and slap their clothes on a slab at the river's brink, where they wash. (here bring in the picture) Cotton clothes bear such washing better than linen. Had I have known of the decided preference to be yielded to cotton worn next the skin, I should have acted upon that principle. I find that linen confines the heat of the body, about it, but cotton conducts it off, in a comfortable manner. This if perceptible on putting on linen after bathing: or at any other time. Four suits of white may be obtained here, for the money requisite to buy one in America. The mosquitoes are very ravenous!

In Burmah, there is no such thing as *Caste*, although there are different ranks amongst them. One servant will do all the little turns for a small family, there. A tailor who has worked for Mr. Judson says, that Mr. J. lives like a poor man. That if he wishes for more than one dish on his table, a fowl must be divided and cooked different ways—that there are no potatoes there. This apparent poverty, is not owing to shortness of means, nor to a want of fertility in the soil; but is owing to an arbitrary government, which exacts almost everything from the agriculturalist; and the ravages of the thieves, deter people from planting.

June 11th. [1816].

Yesterday was a great annual celebration of the Descent of Juggernaut from his seat. An amazing festival it is!! Who shall describe it. [57] His deaf and dumb Majesty is not so august a Deity as might be supposed. His face is a mask, 18 inches long, painted in imitation of—no human being, horribly staring. We saw his eyes half a mile off, as he sat in his seat, in a Cupola on the top of his Car. His arms were without hands, and his lower parts were hid by a full muslin skirt. There is some great ceremony at the time of putting the *hands* on the arms. They are said to be of silver. We walked round, and took a view of things. There were images of indecent form which I had almost come near, not knowing of them, which Mr. M. gently came between me & them, and guided me another way. The heat was so great that we did not stay to see the immense crowd pull the cables and draw the car along, but we saw his empty Majesty, let down by a rope, from platform to platform, with shouts that echo'd from the blue vault of the firmament. The natives cast up offerings of small matters, which the Bramins on the platforms caught, and appropriated to their own use. (here bring in the picture) There were no immolations last year, beneath its messy wheels, of which there are 6 times 6 in rows, if I counted right. It is to be hoped that the tracts and gospels which are every year distributed among the crowd, have had that effect. Many bones, of human sacrifices in former festivals, lie about in the vicinity of the car! Breathe, O holy spirit, on these dry bones, and bid them live!

I shall not be able to note much more in the diary as I am busy preparing for the nuptial occasion, but as I dedicate this scrawl to my dear brother, he must accept it, for an Epistle. He will give my love to all our friends. May God bless you, and them!

I must not only prepare for my own wants but in some degree for those to whom I expect to become a Step-mother. The term has always had something disagreeable in it, but I hope, by experience to find it a pleasant relationship; and that the growing affection of the three motherless little boys towards me, will soon make them think me a mother in [58] the best sense of the word. Time, however, will settle that point between them and me. I have tasted the bitterness of entire orphancy from their tender age—and I can therefore enter into all their feelings. This may enable me to avoid in my discipline with them, what I felt obnoxious to my comfort, in youth. Yet no one perhaps was better guarded and instructed, than I was, and I have only to regret, the thankless return I made to the best of sisters, who was, at the same time, my Godmother,[59] and became my foster-mother. She saw me married to her husband's younger step-brother;[60] she wept for me, when I became a young mother with

[59] The sponsors at Charlotte's infant baptism on October 18, 1782 were Elizabeth Amelia Atlee (her oldest sister), Mrs. Charlotte de la Saussaye Hazen (a friend of her parents after whom she was named), and her father, William Augustus Atlee. Barber, *Genealogical Record of the Atlee Family*, 80.

[60] Charlotte's first husband was Nathaniel Hazen White, half-brother to Maj. Moses White who was married to Charlotte's oldest sister, Elizabeth Amelia Atlee.

a fatherless child. She saw me bury both—and "then she went away"—she followed them, and was laid beside their mouldering frames, in transcendent peace.[61]

Do not suppose that I expect riches or worldly honors—no—we are *missionaries*. We have not seen the *rich* giving up their comforts to combat the trials of a missionary life; and it cannot be conjectured on any reasonable grounds, that missionaries have such salaries awarded them, as to so much exceed their current wants, as to allow them to lay up treasures on earth. *We* expect to earn our living, mostly; by industry beyond our calls for absolute missionary work; until true religion gains upon the heathen. Messrs. Moore & Rowe came from England together, spent seven years together assisting the Mission at Serampore, and then, finding their exertions not absolutely needed there, resolved to try and form a station higher up the country; and accordingly purchased, in the name of the parent Society, an Estate which they saw advertized. It proved just such a Situation as they desired, and there they settled jointly, resolving to aid the Society by relieving it of the whole of their support, drawing from them the amount necessary to support that part of the work strictly missionary. To this intent they opened an English School for the children of the officers in the army stationed at a mile distant from their mission house.[62] In this labour, they and their wives united jointly, and the proceeds went in the support of their families. They buried their wives at Digah. Sisters in all things but [59] consanguinity, they lived in harmony seldom equaled, and were not long separated in their death. They sleep in Jesus. Mr. M. is united to the widow Biss, who with her first husband, were accompanying missionaries from England. Mr. Rowe has a little in Bank in Calcutta,

---

[61] Nathaniel Hazen White died December 25, 1804. Their son, also named Nathaniel Hazen White, died May 10, 1805. Charlotte's sister, Elizabeth Amelia (Atlee) White, died June 12, 1808.

[62] Military regiments of the Crown and of the East India Company were stationed at the Dinapore cantonment one mile from the Baptist mission station in Digah.

which is the patrimony of his first wife—and I have placed the money I brought over with me in Spanish dollars, there also, to provide against exigencies, in future. The house I think, where he has lodged it, is called Messrs. Palmer & Co.[63]

It is four years since the Digah mission was formed, situated on the great and famous river Ganges, 300 miles from Calcutta by the post-path, but reckoned 450 by water, the River being winding. There is not as yet a road open for carriages, thither, and no public houses are erected anywhere out of Calcutta. The Post goes on foot, a line of men are laid by Gov^t^. for a thousand miles up the river. A man has two cane baskets covered with leather, and having padlocks to them, suspended to each end of a pole which he lays across the nape of his neck, balancing the weight; *he* runs five or ten miles; when another takes it from his shoulder, and runs his stage, and so on, there being only a foot path for men and beasts of burden. This is called the Dawk, or Post, or mail, for all intelligence intended to be certainly and expeditiously conveyed, is put in his charge.

Individuals travel this path by Dawk in palanquins, laid by government also; which do not allow of fifteen minutes delay. A cold collection and crackers, and a bottle of beer, must serve the traveler three days or so, until he reaches his goal; where, if there be a Magistrate, he may have another Dawk laid, for as far again. This being known to be governmental travelling, persons are seldom molested by thieves &cc. (here bring picture of Dawk wallee.)

Digah is between the ancient great city of Patna, and the modern military station of Danapore, northwest from Calcutta. Dinapore or Dânâpore means "the place of grain," dânâ meaning grain.

[60] Cheerless as Mrs. Hough's prospects are at Rangoon, she longs to be there—I do not wonder at her anxiety to be settled, at her place of Destination.

The missionaries at Serampore, live in separate houses, but have

---

[63] John Palmer's company combined banking, trade, shipping, and plantation agriculture. Lord Moira, the governor general of India, called him "the Prince of Merchants." Webster, *The Richest East India Merchant*, ix.

set times for assembling at one, and of partaking of a breakfast, a dinner, or tea, *all* together. This is very cheerful.

I have run on just as it happened, but you must arrange for me—it was not all written at once—Good night. Note—in Dr. Carey's garden I see the plants called with you, Thistle, James-town-weed, wild Catmint, Poke, and many wild weeds, *cultivated* with the utmost *care*, as Exotics. There are 4000 different Plants in his garden.

June 13th. [1816].

In a bustle to get parcels ready—Capt[n]. A. sets sail for Phil[a]. much sooner than I expected. That however, does not affect my concerns, as Mr. R. and self must get away from Serampore by the first of July.

On the 15th Inst. *we*, that is Mr. Rowe and myself, and the three pretty little boys, must go to Calcutta, to get things set in order for the final Notification of our union, which can take place no way but according to governmental rules, as before described. So do not think I have turned Episcopalian by it—They are the high church here, and I respect them, for you know that both of us were born in it, as to the flesh, but the Spirit has led us both out of it. Both they and we are right so far as we love and obey the Lord Jesus. I should be glad to see the Sprit leading hundreds of the natives into it.

The distinctions of Cast among the Hindoos, ought to disgust everyone with diversity in religious faith, so at least as to cause enmity. Now these heathen feel no enmity, no questioning as to the entire propriety of the diversity of cast or rank among themselves. It is a system of Braminical policy to answer two ends, first, to provide a revenue to themselves, and secondly to provide for the subsistence of the millions around them, most of whom, they by this means, tackle upon their conquerers[64] to support, and as it is "*the custom*" it has become a binding law upon all alike, whether Civil or Military. Nay, there are no means of avoiding "*the custom*."

[61] Burmah, with all its present wretchedness under an arbitrary monarch, is a far happier country than this, because a change

[64] I.e., the British.

of political affairs would make Religion and morals *free*. Those who labour there now, amidst such appalling discouragements, have hope, for they wait only to see the mind of the *Sovereign* made tolerant, to have *every facility opened* for the Gospel. That day will probably come. The champions now engaged in the cause of Truth, there, deserve great praise, for their stedfastness [sic], faith, and patience. Religious freedom is the thing last and least to be hoped for, amongst the Hindoos. I feel happy however, in the prospect of immediate usefulness to a class of Society who need cultivation and to be wrested from the superstitions of their *mothers*. Under these considerations, I feel that Providence has peculiarly favored *me*, for I shall not have the care of looking after tables, as Mrs. Moore is provider; and my intervals from tuition can be employed in acquiring the Hindostani.[65]

Petty vexations, by being continual, and hopeless of departure, become afflictions. I already feel, in the irritations of mosquito bits and prickly heat, a call for the exercise of patient endurance.

Serampore June 26, 1816.
My dear Edwin,

I have been again to see Juggernaut in parade this evening; and as Adeline Musser[66] desired me to write her, I gave her as full an

---

[65] In applying for missionary appointment, Charlotte stated that she wished "to pursue such studies as are requisite to the discharge of missionary duties;...to apply what talents I possess wholly to the service of the mission, either in taking the management of a school, or to hold private meetings, should there be opportunity, with native females, to instruct them in the principles of the gospel...." White, "To the Baptist Board of Foreign Missions," 112.

[66] Likely twenty-one-year-old Adeline Musser (1795–1839) the youngest daughter of John Musser, Sr. of Lancaster, Pennsylvania. The officiant for Adeline's marriage to Joseph Tate of Richmond, Virginia on September 3, 1818 was William Staughton, pastor of Philadelphia's Sansom Street Baptist Church of which Charlotte was a member. "Married," *Lancaster Intelligencer*, September 12, 1818, 3.

account of it as my wits could afford and as I cannot recapitulate at this hour, I must refer you to her, if you wish to know more about the horrible affair.

We are now pressed for time to write, and must cut something short. My love, is writing to you, therefore I need say but little.

My missionary companions have left us, to take passage tomorrow for Rangoon.

As I was passing a stall where toys were selling, in the fair on the way to Juggernaut, I saw one in imitation of him, which I bought to send you. You will wonder with me, that human nature can be so deceived as to worship a molten image baked in the oven! Yet Aaron made a molten calf for Israel to worship; and that too, at the foot of the mount where God was in conversation with Moses—this reminds me of the world given to fashions, in the house of God.

[62] I have often wished you could be a party in the social pleasures of the mission family, especially when assembled at meals for they seldom meet to converse at any other time, being so deeply occupied in their several engagements. I often think that *their* minutes fly to heaven, like bees, whose legs are loaded with honey, to the hive; and their family order is much like theirs.

I hope Captn. Kenyen[67] will soon arrive with letters for me. There are several ships in the harbour from America. The intercourse between us might be so frequent as to obviate the sense of so great a distance between us. It is not very probable that we shall see each other on earth, but I hope we shall live long, to redeem time. I have not found time to write to my cousins as yet, unless I had broken upon the train of my diary. Do give much love from me to them, and to Mr. P and Mr. I. and E. D.

I am, my dear brother's
affectionate Sister, now
Charlotte H. Rowe

---

[67] Possibly Captain Henry Kenyon of Philadelphia. "List of Letters," *Aurora General Advertiser*, April 2, 1812, 3.

Serampore June 26th. [1816].
My dear brother,

I surmise that with all our writing, you have not been informed, that the union between Mr. Rowe and myself took place at Calcutta, in the Honble. Company's Cathedral,[68] in the Episcopal form, on the 18th Inst. Dr. Carey acted as father to give me away, and the Gentlemen of the *Benjamin Rush* witnessed it; and partook of the wedding supper at Mr. Eustace Carey's.

Yours &cc.
C. H. Rowe

Serampore. June 27th. 1816.

The relation which now subsists between us, is of such a nature, as that I may with propriety address you, my dear brother.

As my dearest Charlotte has communicated the particulars of this event, there is no occasion for me [63] repeating them. The principal object I have in view in writing these few lines, is to introduce myself to, and commence a correspondence with my new Relative.

I trust God has led Charlotte and myself by a right way: our concerns have evidently been under divine direction. All things have been working together in a remarkable way to effect the union which has taken place. I can but look upon my Charlotte as a gift from heaven, and see in her, the full answer of many prayers. Boasting is not a common practice with me, but on the present occasion I must go a little out of the common way. You may rest assured, that your beloved sister has met with a good husband, one who will always manifest the tenderest concern for her temporal, and above all, her spiritual interest. On the other hand, I am fully confident that she will be a real comfort to me, and thus we shall be helpers of each other's joys.

---

68 St. John's Church in Calcutta was built by the East India Company in 1784 and designated as the Anglican cathedral on Christmas Day 1815.

I am glad Charlotte did not proceed to Burmah, for that would have been a very unsuitable place for her, as she would have had but little opportunity of doing good.

My residence is at Digah, which lies between Dinapore, a military station, and the city of Patna, about one mile from the former, and ten from the latter. There we have a Boarding School containing about 20 young females, daughters of military officers and Indigo planters. When we get home, Charlotte will take charge of that department. There she will at once be placed in an extensive sphere of usefulness, by which the desires of her heart in this respect, will be obtained. Our situation at Digah on the banks of the Ganges, is delightful, and we have as much European Society as we can wish.

We have some native christians at Digah, some of whom are constantly engaged in preaching the Gospel to their countrymen. We have 6 schools for natives and hope we shall soon have many more. There is no difficulty whatever in getting the boys to read the Scriptures. My colleague, Mr. Moore, and myself, regularly preach in English at Digah and Dinapore. At the former place, the congregation consists of a few of our neighbours

[64] with our own families and school—and at the latter, of European troops. Charlotte will, no doubt, give you a particular account of these things hereafter, and I have every reason to think, that you will hear of her being exceedingly happy in her new situation. Herewith I send you a memoir of my dear departed Elizabeth. The sweet little girl she left me, died in November last. I also send a Pamphlet, containing a Map of the countries in which we have missionary Stations. The pamphlet will shew you what the Mission was about two years ago. Several changes have taken place in some of the stations.

Your likeness makes me familiar with you in idea. I hope I shall often hear from you, for a correspondence with you will give me real pleasure. I am persuaded we shall have an interest in your prayers. We may never see each other in the flesh, but I do rejoice in the hope of seeing you in heaven. Give my Christian regard to your beloved spouse, and to your friends in general.

I am, my dear brother,
most sincerely your's [sic]
J. Rowe

Continuation of the Journal. On the Hoogly.
July 13th, 1816.

The journalizing remarks in the following sheets, I design to address in much affection to my ever dear brother Edwin. I have already given him a minute account of my new connection. I have now to state the progress of happiness consequent on it. In regard to which I can only say, that I now think the last ten years of my life were spent in under a mistaken sense of the married state. You may perhaps query, knowing I lived a *widow*, but you will not long question, after reflecting under what afflictive circumstances I formed and ended the short career of a married state. These trials arose not out of a want of attachment on either side.

My dear partner and myself (present partner) with his three little sons (the two youngest of whom are 5 and 6 years of age, I call my twins) with the daughter and son of my Mr. [65] Rowe's colleague's present wife, Deborah and Isaiah Biss (the former of whom was born at my friend Mrs. Cauldwell's[69] of New York, while her parents were waiting for a passage to India) and our four servants, 3 men and one woman; left Serampore on the 10th Inst., in a Budgerow, in which we trust by divine Providence, to reach our place of residence, Digah, my *home*. Thus commences the thirty-fourth year of my age, yesterday being my birth day.

A budgerow is a covered boat having a mast, a deck and forecastle, and apartments, very convenient for sitting, and sleeping in, with other conveniences needful about a place of so long domesticity, as they usually are. The rooms are wholly enclosed with venetian windows which lift up wholly or shut down lightly. It is made

[69] Deborah (Lea) Cauldwell.

like all the boats used on these rivers,[70] *without a keel*, and therefore not very safe in a storm, but are easier to get off from Sand beds, on which they often graze, and sometimes lodge, until the poor watermen, push it off with their backs by main strength. When the wind does not serve to propel it along against the stream, the men draw it, by means of a rope, walking on the shore. In this way our progress does not exceed 20 miles a day. With a fair wind, and the assistance of the oars, of which there are many, we make 50 miles per day. We come to shore every night for safety,[71] where we have an opportunity of walking, and the men cook their suppers and the next day's food. It is quite composing to see them enjoy their hookas (pipes) and eat their fill of rice and some vegitables [sic] cooked in a savory manner (here bring in picture apropos). In the evenings, we sometimes obtain milk, and fruit, such as Bales,[72] pine-apples, Cocoa nuts, Plantains, Jackfruit, and pomegranites [sic]. This last I never tasted until yesterday, my Joshua having gone some distance to procure some. He now calls me to walk on deck, the rain having subsided, for we now have abundance of rain, the Annual Rains having set in.

---

[70] In 1815 Charlotte had taken a steamboat down the Delaware River from Philadelphia to New Castle to board the ship *Benjamin Rush.* Steamboats had begun to appear in the lower reaches of the Hooghly River in the early 1820s where they were used as tugs for sailing ships. Not until 1828, two years after Charlotte left India, did the first paddle steamer (the *P. S. Hooghly*) travel up the Ganges past Patna, Digah, and Dinapore to Allahabad. Ivermee, "The Hooghly River, 32; Gibson-Hill, "The Steamers employed in Asian Waters," 120–162.

[71] The Hooghly was a shallow river with shifting sandbanks. Sailboats and steamboats hired experienced local men to "read the river" to locate the channel and avoid submerged sandbanks. Boats stopped overnight along the riverbank as the river could not be "read" in the dark. Ivermee, *Hooghly*, 171.

[72] Bales: also known as golden apples, Japanese bitter orange, stone apple, or wood apple.

July 14th. [1816].

The date yesterday reminded me of my birth day[73] on which account we were all treated with a Cake and a glass of wine. We then went on deck to view a pompous range of temples dedicated to Seib.[74] In the numerous [66] pagodas and temples everywhere to be seen, is very affectingly depicted

> "the madness of a nation
> worse than ocean's wildest roar."

A native who is very rich, lives adjoining the sacred ground. It is probable that he, like some others, acquired his wealth by the offerings made at the temples. He has built a brick house, which displays some attempt at imitating European architecture. This endeavour to emulate their conquerors, has a good effect, as the example of natives of influence or *wealth* which they adore, does much to draw the populace from their govelling [sic] habits of life. The generality [sic] deem Jewels, the greatest earthly good; and all discover a passion for gaudy show. Such as have it in their power to gratify their wishes to the utmost in these things, will I trust derive from them the lesson, which satiety teaches, that there is a principle in the Soul which no attainment of wealth or pleasure can satisfy, which points to a hidden life.

Near to this temple, a lofty spacious house owned by an *Armenian*, presented itself to view, ornamented all round with trees, walks, and groves. His extensive fields of *Indigo* in full growth, and of the deepest verdure, presented a prospect beautiful to behold, and agreeable to consider, since the cultivation of that one plantation furnishes employment to several hundred persons. Perhaps too,

---

[73] Charlotte Hazen Atlee was born July 13, 1782 in Lancaster, Pennsylvania, the youngest of eleven children born to William Augustus and Esther Bowes (Sayre) Atlee.

[74] Seib: another name for the Hindu god Shiva, the Destroyer.

some of this very Indigo, will imbue with clearness, *your clothes*.

The effluvia from it is unpleasant, as the reapers cut it. They bear it away in great bundles as soon as cut, to fill the vats, where it is kept under water until it ferments, and then is beaten in the water with sticks, which break it, and filter out the particles of indigo, which settle at the bottom like potatoe [sic] starch, and is then drawn off and cut in blocks, and dried in the Sun. The plant sometimes yields five crops before its strength is spent.

This place was once infested with thieves, four of whom were taken and brought to justice at Calcutta, two of them were hung on one side of the river, and two on the opposite side: their bodies were put in iron cages, and suspended on the gallows, for a terror to others. It has been found a powerful check upon malefactors.

[67] Quite near the gallows, on one side, stands a temple of note. Those dedicated to Sieb, consist of one large one and generally five or six small ones on each side of it, which make a wide display on the bank of the river. *All for display*, is their motto.

We put to, for the night. A great number of trading boats loaded with rice, cotton &cc. lay along the shore by us. All the boatmen, arranged in companies according to their casts, were cooking their meals. They cook in chafing dishes or ovens as some call them, which they make up themselves of clay and okum. They carry them about with them in the boats. Very little fuel, being confined to one vessel, will make it boil presently. A cake of turf which the women prepare from the dried leaves & chaff they sweep up, mixed with dung and dried in the Sun, keeps fire from day to day, and when ignited yields a powerful heat. This with a few twigs a few inches long, will cook both their rice, and after that, their vegitables [sic]. This is true economy, to which the scarcity of fuel exists. They look, when in their private dishabille, like a flock or family of monkeys, aping manhood. They (the Hindoos) worship monkeys but if in contempt called a *bunder*[75] they feel highly insulted. They spread a

[75] Bunder (also spelled bundar and bandar): an Urdu word meaning monkey.

mat on the ground, and all sitting on it, make up the rice (which they take out of the boiler, into brass plates) in balls like a snow-ball, and without masticating it, gulp it down as a ruminating animal does its cud. They eat an incredible quantity at a time, to provide for fasting the next day until the evening, except tossing a little parched rice into their mouths, as they work at the oar, or draw the boat along.

According to our principles, we do not travel today, as it is the Sabbath. We wish by it, to afford the men an opportunity of engaging it religiously, but they are mostly glad to have the day for making their ovens or furnaces, cut up the sticks they steal or pick up by the river, and pound out their rice from the husk. This they do in large mortars with great poles, three men doing it at one mortar, and afterwards sift off the chaff.

We hope our example in observing this day as becomes *us* on the Sabbath, will lead them to think it a day to be set apart [68] for serving God, and not the world. The family being seated in an orderly and quiet manner before breakfast, a chapter is read, with commentaries is read, and a prayer put up, all kneeling. During this, the servants keep silence among the boat men. We sing a hymn too, which attracts the attention of the people, for they are fond of singing—They however, deem our singing mere baby sounds, believing their own harsh, discordant tones, far more *musical.* After breakfast, I catechize the children. I do not confine myself merely to the catechism, but endeavor to make it a pleasing engagement, by applying the questions to characters mentioned in Scripture, which also, elicits from my little audience, many interesting questions.

At ten o'clock we had worship as if in a congregation. My heart felt the presence of Jesus, whose kind spirit seemed to touch us all; for he has promised, that where two or three are met together in his name, there will he be in the midst of them, to bless them.[76] I felt renewed, thankfulness to God, for uniting me with a family where holy things were not strange, but rather delighted in.

In the evening we took our walk on the shore, observing the

[76] Matthew 18:20 King James Version.

people at their cooking &cc. after they had eaten, they washed their brass pots and plates, and scoured them very bright at the edge of the river, and took them away.

July 16th. [1816].

I have heard of the burning of dead bodies. Yesterday we passed where one was being burnt. It lay on a little crib, which had been made with sticks driven into the ground cross ways. Under it were faggots; it had just been set on fire, and made a great cracking and frying. They bring them as near the water to burn, as then can, so that they may have the less trouble in pushing the half burned body into the river, for the fuel they allow for this office is sufficient only to take the skin off. Thus blackened and disfigured, they commit it to its holy "*mother Gunga*," and to happiness!!

Have commenced my school, with my present inmates both to benefit them, and accustom myself to the heavier charge, before me, on my arrival at Digah. It is four weeks today since my marriage.

[69] Our progress up the Hoogly is very slow. The wind but little in our favour, and a strong tide against us, consequently, the poor boatmen have to tug the vessel by means of the *goon*. Came to, last evening at a large field where the herdsmen were tending their cattle, consisting of small kine, tame buffaloes, and milch goats. We took our Tea on the bank, as the evening was dry.

Although the prospect of native villages set among the trees, is very pleasant, yet if the ground were not so level, it would be more beautiful.

We yesterday passed a large Indigo Factory, to which the water was raised from the river by *china pumps*. They are wrought by men, who turn the beam with their feet, as a squirrel turns his cage, only that they stand on the outside of the wheel. The banks of this river are thickly inhabited. We heard the horrid yell of Idolatrous settlements on the opposite bank of the river, at sunset last evening. We concluded there must have been a great concourse of people. Their noise, with the frequent striking of a China bell, continued nearly all night. The China bell is a brass or bell metal vase which they touch with a hammer.

Today, there has been a great display at the water's edge of Bramins making their devotions, using many gestures. The women were bathing in companies, and casting large red flowers and roses on the water, as offerings to "mother Gunga" who sits on some distant mountain, pouring from her exuberant locks, this transforming stream!

Disconnected from a design *to worship*, the appearance is very imposing, and romantic. At all these Superstitions, my heart sinks—and the immensity of the population makes it appear impossible that by man's means a reformation should be wrought; but we have the belief that "the heathen shall be given Him for an inheritance"[77] "through the preaching of the Gospel."[78]

July 17th. [1816].

Last evening, the moment the boat was moored, we went ashore, and set out on a ramble. A village at some distance attracted our curiosity, and we followed a path, until we met some natives who told us the name [70] of the place was Maniepore.[79] A wind and winding road with shacks planted all along on each side, presented a delightful change. There were some tall trees on which the hang-birds had built their nests in great number. We were allured forward, until we reached the village. It presented the most rural view of peaceful domesticity I ever beheld. It consisted of mud-built huts, each having a considerable lot of ground allotted it, and divided from the next neighbors by a line of hedges, of *Mehindee* or wild myrtle,

---

[77] Psalm 2:8.

[78] Mark 16:15.

[79] This village south of Nuddeah (now Nadia) in Bengal on the Hooghly River is distinct from Moinpoora (now Mainpura) in Bihar on the Ganges River between Patna and Dinapore. Charlotte would start a school in Moinpoora.

the air from which is very fragrant. It has a small leaf and when kept trimmed square as is done at Serampore, it so resembles box, thus it has gained the name of the Indian box wood. Some of these green enclosures were vacant, designed for cattle to graze in. Most of the yards, or compounds, had a wicker gate in the hedge front of the hut.

I felt deep regret at not being able to do them any good. The whole village was immediately around us, for that a Sahab and bee-bee-Sahab (lady & gentleman) should visit them, was a wonderful thing. Mr. Rowe inquired of them, if they could read? They replied that not a man in the village could read. He had some pamphlets which he gladly would have given them, but they said in their language "What good will they do us, we cannot read them."

I felt a willingness to spend my time in teaching them, but I had first to acquire their language. No one can tell my feelings (except such as have trodden these steps) when I cannot speak a word to their Souls. The field is wide—but alas! labourers are too, too few! There are native schools, but not in country places, O! that these people were favored as the country of New England is, with respect to schools. Christ must be taught in schools for youth, before the Truth can take hold.

Rice while growing resembles young wheat. There is a variety of kinds of rice. The table rice varies in price from 16 to 20 Seers[80] or double that many pounds, for one rupee. That kind which the low natives live on, is had from 40 to 60 Seers for a rupee. Mr. Rowe has told me, that when fields of rice are cultivated in the *best* manner, every *root is transplanted.* How numerous must be the culturers, to do that—It yields much more abundantly.

[71] Today we have passed *Nuddeah* where stands a temple famous both for its magnificence and its gross idolatry.

---

[80] Seer: a traditional unit of weight that had many local variants. The Standards and Measures Act of 1956, amended in 1960 and 1965, designated one seer equal to 1.25 kg (2.75+ lbs.).

We expect to pass this evening at Mr. Johnson's.[81] He is a great Indigo planter: He is a friend of the mission family. Indigo planters of renown, are admitted to dine with officers of the army & of the Civil Service. Merchants are not!! Except they have acquired such wealth as to enable them to support great style, or to do favours to the others. So much for importance, in this country.

July 19th. [1816].

Arrived at Mr. Johnson's ghaut[82] or landing place as we expected to do, and sent a man to acquaint him with our intention to visit him. In a little time he came to the landing, bringing two palanquins, a buggy or gig, and an Elephant to convey us all to his house, (for such is the kind of hospitality between gentlemen in this country). I chose to ride on the Elephant, and my little Josiah chose to ride with me, and Mr. Johnson. I found its gait very unpleasant, jostling beyond endurance for any great distance. The creature stepped widely with a quick walk, which is the only gait it can take. William and Joshua Rowe, being small, went in one palanquin, and Deborah and Isaiah Biss, in the other. Mr. Rowe took the gig alone. The Elephant reached the house with the horse, which had trotted all the way. The palanquins came up, five minutes after. The house being two miles from the river, Mr. J. sent an ox cart to bring the Iah or woman servant.

We left the Dirzy or tailor of the family; the *Khidmutgar* or server, the *Boverchee* or Cook, and the *Bearer* or body-servant, to hand drink do errands, dress the boys and walk with them &cc.

---

[81] Arthur Johnson. Young English owner of Indigo Plantation and factory, at Soojenpore (Sujanpur) along the Hooghly 20 Miles before Cutwa (Katwa). Johnson was baptized by Richard Mardon and was a great friend of the mission. He was married to Maria Derozio, who had been baptized with her parents by the Serampore missionaries. I am grateful to Peter de Vries (Serampore College) who identified Mr. Johnson.

[82] Ghaut (also spelled ghat): a broad flight of steps situated on the riverbank providing access to the water, especially for bathing.

These were to take care of the vessel, and lay in a fresh stock of provisions. This will give you some idea of the household of *plain* folks in India.

Mr. J. cultivates an Indigo farm of plantation of *four* thousand acres, employs six hundred men; he shewed us the whole process of extracting the indigo from the plant, and preparing it for sale. He says, the *palest* indigo is the best.

Mrs. J. was in Calcutta, which we much regretted, but Mr. J's mother was at home. I was much pleased to see her feed her beloved pet from the palm of her hand, as she sat in the piazza; *her pet* the Elephant we rode. Mr. J. being a [72] man of taste, his house is furnished with everything for both comfort and amusement. We are now returned to our marine abode, where Mr. J. has taken tea with us, and we have bid farewell, much refreshed by our intercourse. I find, notwithstanding as much pleasure today in resuming my little family school.

We have seen several deserted villages on the bank of the river lately. The water having undermined the bank has caused many huts to fall into the river, and several are standing with only the back wall on the brink, ready to fall with the next mass of sandy earth. When a Sand-bed forms on one side of the river, the stream is naturally driven more on the other side; hence the boundary line alters as the stream inclines. On this account no permanent water works can be erected. Consequently men perform by manual labour, what it is customary for horses or steam engines to effect in our country. And men may be found in any number for any purpose, at a low rate. The valves of the china-pump wheels catch the water and throw it into a trough which conveys it into the vats of indigo—which I have described heretofore.

Monday. July 22nd. [1816].

Saturday afternoon brought us to *Cutwa* where William Carey, Dr. C's son, is stationed. He and his Mary have been six years there. Not more than 30 persons have been openly Christianized in that time. But William is not disheartened—he says he believes the good work is secretly going on, amongst the natives around him, and that it will break out all at once by and by. I think so too; for the people all round Cutwa send for the native brethren to come and read and talk with them about Jesus Christ's religion. The influence of the native brethren, he says, is great, because it is known that they have sacrificed all their social and legal privileges for the sake of Christ. They may well shew to them how Christ forsook all *his heavenly* delights, to serve out a life of probation and at last give himself a sacrifice for them. In a country where human beings are sacrificed to the gods, one would think it not a hard doctrine to comprehend. It is the purity which it enjoins, that make them reject it.

[73] The Christians have taken shelter in William Carey's premises, where they have built themselves huts. We derived much pleasure from spending the Sabbath at Cutwa. Not only in exchanging hospitalities, as our boat affords a table, but in social worship, morning and evening. Services in the Bengalee language (for we are not yet out of Bengal) were held at his house, where a congregation of natives attend. It was delightful to witness. Sacred songs impressed on the memories of the young may furnish them with christian knowledge, and afford unspeakable consolation to their hearts, should they be brought to know the truth in the Spirit of it. We shook hands with then all. The women tried to make me comprehend, that they were glad I had come to visit Mr. Carey, who they said, is very lonesome.

A native woman was baptized by Mr. Carey, on Sunday in a large square reservoir of water, dug in the earth, called a tank. It appeared as if all the city had collected to witness the scene. They offered no opposition, but gabbled among themselves. Those who seemed to feel any reverence for the ordinance, formed themselves into a phalanx around the baptizing place. They do not baptize in the river, for fear of the alligators. Many of the people made their *Salam* to us. This they do, from various motives, to be noticed themselves, as well as to shew others respect. Query: Why should we *expect* respect unless we shew it. I looked round upon the countenances of the females at the Ghaut or steps of the bank; and observed how evident is christianity in the countenance of those who possess it, softening every feature, and making "*not ashamed*" while others look wild and shy.

William Carey says that his wife has more to do in a missionary way than he has; since she has a little congregation of females, who come to her to hear her read and talk, every afternoon. They say they are too poor to afford time to learn to read, but they like to hear reading.

Cutwa contains fifteen thousand native inhabitants—what a field for gospel labours. The school there, has depreciated for want of means to support it: consequently, Wm. C. has undertaken to rear a small plantation of [74] coffee trees, in hope of realizing some profit from them. This is the third year of their growth. The plants were brought from the Company's botanical garden near Calcutta. They form a beautiful thicket, and thrive best, when shaded by higher trees.

O! what a scene have I just witnessed—the children roused my attention from school duty, to look at a man, carried on a bier, whom the people were taking to the river side, to put a finishing stroke to his misery by stuffing his mouth and nose with the mud of the Ganges. The poor man *was not dead*, nor to any appearance dying, as he kept kicking off the sheet, which it required a person on each side to bier to keep over him. The bier was followed by a small procession of barbarians, beating drums, sounding horns and pipes, and singing monstrously, in order to drown any noise which he might make. Nobody can prevent his being in eternity in another hour, and his poor singed body floating down to meet hundreds of kindred victims, at the tide waters. Yes, nobody either civil or religious, can hinder them, for Gospel, they will not hear, and there is no law in the land to act against it.

The natives make great parade in *marrying* two trees! The Peepul and the Bout, or

Banian tree[83]. The Banian tree I have already described. The Peepul is considered to have a spirit dwelling in it, and is thence considered Sacred. The Hindoos never pass one, but they make a Salam to it. The leaves are almost three-cornered and large, hanging by a stem several inches long, and very slender, similar to our aspen tree, which is known to be always in motion from the slightest undulation of air—hence the Hindoos imagine that a demigod resides in it, not knowing the real cause of its leaves moving more than those of other trees.

The boatmen sometimes amuse themselves with singing a sort of tune, which, from the rise and fall of the notes, reminds me of the howling of the winter north wind in America, when it whistles in the windows of your chamber.

[75] To resume the subject of the poor man doomed to die by the hands of his *friends*—the Hindoo faith in the holiness of the water of the Ganges, and the several branches which it supplies towards the Sea, making so many mouths of the Ganges; affords them a pretext for getting rid of the leprous and those who have been long sick, without giving signs of speedy recovery. Hence, they make it an article in their religious observances, that to die by means of those waters, is blessed; and the released spirit goes at once into a state of happiness, if they have been good, but if not, they undergo a transmigration, into animals, most congenial with the characteristics exhibited by them during life. This has a retributary effect upon the living; for instance, if two persons have quarreled, and one of them has threatened to be revenged, if he die, his antagonist on hearing of it, will expect his spirit to come back to him in the form of a snake or other evil beast, to torment or injure him. But if any two are friends, and one die, the survivor expects to see the spirit of the other, in the bird that charms him most, or in a cow that feeds him with milk.

---

[83] Banyan tree.

They do not always *burn* the body which they have suffocated with the heaven-securing water—they leave it on the brink, so far in the water, as that it may chance to be washed away. It so happens that, sometimes the poor creature, not having expired, is cleansed by this washing, from the mud, and surviving the struggle, crawls back to shore—but alas! he is forever proscribed by all who knew him: and if there had not been a village set off by the English Gov^{t}. here, for a city of refuge for such in particular, they must wander about, homeless and pitiless, no one giving them a morsel. I do not remember the name of this village, but I have been in its narrow streets, which are now very well peopled, from the devoted dead—and they are supported chiefly by Government, it is said—thus the Company, though they do not prevent death by their vile rites, provide for the welfare of such as accident, or providence, rescues from supposed death and utter desertion.

[76] July 23rd. [1816].

While we were at breakfast, going close along the high, perpendicular bank, which is continually letting fall its sand, we found *a cow*, which perhaps had fallen down from the margin of the land, on a body of the falling bank. The bed being shallow there, she kept above water. It must have been some days since, as she is wasted to skin and bone. Altho the cow is a sacred animal in the Hindoo faith, and whoso injures her, must suffer bitterly for it, yet she could not but have been seen in this situation by many of the devotees. I am not surprised, however, at their indifference towards her, after what I have seen, in their acts to men. I took it upon me to have her hoisted up by ropes, upon the bank, and set free to graze on her native fields again.

We are now opposite *Plassey*,[84] where the great Battle was

[84] The Battle of Plassey took place as the British were fighting the French to dominate trade from India. On June 20, 1756, Siraj-ud-Daulah, the pro-French Nawab of Bengal, captured Calcutta's Fort William. Prisoners

fought which decided the conquest of India—the natives themselves being enraged at the cruelties of their Raja or king, contrived by a well-concerted plan, under the appearance of defying the English, who were privy to the intended cheat on their Sovereign, gave themselves and their King into the hands of their conquerers, by suddenly wheeling about and joining the English. A terrible Slaughter of their own countrymen about the palace, ensued, among whom was their King.

We have now come a hundred miles up the Hoogly, and have not seen a rock, nor a barren piece of ground.

July 24th. [1816].

Began about the 10th Inst. to learn the Hindee alphabet, under the instruction of my beloved husband. Can now read words without spelling them, but understand nothing of their import. Find it less arduous than I feared. My anxiety to become mistress of it, outweighs all difficulty. I long to be the missionary in it. It is grievous to me, not to be able to throw one drop of religious instruction into this stream of superstition and barbarity.

---

of war were crowded into the fort's small prison dungeon where many died overnight from suffocation and heat exhaustion. A survivor claimed that 123 of 146 prisoners had died, although some modern historians dispute that number. The infamous "Black Hole of Calcutta" incident spurred reprisals. In February 1757 the British regained Calcutta. They then advanced toward Murshidabad to overthrow Siraj in his capital. British, Indian, and French armies converged at Plassey, a small village on the east bank of the Hooghly River about one hundred miles north of Calcutta. The British were vastly outnumbered but won the battle on June 23, 1757, having bribed Mir Jafar, one of the Indian army commanders, to turn against Siraj. After the Battle of Plassey, Mir Jafar was appointed the new Nawab of Bengal and the British gained the right to collect tax and customs revenue in Bengal. This began the East India Company's transition from being a purely commercial organization to becoming a governing body.

[77] July 25th. [1816].

In sight of Berampore, the great military station of the East India Company. It is a grand city, as we view it from the water—but we find that the native buildings exhibit nothing but outside show—they are without comfortable apartments and without furniture within. But when we make this remark, we forget that they require much less furniture than we do, from the nature of their *low* habits.

The views on the River, are picturesque; changing from rural nature, to pompous art. The natural reflections excited by each, in the mind, keep up a constant action in the mind, favorable chiefly to its support under so long a delay in accomplishing our journey *home*, the good man's sanctum, and the female's fort.

"There, Peace with silver streams reflects the heart.
If tis not there, where does she build her cell?
For only *there*, she finds with Love to dwell!"

Monday morning, [July] 29th. [1816].

Having on Friday arrived at Berampore, Mr. Rowe sent a servant with a Note to his friend, Major Latter,[85] to acquaint him of our arrival. We were soon conveyed to his house, where everything

[85] Major Barré Latter (1777–1822) distinguished himself in the Company's 1814–1816 war against Nepal. His Majesty's Twenty-Fourth Regiment had been stationed at Dinapore in 1814 where Joshua Rowe preached to them. When the Twenty-Fourth proceeded to Nepal, Joshua Rowe followed and spent three weeks ministering to them on the Nepal border. Maj. Latter was an evangelical and in September 1816 invited CMS missionary Frederick Christian Gotthelf Schröter to his headquarters at Titalya to begin study of the Tibetan language. After the deaths of Schröter (1820) and Latter (1822), Schröter's draft dictionary was brought to William Carey and John Clark Marshman, who edited and published it in Serampore in 1826 as the first-printed Tibetan-English dictionary. Trulson, *Charlotte Atlee White Rowe*, 109–110; Bray, "Captain Barré Latter," 2:11–12.

except a wife, waited to make us welcome. Major M.[86] is *pious Bachelor*. An arrangement was made for us to meet at Mr. Money's[87] to Tea. Mr. M. is also a very pious man. He is in the Civil Service, that is, employed by government, in some way not military. Hs is blest with a lovely young wife, exemplary for the love of piety. Two young Lieutenants, who prefer Mr. & Mrs. M.'s company to spending their evening with the gay, were of the company. Thus, as we pass along, (but at great distance) we are favored with the choicest of associates. Persons in the midst of an enlightened society, know not how to reciprocate our feelings, at meeting an intelligent, and especially, religious friend. These gentlemen are Evangelical Episcopalians. They prefer meeting together round a private table, and holding social worship in a spiritual way, to attending the Services, where an interest-made Chaplain officiates, and where the Soldiers are obliged to attend, once on the Sunday; but they are not prohibited from attending elsewhere afterwards. Mr. ____[88] would consider it cruel to frighten people with preaching *vital* [78] religion. They pressed us, so much, to continue over the Sabbath, that we consented, for they desired Mr. Rowe to preach to them. This he did, sitting at the head of a long table all the audience sitting round it, as is the custom here when the party is not so large as to prevent that mode of placing themselves.

After passing some days with them in the happiest manner (returning to our boat at night) we parted last evening, acknowledging our vital affinity in the Gospel bonds. They pursued us with benefits, their servants bringing comforts until midnight.

---

[86] Likely Major Bennet Marley who led the first division of British troops from Dinapore in the Nepal War in which then Capt. Latter provided flank protection to Marley's troops.

[87] William Taylor Money, East India Company civil servant and later an East India Company director and Member of Parliament, was an evangelical Protestant who in 1812 assisted the American Congregationalist missionaries Gordon Hall and Samuel and Roxana (Peck) Nott on their arrival in India.

[88] Charlotte left the chaplain unnamed.

Reflections on the happiness of *home*, and the Society of congenial friends, excited the following metrical ideas, on the subject, which I copy for my beloved brothers.

> There, Hospitality with flowing breast extends
> Th' inviting hand and Smile, on entering friends;
> Theirs is the shrine, by welcome footsteps press'd
> And social ease, sets there a genial guest.
> Domestic piety her lamp illumes,
> While sham'd, retiring Demons feel their dooms; –
> There, buds of Love's own blossoms cheer the scene;
> While culture mild, and pleasures intervene.

Still pursuing our watery journey, we have come in sight of the famous city of Murshudabaud.[89] It was the residence of a former Raja, but since the conquest of India by the English, it has fallen to ruins. The palace is standing, where the Tyrant Nabob lived, who was conquered by them in 1755 [sic].[90] His cruelty was such, he would have boats loaded with people, and then order them to be sunk in his sight, that he might be amused with their confusion and attempts to save themselves from drowning. He has ordered childing mothers[91] to be cut open in his presence, that he might gratify a hellish curiosity. Moorshudabaud and Berhampore, almost join at their suburbs, extending many miles. The Barracks erected by the Company at the latter place, are very extensive, and handsome. We are now opposite the Palace, which is a two storied building, having a portico on every side, the pillars of which are round and plain, with

---

[89] Alternative spelling for Murshidabad. This city, formerly Maksudabad, was renamed when Murshid Quli Khan (d. 1727) made Bengal an independent entity from the Mughal Empire and made the city his capital.

[90] Siraj-ud-Daulah, the last Nawab of Bengal, was defeated by troops of the East India Company on June 23, 1757.

[91] Childing mothers: women in advanced gestation.

a curl [79] at the top, very much like those of Gerards Bank[92] in Phil[a]. The walls and pillars are of brick, covered with plaster in imitation of marble. There is no appearance of grandeur existing at present. The only token of state, was a man clothed in white who kept before the palace, holding a silver or silvered mace in his hand—the ensign of dignity in this country. The palace is now occupied by a petty raja[93] who is a mere vassal, tributary to the present government.

The power of the ruler being despoiled, his residence has lost its éclat among the places of commerce. The river passes through the site of the city; but the part lying on the south side of the water consists of huts, and mosques, temples and trees. Multitudes of the natives stand on the shore gazing at us, though it is no novelty to them to see a budgerow pass. We pass near enough the shore, to toss an orange into their boats. The only things doing in sight, are men filling large leather bags with water, as they hang on each side of an ox; others selling bags of Rice; others weighing wood; others bathing, and washing their garment, which some having done, have slung the wet cloth about them, and walked out of the water, letting it dry on them.

I was pleased to see that curious *sheep* spoken of in Asiatic history, having a tail as large as a saddle bag, which flaps from side to side as he walks. The tail affords a delicious dish. This singular animal is covered with black wool, and is large and handsome. You would from this imagine perhaps, that India mutton is very large

---

[92] Gerard's (also spelled Girard) Bank was housed in the Greek Revival, temple-style building at 120 Third Street, Philadelphia, built in 1795 to house the First Bank of the United States. When the First Bank's charter expired in 1811, French-born Philadelphia merchant Stephen Girard (1750–1831) bought most of First Bank's stock and facilities and reestablished it under his personal ownership. One of the nation's wealthiest men, he provided crucial financial support to the U.S. government during the War of 1812. The bank building was designated a national historic landmark in 1987.

[93] Zain-ud-Din Ali Khan (a.k.a. Ali Jah) was Nawab of Bengal and Bihar from 1810 to 1821.

and fine: this sort of sheep is not for eating uses in common life.

Passing farther on, the prospect is dreary enough in itself, owing to the many brick walls falling from decay and neglect; but connected with the idea of departing idolatry it is pleasing. The Mahometons were the former Masters of this city; whose religion is even worse than idolatry, as less susceptible of reform. Moss, shrubs, and even trees, are growing from the tops and sides of the mutilated fabricks. Ranges of heaps of bricks covered with moss and thorns and prickley-pear, indicate their [sic] once having been garden enclosures. Several native women are now peeping out at us from a door in the wall, whom I take to be some of the petty raja's concubines; perhaps the habitation within is his bagnio.[94]

[80] Their dress is a purple petticoat and white mantle or sheet going over the head. We passed a very grand pleasure boat belonging to the petty raja. It had a gilt eagle at one end, and a dragon on the other: to both of which they pay adoration.

When we set out on our voyage, our head boatman, called a Maungee,[95] poured out a libation of milk upon the deck before the figure of a great bird at the head of the budgerow, and made Salams and prayers to it, for success on our journey. Unfortunately, not long after setting out, a barge loaded with cotton, struck it, and knocked it into the water. The man plunged in, and recovered it, expressing great anxiety on its account, and spent a day on the shore to replace it.

Now we see, on the south bank, a long palisade, resembling the fence round the state house yard in Phil[a]. It encloses a building which one would take to be a college, but it is a mosque, with the dwelling of the Moola or priest beside it. All else about it looks in a state of ruin. Nothing but the palace before mentioned, and a few houses of business on the river belonging to the English has any appearance of escape from ruin. Here, within the grasp of the eye are renowned edifices, and thickets with now and then a straw thatched

[94] Bagnio: brothel.

[95] Maungee: a boatswain in charge of boat and crew.

hut among them. If the simplicity of the latter, were that of primeval *innocence*, how enchanting would it appear! And were the former, sanctuaries for the worship of the living God, how different would be our feelings at the sight! O that God would look down and see, and convert these deluded mortals! Then should songs of redeeming love echo from shore to shore, instead of the idolatrous shouts which rend the air, at times of their festivals.

When we get near the bank, which is very high, we are almost suffocated with heat, and smoke of pipes and fuel, with stench. We are now suffering for a day too many, spent among our friends, when if we had improved the wind, we should have cleared this noisy, noisome place.

I [have] been amused with looking at three more pleasure boats which betray great pride and barbarism.

6 o'clock—Fortunately a shower accompanied with wind [81] has lasted just long enough to take us across the river to an open bank. There are hundreds of boats constantly passing, manned with from 10 to 20 men. They sing a savage roundelay, rowing famously, and at stated intervals shout in response.

[July] 30th. [1816].

We have come not more than three or four miles up the river today, since we entered Moorshudabad. The part we saw yesterday was the court and the town, the part we see today, is the merchantile. The boats of transport, thatched, are innumerable at the shore. This part has more the common aspect of a city. The white domes of temples, rise here & there, with spires which once have been covered with gilt—would that they were washed from *guilt,* by being dedicated to the Healer of the nations! The greater number of inhabitants live in huts. The city stands on a curve of the river, which displays it to great advantage. Spires in the background, and fair white-washed mosques & temples on the shore, interspersed with thick green and ordinary dwellings—some bungalows are covered with earthen tile. The articles of trade here are rice, oil, grain for cattle, wood, cloth and indigo.

11 o'clock—The Raja's family boats made in the Chinese style are gaudy beyond description.

12 o'clock—have passed the city, which is seven miles long.

The pleasant society we met with at Berhampore, expressed their regret that the E. I. C.[96] should support idolatry, by receiving revenues from their temples. They were surprised that they should not discern, that to christianize the nation, would be the most effectual way of preserving subordination. They extract the support of the standing army, chiefly from taxes, and taxes too, laid on their consciences—for the heathen will bathe once a year at an esteemed sacred place, though they have to pay five rupees to get to the place—one said he *had a right to immolate himself in the holy stream, because he had paid five rupees to get at it.* They have promised not to interfere with their religious rites, but it seems have endeavored to sicken them or deter them from them, by imposing a toll at the main entrance to them. [82] This however has not diminished the number of objects to pass—for a man will starve himself rather than not find means *to do as others do* in matters of their religion. Thus, a handsome revenue is the result.[97]

[July] 31st. [1816].

Here we are aground on an inundated field of rice—with a fine wind that would take us five miles an hour in the open river. The natives are lazy, and in going shortcuts, sometimes have to go round

---

[96] East India Company.

[97] In 1805 as a response to perceived corruption and mismanagement, the East India Company stopped local Indian guardians of holy sites from charging entrance fees. Instead, the Company began collecting a pilgrim tax as a function of government. The Company used the income to manage and maintain the sites and for other governmental expenses. It continued collecting the pilgrim tax until 1840. Carson, *East India Company and Religion*, 62, 216.

Robin Hood's barn.[98] They have turned the boat into an untried place, because they thought to save a curve of the river; sometimes it proves successful, but in this instance it subjects us to delay. We have only, while they tug and push the boat, and make a bobbery,[99] to look at what is around us. A herd of tame buffaloes are enjoying the water—they stand in it, and lie down in it, only letting their eyes and noses appear.

8 o'clock—We now have at length got the boat off so as to go by the sail, through a pass between ploughed ground, just wide enough to admit the boat. The low lands are always inundated for months during the rainy season, which generally commences in June. On the ploughed ground are a great number of those birds which the English soldiers call Adjutants. They are picking up worms or small fish, which may have been washed thither. One great fellow that stood with his back to us at some distance off, I at first sight took to be a lad, dressed in a long bluish coat—but observing very slender legs, I began to compare with other birds, and found him to be a very bird. They are the ugliest things I ever saw—They are of the vulture kind, feed on carrion, and pick up all the offal that is thrown into the streets in cities, keeping watch for it, on the tops of the houses. On this account, they are protected. They make no noise.

Evening—the scene is always changing—we have, since our boat put to, walked through fields, where are growing most luxuriantly, Rice, Indigo, Wheat, and mulberry plants designed to feed silk-worms. The latter are cultivated from the slips taken from a tree. We are not far from a great manufactory of silk.

[83] The reason that this ground is not overflowed is, that it is important a plantation, yielding a revenue to government, that a mound has been thrown up along the bank of the river, which has prevented the water from overflowing the land.

---

[98] Go round Robin Hood's barn: to reach a destination or conclusion by a roundabout way.

[99] Bobbery: turmoil, noisy disturbance, hubbub.

August 2nd. [1816].

Yesterday, the wind favoring, we made more way than on any previous day. Passed many large villages, and an extensive silk factory, near which the owner or rather the manager, lives in unusual style and splendor.

The natives sow two or three kinds of grain together lest the main [crop] should not spring up—if it do, they pluck up the others, which serve as grass for their cattle. There is some penetration in this. These cows give but one pint of milk at a milking. They are small and lean.

Today, we have entered and crossed the *Ganges*. It is very wide here, where it gives part of its waters to the Hoogly. A long range of mountains, called the *Rajmahal* hills, appear veiled in the blueness of distance. The boatmen intend still to shorted [sic] our rout [sic] by navigating inlets.

9 at night—Seibgunge being an inland village and not exposed to strangers except but this season, the villagers flocked out to see our boat pass. The place has a pretty appearance, being laid out in lots appropriated to families, and divided from each other by hedges. The eldest of a family is the patriarch in it, and when he dies, the next eldest male takes his honours. It is said that all the younger branches of their families bring their earning to their Patriarch called "*Booda Sahab*" or the Ancient Sire or gentleman. This custom is common amongst the best Hindoos. It betrays much of filial duty. Yet there is very little of this virtue exercised in the daily conduct of children to the aged Hindoos.

Bamboos are used for hedges, as swamp-willows are in America—but the former is far more beautiful. It grows in long poles, bending gracefully, and is clothed with [84] long dark green leaves similar to peach leaves. The poles are used in making roofs—they are split up into thin strips and woven into mats to cover floors, which here, are never of boards—but bricks or plaster. The Bamboos on each side a road, close their tops over it, and form an arbour as far as they go. Grateful to the traveler, is such a cool shade.

Seibgunge, is a place dedicated to the demigod *Seib*, near his temple, is a summer retreat made of trees & vines, in constant growth. O that it were a place where Christ was owned! If Mr. Rowe had brought a native brother with him, who would communicate truth by means of the figures used in Hindee Rhetoric, he would try to preach to them; but dialects differ so much in different provinces, that he cannot be understood, by means of common plain speech, in Hindostanee neither does he understand it, so well as Bengallee, having spent seven years first at Serampore, where Hindee is not the common talk.

On a plain, on the opposite side of the Nulla or Inlet is a village of huts, resembling a clump of hay-stacks, and having no trees among them, and no order in their situations. We have been almost distracted with the yelling of the boatmen, for when the boat gets aground they push, pull, and some of them halloo to their gods in a kind of Rosary, while other respond by a shrill yell.

August 3rd. [1816].

Just getting out of the Nulla into the great river again. We lay all night by the village without fears, except that they might lift the venetians in the night and take off something.

While sitting at breakfast, the boat being drawn close along the shore, I observed three men whose complexions were fairer than other in general, walking. They were dressed in long white garments, and looked very stately. Presently a poor man came along with a great parcel on his head. They stopped and he stopped, he then let down his budget,[100] laid it beside him, and prostrated himself to the earth, his head almost touching [85] their feet. He bowed first on his knees, and then kissed the ground! I looked about to see if there was a temple near which should make him think it holy ground, and seeing none, I enquired wherefore he had done so. Mr.

[100] Budget: quantity of material (archaic).

Rowe then informed me, that those three men were *Bramins*, and the poor man a *Soodhra*[101] or man of a particular low cast. Such is the reverence paid to them!

A little farther on, we came to a temple, and a large, spreading mango tree, near it, around the trunk of which was a seat built of brick & mortar, to afford a resting place for travellers. This is the only known public house if it can bear the name, that we have seen since we left Calcutta.

Providing this accommodation, was an act of self righteousness in some wealthy native. It was sufficient to deify him after death. As much evil is perpetuated behind the veil, as so great an act can absolve. Mr. Rowe endeavored to enter into conversation with some of the people here, but could not be understood.

August 6. [1816].

Arrived at Chaundney—went to see Mr. Andrews, another pious man, engaged in the Indigo business. His house stands near a monument called "Chaundney peer" (not *pier*). Peer means Seer or prophet. A Mehomedan Moola by the name of Chaundney was buried there. His devotees come nightly to pray divine honors to his spirit supposed to dwell there. They light a lamp and leave it burning in a niche in the tomb stone. This act, they imagine, will ensure future prosperity. A young man, newly married, was anxious to have a *Son.* He therefore visited the tomb and lighted up the taper regularly, praying also to the lingering spirit in the tomb. In due time he had a son; but after some months the child died, which caused the father to leave off the nightly orgies of thanksgiving for the gift of his son. He has never been seen to visit the place since. His confidence in the prophet, seems to have fled.

Mr. Andrews took us to see the mosque which is [86] renowned for having once been overlaid with pure gold, (as the story goes). It

---

101 Variant spelling of Sudra or Shudra: the lowest of the four Hindu castes, normally artisans or laborers.

is still known by the name of the "golden mosque". It stands on the site of the ancient city of *Gour*,[102] now laid level almost. We walked through weeds and brambles which have sprung from the Soil made rich by human voluptuousness now no more. This mosque once the Glory of Gour, is now the habitations [of] bats and ravens. Trees are growing out of its very walls, whose roots and suckers intersect the stones, and force them out of their places, where they have stood for centuries.

The God of nature seems to have given command to inanimate nature, to conspire in the conquest over both Mehomatonism and Idolatry. The trees, as high as forest trees, raise their heads triumphantly to heaven, from the remaining roof and tops of the battlements. Mr. A. had cut down some of the trees from *the top* of the building which had grown as high as a Lombardy poplar. He cleared out the inside which had become a thicket. The peepul tree seems to possess a sensitive power, like the finger, its young shoots adhere to whatever it grows near, feeling its way to every interstice, and to whatever may become one by its gradually insinuating itself into a joint between two messy stones of a building. They must ere long, tumble out of the places they have held for hundreds of years.

The mosque has five rows of domes, three in each row. The domes were supported by 20 pillars. The remains of the platform or rostrum, still stands in one corner. The mosque fronts the East, and has three nitches in the west wall, where the Mussulmauns go to pray, facing the west, as Mecca lies in that direction, towards which they pray, because Mahomet was buried there. These crannies were beautifully ornamented with carved black marble arches, one of which Mr. A. succeeded in getting out and has placed in his front

---

[102] Gour (also spelled Gaur), located on the eastern bank of the Ganges, was one of India's largest medieval cities and Bengal's capital under several kingdoms. Political instability in the 1500s weakened Gour's economy. When the Ganges gradually silted and changed channels westward, the remaining stagnant water may have caused the severe outbreak of plague in 1575 after which the city was abandoned. "Gaur, City," *Banglapedia.*

door as a frame.

[87] The whole outside of the building is finessed with stones 12 inches cubic, and 2 feet long, being carved with the Persian and Arabic letters. The Lotus flower is carved with other sacred flowers, on every part of the building. It is singular that *they* should employ the *Lotus* as a sacred emblem, when it is adored by the Hindoos whom they despise. This flower grows in pools of water similar to our water-lily. The leaf and flower spread themselves on the Surface, and are much used by the natives. The poor eat their rice on the leaf instead of a trencher, and make an offering of the flower. They are not so numerous as to be always obtainable.

The bricks which fall from the temples, are much prized by modern builders, being superior to any that can be made now. The part of the Golden Mosque, is the gate still, but the wall has fallen away, or been picked away from it. East of this are the vaults and monuments of the deceased kings and prophets. Near it is a tank or dug reservoir for water, which is *full* of fish. It is larger by as long again, as the reservoir which supplies the city of Phil[a] with water; In our walk to view other antiquities, we met with several other tanks of less magnitude. There is one, on the City ground, which is said to be a mile long—this we could not reach.

We went to a temple where the Koran is yet read by a few re-cluse Mehometans who dwell by it with their women, surrounded by high walls. As the gate was shut for vespers, we could not enter it, but passed on to the mausoleum, where many of the great lie gor-geously entombed. We were just in time to see a lad light a taper in each of the monuments. Several men came forward to open the door of the tomb of the great King. It had a verandah all round it in which we were permitted to walk, but into the sanctuary where the body lay, we might not enter [88] unless we would *take off our shoes*. That I could not do, for conscience sake. We however saw all worth knowing attached to it, which was a plain marble slab that covered the grave, and a fine muslin canopy over it, clearly discerned by the light of the lamp placed at the head. A *Hindoo image*, having its head broken off, as large as a stout man, stood in the verandah, facing a small mosque without. This was but making Hindooism bow before Mahometanism.

Night coming on, we could not penetrate any further into the ruins of Gour. It would have been perilous, owing to the wild hogs that infest the place. Those who go deeper into them, go on Elephants, and even then they are not out of danger from other wild beasts. They often come out, round the houses on the bank of the river.

Dwellings, palaces, theatres, and circuses, lie in heaps of bricky [sic] earth, grown over with wild weed: the unevenness of which, makes it very difficult to examine the site of this once the Glory of the Heathen world.

On the 2^{d}. day after leaving there, as we sailed up the inundated way to *Goamalty* which is about ten miles distant, the fallen walls of the principal palace, the horserace and its Gateway, were distinctly seen, shrubs growing on the tops of the walls, with trees wildly interspersed.

Having reached Goamalty, ruins of a similar character present themselves, of which the same tale of fallen power might be told. Mr. Ellerton,[103] who lives here and is another valuable friend of the missionaries, has formed a beautiful fireplace in one of his rooms, with carved stone taken from a temple close by his house. Though

---

[103] John Ellerton was an indigo planter at Goamalty near Malda. Charles Grant, an Anglican evangelical, had been the East India Company's commercial Resident at Malda. After returning to England, Grant unsuccessfully urged that responsibility for education and evangelism be included in the Company's charter when it was renewed in 1793. Grant gave positions on his Goamalty indigo plantation to Henry Creighton and John Ellerton, who were also Anglican evangelicals. By 1806 they had established twelve elementary schools in the area, each with an average of thirty boys. Ellerton encouraged and supported missionaries of various denominations. He translated the New Testament into Bengali, seeking to improve William Carey's Bengali translation. "Death of Mr. Ellerton," *Friend of India*, September 1820, 271–272; "Deaths," *Friend of India*, May 1818, 393; Laird, *Missionaries and Education*, 60–66.

fires in a sitting room are rarely seen in India, he has built it, more to remind him of the social firesides of England, than to prepare for one at Goamalty, the weather seldom requiring any modification of heat. There are three columns of entire stone 12 feet high, still standing between the broken vacancies, on the top of one of which, Mr. E. has erected a handsome pigeon house.

[89] There are many square tiles of bricks lying about on which are beautiful inscriptions in Arabic, and flowers raised like embossed work, as if they had been made in a mould, and afterward polished. A square of which, I should much like to send to America, but don't know to effect it. From one inscription, it is found to have stood five hundred years!

When I stand on these grounds, I feel a holy awe; the power which time has on all things; the truth of Scripture fulfilled in what I see; the belief that the Religion of Jesus will prevail; and the way which appears to be making for it in this idolatrous country by the extinction of its national Power, the destruction of its cities, and its hapless inhabitants, ignorant that they are unhappy: all cause my heart to exult; for hope speaks loudly from all these things, that the feeble beginnings of the force of Truth will gain strength, and bear sway. The iron hand of superstition binds down the struggling infant of Reason, palling its every energy; but that hand shall be taken from its place, as is the *Silver hand* of the Horrible Juggernaut, when he returns to his accustomed residence after his *annual visit to his Brother*!! Yes! er'e long, triumphant *Truth* like the *peepul tree* about these sturdy edifices, which, sending forth its fibres in a *feeling* search after roughness and joints, cleaving them asunder by a Secret growth as with a wedge of Iron, bidding *make way*, that the root may become a branch, and the branch a tree—even so, truth shall one day wind its influence round the hearts of these [sic] Idolatrous nation, cleaving asunder the thoughts of their minds—Then shall they cry out with one consent, "Come bow before the Lord, the God of Israel, all ye, who with us, have bowed before the Peepul Shrine."

Mr. E. says that the most that can be found at this day on the subject of *Gour*, is contained in a Circular letter, and is strictly true as far as it goes.

The natives make offerings still to the Alligators that infest the tanks among the ruins, one alligator [90] in particular, has become so tame as to come out at their call, and take their offerings from their very hands. He has consequently become very large, and they believe God resides in him! Mr. E. shot a crocodile (a young one) in the tank which is so near his house that I could cast a pebble into it from the window where I write. It measured six feet round. It had strolled there from a thicket in the ruins of Goamalty, in the site of which he lives. Mr. E. shewed us the jaw bones of a Tyger which was shot on this spot.

[August] 7th. [1816]

Mr. Rowe and I walked with Mr. E. and Mr. Andrews who came over from Chaudney, to join us last evening, who led us to see where the late Mr. & Mrs. Marden [sic] had lived. They were two of the nine missionaries who came to India when Mr. Rowe did.[104] Five years ago he was in florid health, having a wife and four children. In the space of a few days, himself, and wife and two children died! They now lie entombed in a corner of Mr. Ellerton's compound. Their Monuments presenting continually to the mind, the brevity of life and the certainty of death. Their dwelling house is now grown defaced and is surrounded with weeds. Thus has this missionary station dropped from the place it bore in the Periodical accounts.[105] Mrs. Marshman has taken their daughter Rhoda to bring up as her

---

[104] The British Baptist missionaries were Richard and Rhoda Mardon, Joshua and Elizabeth Rowe, William and Eleanor Moore, and John and Hannah Biss with their daughter Mary and their infant Deborah, who was born in New York City.

[105] *Periodical Accounts Relative to the Baptist Missionary Society* were issued irregularly as the society's official publication. They contained letters from missionaries and contribution lists.

own child.[106]

Mr. Ellerton, having acquired a correct knowledge of the Hindostani Language, has kindly undertaken to give me a few lessons. While I was thus engaged today, *Creeshnu*,[107] the first Heathen *convert*, was introduced to me. He is on the decline of life. He lives near here, and acts as missionary to his Hindu Brethren, instead of Mr. Marden. We are now out of Bengal, and enter Hindostan.

Beheld this evening in the west after Sunset, what is very common in the Eastern hemisphere, but what I never saw before; the beams of the Sun assume the colours of the Rainbow, diverging from a focus, just below the horizon.

[91] [August] 9th. [1816]

Being still at Mr. E.'s, his gardener brings me, as soon as I leave my chamber in the morning, a green plantain leaf done up full of fresh almonds from the tree; and another full of flowers—The kind of almond he brings, seem to be like white paper wound up into a kernel. They are exceeding crisp and delightful. An act like this, some years ago, would have shocked his delicacy—but Mr. E's manners

---

[106] Richard and Rhoda Mardon's daughter Rhoda married Charlotte's stepson Joshua Rowe in 1830.

[107] Krishna Pal (1764–1822) and Felix Carey were baptized by William Carey in the Hooghly River on December 28, 1800, the same day on which John Saffrey baptized Joshua Rowe in Salisbury, England. Krishna was a carpenter of the Sudra caste. He was a follower of Ram Churn Pál (also spelled Ramsharan Pal) of Ghospara some forty miles north of Calcutta on the west side of the Hooghly. Though low caste and a guru in the Korta-Bhoja (Kartabhaja) sect, Krishna Pal sought and received medical attention from the Serampore missionaries after an accident dislocated his right arm. Conversations with the missionaries led Krishna to become a follower of Jesus and to eat with the missionaries. News that he had broken caste led to strong opposition. An appeal to the magistrate was deferred to the governor general who affirmed Krishna Pal's right to become a Christian. From then till his death Krishna Pal worked with the missionaries as an evangelist. Carey, *Oriental Christian Biography*, 1:133–136.

have taught him, that it is neither unmanly nor indelicate to be courteous to *females*. He seemed to feel much complacency in doing so, as it won a "Salam" from me in return—the usual mode of saying, good morning or evening, how do you do, I thank you, &cc.

Today I have begun to *write* Hindee, or rather the Nagree character, in which accounts are kept. I enjoy the best of instruction, from Mr. E. His learning is general in it, having to transact the business of an important Estate, in this language, to the owner in England. He says the Hindostani is the language most generally spoken in India. That the Bengallee is so much like it, that they may be acquired together. He respects it rather more than Dr. Carey does. The Hindostani may be written with most ease in the Bengallee character, he says. The Nagree character is to me like joiner's work, it is so stiff and jointed. The Kythee character, from Kyat a Scrivner, is quite different, and unites the words from the beginning to the end of a letter or account. How ardently I long to understand enough of it to communicate my thoughts in it. I pray earnestly to God daily to aid me in the acquirement of it; I hope my motive is in a desire to be useful, rather than to serve my own convenience. Truly, when I cannot give a direction to a servant in any other tongue, it must be essential, but I trust that my first wish is, to communicate Christian instruction to those *might never know it*, but from me. The medium of a female instructor is all important here, where the native females never go out, to be seen by males—that is, none who feel themselves of good rank, as none appear abroad except those who go out to service.

[92] I saw two women, the wives of one man, one of whom was older than he, the other only 16 years old, who live harmoniously together, and it is said, love each other; which is extraordinary among this people; but they yesterday happened to talk while he lay sleeping, and disturbed him, consequently he rose and beat them unmercifully. He answers, "must I not chastise my wives when they disobey me?"

[August]15th. [1816].

Left Mr. Ellerton's beautiful place yesterday. Our stay was very profitable to me as Mr. E. so kindly gave me many lessons in the language. And I reason to think, it was satisfactory to him and his friends, as our time of evenings was spent in social music, and pleasing conversation, prayer and exhortations. Mr. E. lost a lovely wife some time ago,[108] and now feels his condition very solitary.

Today at 9 o-clock passed *Rajmhal*, the meaning of which is, Kings-palace. Here are hills in sight—the first I have seen in India. They stretch along not far from the shore, give grandeur to the prospect, no where else to be seen between this and Calcutta. These Hills are known by the name of the Rajmhal hills. The city formerly the residence of another native king, presents no more of state than a stately block of ruins, with thickets growing from the tops of fractured and neglected Seraglios[109] &c. the gardens attached to which, extend far back. The "Gardens enclosed" of Asia, when in their prime, are delightful and extensive places of retreat, resort and exercise for females especially, who are, from the ancient prejudice, excluded from going out of their homes to be seen of men—but when they visit or go to bathe in the Ganges which they must do sometimes to keep holy, they are carried in little "*Doolies*" which have a scarlet cloth cast over them, as closely as they confine their singing birds. (here bring the picture). The cloth has a place left in one seam, which she may peep out of when no man is near. All the ancient

[108] John Ellerton's first wife, Elizabeth Catherine Brewley (1773–1796), died seven months after the birth of their only child, John Frederick Ellerton. The son later served as a civil servant in the East India Company and became a judge in Madras. Charlotte's journal refers to Ann (Potenger) Gunn (1784–1809), John Ellerton's second wife to whom he had been married less than a year. Ann was the widow of William Gunn, an indigo planter and manufacturer. In 1818 John Ellerton married his third wife, Hannah (Ayres) Myers (1772–1858). Hannah was the widow of William Myers, a whitesmith. John Ellerton died September 17, 1820. India Office Records

[109] Seraglio: apartments or rooms in which women lived in seclusion.

gardens were furnished with pools & tanks where people might bathe at their pleasure; but then those waters cleansed only from dirt, not from *sin* like the Ganges! The gardens now in our view, are inhabited only by reptiles and birds

[93] There is a white monument on the site, which was erected in memory of an Englishman, who curiously viewing the ruins, pressed too far forward over a precipice connected with water below, and falling, was drowned & mangled amongst the rocks. It is probable, he was penetrating through the wild shrubbery which had sprung up over the ruins, not suspecting the bounds were so near.

The Ganges, into which we have several times entered avoiding curves by sailing over the fields and through remote villages, is at this view like a Bay for width.

The reason why shrubbery so soon springs up, upon any place is, because during the monsoons the wind carries such a quantity of earth with it, and seeds of all descriptions which are light enough to be bourn [sic] along with it, settling on the tops of everything, that when the rains come on, they take root, and thrive undisturbed, because the natives for two reasons will not molest them, one, that should the *peepul* or *Tulsee* be there, they are sacred and must not be displaced, and that the country being subjugated again, they feel no interest in keeping their former places of worship entire.

19th August. [1816].

Have observed nothing worthy of remark today except the *field White ant hills*, which in particular places rise over the plain in a way to resemble hay-cocks; and had I not have been assured to the contrary, I should have set it down for a meadow, the mounds being *quite* as high as those thrown up by hay makers. Mr. Rowe says they have their commonwealth and Soldiary [sic] like bees, and that when they are invaded, their armies arrange themselves to defend the state. I have little doubt of this, since I have seen much of the ingenuity of the *house white ants* in Calcutta. They cover the native huts outside with little mounds like mole-hills through a garden, and find their way unseen through them up to the wood or the roof, which they devour, unless the ends which touch the wall be first singed to a charcoal coat. This is one reason why so little flooring, and so few two story houses are seen here.

[94] These little creatures build like masons at the top of a chimney; but they carry up their mud inside; and will build up pipes the size of a white smoking pipe so high, that its own weight throws it down. I have seen branches of these sticking out of the walls of a house, that I thought were a twig, until I touched it, and it fell, exposing all the busy workmen on the ground, like so many white lice, and were out of sight in an instant. In one house in my immediate neighbourhood, they destroyed in one night, a landscape [painting] which hung against the wall. In another house as near us, they destroyed in a few weeks, a large Brussels carpet which had been taken up and stored away to be ready for the ensuing cool season. They left a piece an half yard square, just to shew that *they* had *stolen* it, and not the servants. They had eaten it up. Whatever they destroy, they first cover with a coat of mud, that they work unseen. It so happened when I arrived in Calcutta, that the servants set my little trunk of clothes *on the* floor. They knew it was wrong to do so, but I did not know it, and not being ordered to get bricks and feet under it, they left it to its fate. The next day, when I went to get something, and opened my trunk, behold, the top of the things was quite secluded from my view by a coat of dry earth. I called Mrs. Carey to look at it, quite astonished—she was well aware what it was, and reproved the servants. The little white ants had all made their escape, hearing some noise about the business. Nothing was as yet eaten to injure it much. They had, begun to perforate a garment. This is truly a land of thieves. I do not say so from *not having* lost things, fingered away by higher intelligences. The latter may be reformed, the former must be endured.

We arrived at Mongire[110] yesterday morning, it being the Sabbath, we made a little advance to get where we might unite with

[110] Usually spelled Monghyr in British India. Now Munger.

Christians in public worship. Brother Chamberlain[111] is absent on a Preaching tour, he being the Gospel hero in the Hindoo's cause. No weather keeps him from improving all his talents in their Souls' [95] behalf. I have therefore to lose the satisfaction of seeing him now. There being no minister but Mr. Rowe present, Mrs. Chamberlain invited her neighbours, and Mr. R. gave them an address.

On the 17th Inst. I made my first attempt at rendering the Hindee into English, a very childish attempt truly, but from little things, greater are made to grow.

I forgot to mention the two piles of rocks which we passed near Mongire, in the midst of the Ganges calls the Faquers[112] Rocks. Faquere means Religious beggar. Two of them live on these rocks, very romantically. They make a point of keeping a lookout for boats, and of all that pass, if they can reach them in time, they demand money. Their brethren, believing these men very holy, never refuse them, but grant, either at once, or by promise. They even are adored by the Hindoos. Europeans who are not acquainted with them, generally give them a penny but those who know them, these in particular who have grown rich, turn them off without bestowing anything, it being more a sin than a charity. In such cases, the Faquers never fail to call down the judgments of heaven or the gods upon them. The natives do reverence to their temples on the rocks as they pass in their boats.

Sept^{m}. 2nd. [1816].

Have been detained twelve days at Mongire, in which tine we have enjoyed much hospitality from several families. Those of Mr. G. and Captain Page,[113] with Mrs. Chamberlain, meeting at each other's

---

[111] John Chamberlain.

[112] Faquer (also spelled fakir, faqir, faqeer): a Muslim or Hindu religious ascetic who lives solely on alms.

[113] Capt. Henry Edwin Page (c. 1784–1829) arrived in India in 1803. He was stationed at Cawnpore, then Dinapore in 1814. He accompanied his regiment's surgeon during visits to Digah to attend to Joshua Rowe's first wife,

houses alternately. Mr. & Mrs. G. have a fine garden from which I picked a Jessamine. There were several buds not blown on the sprig when I put it to my breast, and I was much surprised to see at night that had not withered, but had all blown out.

This bloom that *lives* upon my breast
And sweetly balms the air,
I took e'er blown, from its rest
mid Kindred buds as fair.
It felt the glow, so near my heart
Which admiration threw
And caught the sympathetic art
And spread its fragrance too.
[96] Strange that a flower, so prone to fade
When sever'd from its stem
Should wait to grace a Stranger's side
E'er it would wake and bloom!
Here, live and smile, sweet Jassamine,
Emblem of spirits risen,
Which snatch'd from earth by hand divine
Eternal glow in heaven.
Here, virtue half her charms conceals,
But placed in that bright Sphere

Elizabeth (Noyes) Rowe (1785–1814). Her witness of peace during the illness leading to her death as well as conversations with Joshua Rowe and William Moore led Page to regularly attend the Baptist chapel (the "Grass Tabernacle") where Rowe and Moore preached. Page became a Christian after reading a book (possibly *The Saints' Everlasting Rest*) by Richard Baxter (1615–1691), an Anglican clergyman who was expelled from the Church of England for refusing to conform to all its rites and ceremonies. Page met John Chamberlain at the Baptist Chapel in Dinapore, at whose urging Page moved to Monghyr. The Pages opened their house to Chamberlain, whose preaching led to the Monghyr mission station and the Baptist congregation with Henry and Jane Page as its first members. Page supported a school in Monghyr for the education of native children. Carey, *Christian Biography*, 2:106–120.

Where purity no Anguish feels,
She owns her Godhead there.

Sept. 7th. [1816].

Yesterday completed my first rendering of the first chapter of St. John's Gospel; not without many errors in the Hindee.

We have come to a dangerous part of the Ganges where we see wrecks of boats driven on the beach, that happened in the gale while *we* were at Mongire. Thus we may have been preserved, owing to the importunity of myself and some friends, to induce Mr. Rowe to pass a day or two longer there. We have heard of several families that were sunk with their boats, during a storm which blew while we were comfortably housed, and enjoying the pleasures of enlightened friends at *Berhampore*, where too, we continued longer than Mr. R. wished. But it is now evident, that a kind providence watched over our welfare in keeping us there by such gentilities.

Sep. 9th. [1816].

Opposite the city of Patna, the emporium of the district of Behar; the appearance of which from the river is better than that of any city from Calcutta thus far. It looks more modern and less in ruins. The English have erected handsome factories and warehouses there. The Opium House on the bank of the river looks well. The whole, as it stretches along the bank, resembles the city of my brother's residence, Philadelphia. The scenery all along the bank for miles past, has been very beautiful. We have come out of our boat and are enjoying the view.

[97] We are now so near *home*, within twenty miles of it that we feel unwilling to suffer delay. I never have been more uniformly healthy, than since I embarked on this journey. It is now two months nearly since we came on board the Budgerow.

3 o'clock. Joy! Joy! I dreamed all last night about being with my brother and sister Atlee at Phil[a]. On waking this morning I told my

dream to my companion, and affectionate partner—and just now, a boat arrived from Digah 12 miles distant, bringing a supply of good things sent by brother & sister Moore to meet us, with a basket of roses, and a *packet* of letters and one separate, from my ever dear brother Edwin in answer to the one sent him from the capes of Delaware. It is a welcome and sweet messenger from my native land.

I regret having not seen Captn. Kenyon, but shall forward from Digah, a budget for my dear brother, if he will promise me to deal out verbally what he thinks suitable to be communicated in parts of my journal. It contains more things than I would comprise in a letter, and such as I feel sure my friends would like to hear of from my hand. Let them rejoice with me in my welfare, so far I am yet acquainted with my state, or can foresee it. I have been too studious of late in the acquirement of this language, feeling more pleasure and interest in it, than in any other engagement: this with my little Budgerow School, has occupied me very closely of late.

During our passage, we have seen many Crocodiles and Alligators in the river, which we judged to be from 20 to thirty feet long. The Crocodile has a green head and curling snout, and great eyes, which it keeps out of water a long time together as it swims. They lie on the edges of the Sand beds in the river, basking in the Sun.

Letters from Mr. Marshman to Mr. Rowe, and one from Mrs. Marshman to me, speaks of Mrs. Hough having been at the point of death at Calcutta since their return from the ship in which they took passage to Rangoon.[114] I am now 400 miles from them by the

[114] Phebe Hough was deathly sick following the Houghs' abortive first attempt to reach Rangoon. The Houghs had departed from India in late June 1816, but soon made their way back to Calcutta as the ship proved to be dangerously unseaworthy. The captain and pilot were equally problematic. They were drunkards "who anchored opposite every tavern along the Hooghly and usually had to be carried back to the ship." It took another three months to find a ship that could take the Houghs, the printing press, and type to Burma. Departing again in late September, they arrived in Rangoon on October 15, 1816. Anderson, *To the Golden Shore*, 195–196.

river course, and fairly in Hindostan. Here I cannot lay by my pen without reflecting on the goodness of God towards me in all things: and especially in [98] preserving me alive, on this boisterous river, in a keelless boat, during a voyage of eight weeks, four of which have been spent at different halting places.

Somewhere not far from Mongire, we went to see the hot well and the cold well, or rather springs, at *Seetakoon.*[115] They are only a dozen steps or so from each other—one boils up hot enough to cook eggs—the other, as cold as ice.

People who provide for *invalids* going to England for their health, send quantities of bottles there to be filled with *Seetakoon pauny*. It is cooked and sealed, and keeps good long after being in England. The springs are both in a place twelve feet square, having stone steps on four sides to lead down to them. Not less than 20 Bramins live about them, to collect vails[116] from visitors; *all* of whom followed us back to our boat, urging us to bestow money on them, assuring us, we should consequently escape all affliction for life if we did. Mr. Rowe, with his good-natured talent at foiling such persons, told them he too was a poor Patriarch, and need their bounty. The Residence of the Bramins there, renders the hot springs a holy place in the estimation of the Hindoos, and crowds of them go there to be powwow'd and pooja'd by them which takes away all their sins!

We often have seen Bramins standing at the brink of the River, touching over their beads and calling aloud the names of their Deities. I cannot but draw a great comparison between them and the Roman Catholics. When we were at Mongire (brother Chamberlain's Station) a poor pitiable man presented himself at the gate, to excite charity. He had, to do penance for his sins, held up his arms

[115] The Sitakund (meaning "spring of Sita") at Monghyr was one of several places called Sitakund. These included springs on the River Gandak in Tirhut, Bihar northwest of Patna, and those in Benares, Gaya, Brindavan, Puri, Chittagong, Kelat, and Ceylon. Pilgrims were attracted to the springs as well as to the shrines often found at the sites. Sen, *Shrines of Sitakund,* 23, 54.

[116] Vails: proceeds or gratuities.

until the weight of the arms below the elbows, had turned those arms downward from the Elbows, and they hung dangling and withered, having only so much power left in them as to touch his stomach with his finger ends, in token of hunger. He looked like those scare-crows in the fields, made by putting a stick half through the sleeves of an old coat, to frighten the birds away.

All along the coast from Mongire, were erected little temples, where widows had been burned with the dead bodies of their husbands. They are kept very well white- [99] washed, so as to make a show from a distance: they are called *Suttee-gah* or the *shrine of truth*. These objects excite very sad feelings. I felt some little triumph over Idolatry when old *Vrinda-Bund*[117] came out to bid us *good by*; he waded some distance into the water to shake hands with us—I was glad to have so good an opportunity, in presence of many heathen spectators, of handing him a loaf of our bread, which he tasted—a thing that is an abomination in their sight. To eat a crumb of Christian's bread, would be the means of banishing them from society here, and in heaven, forever. He was one of the earliest converts.

I cannot help adverting to times past, the mention of which I neglected when on the appropriate topic, but which I feel pleasure in reflecting upon aloud, as it were. The octagon in Captn. Page's garden at Mongire, has long served for a place of Christian [worship] for those who desire to repair to the house of prayer. Mr. Rowe preached in it, as Mr. Chamberlain was absent. About 20 sincere worshippers of Jesus Christ assembled—a great congregation for

[117] When Charlotte was writing in 1817, Vrinda-bund (more often spelled Brindabun but also Vrindavuna and Brindabund) was sixty years old. He was a Byragee, a high-caste Brahmin, who had wandered for years before he was baptized by John Chamberlain on April 4, 1807 at Cutwa. He read Bengali and Hindi and worked at Digah with Moore and Rowe from 1812–1816. He then moved to Monghyr where he worked with Chamberlain. Brindabun died in 1821 Chamberlain, *Memoirs of John Chamberlain*, 368, 412.

such a place in such a country. The octagon[118] is within the Fort, and overlooks the river, commanding an extensive view. It appears to have been erected for an observatory, by a former and native power. Christians at Mongire have sometimes met to worship the true God in a large mosque, where Mahomet was formerly adored. The Mussulmans do not worship a triune, nor a unique God, but a God in two persons, as in their ejaculations they say "Ulla-mhum-mud" God-and-Mahomet.[119]

Mongire is full of temples, and tombs. One temple is built on a high mound of craggy rocks, so as to be difficult of access. The old Fort walls enclosing the place where the palace stood, was built 300 years ago by the then presiding *Nawaub* or Nabob. The Hon[ble]. Company keep[s] a few troops within them, and sentries at the gates.

Mongire, is without exception, the pleasantest place I have seen in India, as to its natural appearances, being pleasantly swelled with hills, on which the English build their houses. It commands a view of the noble river, and of the continuation of the mountains on the opposite side. It is the chosen place of retreat for invalids and persons retired from public life.

[100] Mrs. Chamberlain having been many months in Phil[a.] on her way to India, became acquainted with several persons whom I knew there; consequently we were fond of holding chat together. She was then known as Miss Underwood. Mr. C. had paid his addresses to her before he left England, and some time after being in India, made proposals to her to come over and complete his happiness.[120] She has become very stout, in body, heart, and hand, in the

---

[118] The domed octagon, dating perhaps to the fourteenth century, was a mausoleum honoring a Muslim saint, causing the site to be called Pir Pahar, or "hill of the saint." Joshua, "Munger: Yoga and Guns," *Outlook.*

[119] Charlotte was new to India and mistakenly thought that Muslims worshipped Muhammad.

[120] Miss Mary Underwood and John Chamberlain married in India on September 18, 1809.

good cause before her. At the same time, she is the most cheerful woman I know of.

Evening—this afternoon finished reading, and giving the literal translation sentence by sentence, of the 1st Chapter of St. John's Gospel, to Mr. Rowe, who is my sole teacher as yet.

September 10th. [1816].

At last arrived at that spot, which in providence I may consider my proper temporal home! I shall narrate circumstances, scenes, and my feelings on entering upon it. Our Budgerow arrived before the Digah Mission Station at 4 o'clock this morning. The full moon shone *resplendently*—It seemed like a nocturnal day. We put to, and Mr. Rowe led me up a steep path under the great Tamarind tree, from under which I first spied the two bungalows or houses,[121] separated by a long Arbour. Mr. Moore soon made his appearance: but as Mrs. M. did [not] relish so early an exit from her quiet repose, he took us into the fruit garden to walk about until day light should better shew us to each other. Much delighted with the romance, my mind was absorbed in contemplation and thankfulness, as Mr. M. and my partner were deeply engaged in conversation, which I did not hear, though arm in arm with them. The Garden had three long parallel walks, at the end of which were grape arbours, of considerable extent. Unfortunately, the grapes were all over, flowers perfumed the air, from various trees in the walks, which formed an avenue. Morning had not yet cast aside her starry mantle and the moon threw out shadows darkly about us. My heart reiterated continually, "O God, thou has brought me *home*." I bethought me, that here I am nearer to my American friends by some hundreds of miles on the returning side of the globe, or rather [101] on the other side of the meridian.

As the morning resumed her golden bracelets, her rosy cheek

[121] A third bungalow had earlier collapsed and been swept away by the encroaching Ganges.

and cheerful eye, peeped over the thick green hedges—there came running out to see this new preceptress, the inquisitive little throng, clad in white, and sweet as the morning breeze—but not so *fair* as Aurora. At once I beheld my duty and my delight in them. Seventeen young ladies, will form my family and my School, together with the little family I had on board the budgerow.[122]

A School of about as many boys, many of whom are the brothers of the little girls, is taught by Messrs. Moore & Rowe, at intervals of missionary labours, having an usher to be constantly in the School.

When the light of the morning was sufficient, *our bungalow* or house, was opened for my reception; it was nearly empty, the furniture being on our boat; and seated at my *own door*, I received Mrs. Moore, who welcomed me to Digah, very affectionately. You may wish to ask, what sort of a house is a Bungalo? [sic] It is a one story house, with a roof falling low from a great height, descending on four sides from a point at the top. It has three rows of rooms, which leaves one large hall in the centre; this is very high, shaded, and airy, having several large doors opening into the connecting rooms, through which it receives all the light it gets. The house is shaded all round by eaves which are supported by brick pillars; and a pavement makes them comfortable in all weathers. All the windows have green venetians. All the apartments are large, and there [are] bathing closets connected with each corner-room, which are supplied from the outside by a man who brings water in a great leather bag on his back, from the river, daily.[123]

---

[122] Most of the students at Digah were Eurasians whose mothers were Indian or Eurasian and fathers were generally British soldiers who wanted their children taught in English.

[123] Bungalow: an anglicized form of *bangla* meaning "of Bengal." The bungalow was based on a traditional Bengali structure of mud walls and thatched roof. "Up country" bungalows functioned as "stationary tents" for soldiers. They became the typical housing for British traders and managers of plantations and factories, as well as overnight accommodation for travelers. King, "The Bungalow, 1600–1980," 53, 55, 88.

Mr. Moore's bungalo is much larger than ours. Thither we are all to repair to the mess-table.[124] *We* only are privileged to *take a cup of tea* at home, by ourselves.

Mrs. Moore has handed me another packet of letters from dear America. My pleasures this day, are great.

[102] I desire to be thankful, instant in prayers, and to fulfill my obligations as a parent, wife, and instructress. I wish my dear brother Edwin and my other friends, could reciprocate my *comfort come at last*. His pleasant portrait which has come the mazy rounds with me, hangs before my eyes and seems to comprehend my circumstances, and to smile gratefully, upon me. I am writing while my husband is busy in putting things into their places, as they are brought from the boat.

I was much shocked this morning by hearing Mrs. Moore relate the circumstance of old bowed-down woman, being *got rid* of by her relatives with whom she lived, recently. They took her out one dark night, out to the middle of the river *alive*, and tying two earthen jugs to her shoulders, let them fill with water, and then let her sink with them! She *crying out for mercy* so loud that she was heard on shore!! After which, there being a great gang of them, they set up a shout or roar of lamentation for her decease. This they did close by a missionary's house, where no doubt many of them had heard the Gospel, for the poor woman was connected with some of their servants, and she with her family used to come to their house to weave up breaches in the floor mats. She was one of the lowest casts called Dooms. A Doom, means a *tail* of anything. Oh! how does my soul long to be able to speak to these poor deluded females; for though their fate *here* might not for a long time be meliorated, they might have the hope of Salvation by Jesus Christ, in their breast, when

[124] The missionaries at Digah ate together, similar to the practice of the Baptist missionaries in Serampore where the Careys, Marshmans, and Wards lived in separate houses but shared meals in a common hall.

hurried thus into eternity.

Nine at night—Mr. Rowe could not think of taking rest until he had been to visit his little flock of soldiers at Dinapore; a church of Christian brethren being formed in the 24th Regiment. This is their regular Lecture evening. A gig and two horses are kept by this station.

Mrs. Moore and I have spent the evening together. We were prompted to remark, how agreeably disappointed we were on our arrival in India, to find a green country, a plentiful table, and many Christian people. This country enjoys perpetual spring, for a field yields four crops of things, one sort [103] after another. If it were not thus, so great a population could not be supported. They have most of the kinds of grain that we have in America, and some which we have not. This my eyes have seen. We have beautiful wheat bread, and we have brown bread, but it is not rie, [sic] it is made of the coarser particles of the wheat, after the heart of it is taken out. The beef, veal, mutton &c. are indeed, far inferior to ours, unless great pains is taken to stall feed them on grain, which cannot be afforded by common butchers, nor can common purchasers afford the price for stall fed meats, every day. There is a change of fruits ripening, all the year.

Sept. 13th. [1816].

Rode with Mr. Moore this morning early, to look at the scenes abroad. At Dinapore, within two English miles of us, the Cantonments enclose four large squares of grass, which is kept very clean and short, to afford parade ground for the Soldiers. The whole view round is very handsome. Companies were on the ground exercising and the Band played cheerfully. Beyond these Cantonments are barracks for *native* Soldiers. They consist of picked men, and are tall and majestic in their mein. They have given evidence of their firmness in battle.

I never have rode [sic] out, in this country, but I feel my heart ache sorely. The miserable appearance of the native women and their half-clad bodies, and their filthy habits about their own little dwellings, disgusts me. None of respectability allow themselves to be seen. They live secluded from public view—they are distinguished from those that walk abroad by the term "Purda beebee" or *Curtain Lady.* There are no wooden doors to the inner rooms of their houses, but a cane blind or a cloth hung in the door-way, is as impenetrable as an iron door—for custom excludes all males except the husband, from entering at pleasure. And he never presumes to surprise them, without hem-hawing outside, to give notice of his intention to enter.

The Baptist Chapel at Dinapore is built of bamboo posts, its walls are coarse mats tied up—and its roof is thatch.[125] The word of the living God is sweet there, to such as go to hear it.

[104] There are Military Stations at about 200 miles distant as far as a thousand miles up the river, and in the interior through to Bombay. The armies consist of men from England, Scotland, Wales, and Ireland.[126] Of course, there is no want of society to persons in similar standings, but we are dissimilar in our habits, to the people of the Army—notwithstanding the intercourse of a *Country* subsists between them & us.

I will send my dear brother a few sentences of my attempts at transposing Hindostani. I dare not say *translate*, for that sounds too high for a beginner at least. They will at any rate, prove me to be [a] fibber about trying to learn this language. They will give you an idea of the appearance of the Alphabet, and expose the difficult and reversed idiom of the Hindosthanee, as I have set the literal meaning

---

125 The chapel was thus called the "Straw Chapel" or "Grass Tabernacle."

126 From the Battle of Plassey in 1757 to the Charter Renewal Act of 1833, the East India Company gradually transitioned from being a trading company to an administrative body that governed India on behalf of the Crown. This new function required a significant increase of British troops. Their presence led to a rapidly growing Eurasian population that in turn provided a preferred labor source for the army and all branches of the Company's work. By the 1750s Eurasians outnumbered Britons in India. Hyam, *Empire and Sexuality*, 116; Anthony, *Britain's Betrayal in India*, 17.

under each word.

I will add one thing more to amuse you, and there close my parcel to have ready to send down, to go by the *Neptune*.[127] As I patted little Josiah on the cheek one evening lately, my beloved partner desired me to make an acrostic on him, and here it is.

Just like a flow'r that hails the day
  On yonder spray so green,
Soft, opening, fragrant, mild, and gay
  Is my Josiah seen;
And soon like it, must fade and die—
  How transient life's cold beam!

Reflect dear boy, no sense nor hope
  Of heaven, have fairest flowers.
With'ring they fall upon the slope—
  Eternity is *ours*.

As I wished my little boys to *feel* a partiality from me, I feared William might think me so, if I neglected him; and therefore I endeavoured to prevent such a suspicion, by conjuring up the following rhymes; though the topics stated were just to his praise.

Acrostic on William Carey Rowe
With various flowers together tied,
[105] I'm met by my sweet William;
  Love places a nosegay where I ride,
  Looks, prove me homeward welcome.
  If but a Butterfly be found
  As o'er the Lawn he ranges,

[127] The ship *Neptune* commanded by Captain Fisher sailed from Calcutta to Madras before sailing on to America. It arrived in Philadelphia on May 7, 1817 after 105 days at sea. "Philadelphia," *New York Evening Post,* May 8, 1817, 2.

Much pleas'd pursues its devious round—
Comes telling all its changes.
As objects offer every hour
Replete with warm conceptions,
Eager he strains his infant power,
Yielding to young impressions.
Religion is the theme, dear boy,
Of early thought most worthy:
When piety refines our joy,
Each object beams with glory.

Dear Edwin, that both the above were obligatory you perceive, and therefore, no wonder if not very enchanting. I must add that the eldest Son, Joshua, is as great a favorite, but not as great a pet. Indeed, his assumed manliness would shrink from the idea of being petted. I know not whether it is owning something better and more refined in their dispensations, or whether it is the quieting effects of this climate, that they are the stillest little fellows I ever knew, always.

Please to send me the life of Harriet Newell. I felt my native (from new birth) disposition to disseminate the knowledge of the love of Christ to sinners, rekindled and strengthen into an unextinguishable flame by the perusal of her life. Her tragical and short career in India did more for the cause of the heathen, than many entreaties sent to government for freedom to missionaries.

Christian worship was held in our hall this afternoon for the natives in their Language. About 40 attended. The songs of grace from such lips are what I most wish to hear under our roof.

9 at night—it passes as if I could not cease communing with my dear brother—I love thee for thy prayers—I need them for I possess a very sinful heart and a frail [106] body. I feel that the work, which lies before me will require the peculiar help of a divinely sustaining hand. I feel inspired with good courage however, in the expectation of commencing my school tomorrow, having written out my Rules. This is the fifth night since I arrived. I find sister Moore to be very

kindly disposed to aid me in all my plans for good government. I promise myself a friendly neighbour in her. She also, was one of those who passed some time in Philadelphia when the Embargo was on,[128] and mentions several persons whom I know.

Dear Edwin, as I have come on thus far successfully, let thy prayers facilitate my progress, helping me to fulfill all the Lord's will concerning me. I desire to glorify him by my life, in my individual capacity. May His eye love to dwell on thee, and his hand be prone to bless thee and thine!

I will give my Joshua's love to you, but I think he will write to you. He is not yet returned from his evening Lecture to the Soldiers in the Straw Chapel, which God has greatly honor'd—Thine, C. H. Rowe.[129]

[106a] Digah, September 14. 1816.

After a day of lassitude, not being very well, but now feeling revived, I will try to begin answering your letter together with that of other kind friends.

I have been only five days *at home*; the following week will engross more of my time from writing, as I expect to commence my task as governess. The young Ladies will lodge under the same roof with myself and the partner by whom, in the providence of God, I am brought into the sphere of respectfulness at which my desires

---

[128] The East India Company banned unlicensed passengers, including evangelical missionaries, from sailing to India on their ships. Undeterred, some missionaries secured passage on ships of other nations that stopped in Britain. The first British Baptist missionaries William Carey, John Thomas, and their families sailed to India on the Danish ship, *Kron Princess Maria*. Many other early Baptist missionaries sailed first to the United States and then proceeded to India on American ships.

[129] Here Charlotte wrote in the margins, "Note the letter dated Sept. 20 must come in between these two last. Also Sept 14 first." Those two letters were inserted here in the journal on unnumbered pages. They appear in this transcription designated as pages 106a–106f. This transcript then resumes the journal's pagination at 106.

aimed. I shall henceforth have little time for pleasure, separately from my duties: I pray God daily, to make those duties pleasurable; and I think I feel my mind in a state to find enjoyment in them, from a desire to redeem time, and glorify the holy name, as well as to spread the knowledge of the truth by quiet means. In four days more, I shall have been three months a wife in India; I have passed those months, as much more happily than the preceeding [sic] three, as the Zenith is higher than the Nadir: Yet I am not without moments of looking and longing to join in the delectable and uninterrupted Songs of the *glorified* at the right hand of The Blessed. I must not however, dwell on self until I have duly thanked you for the sweet letter which has cheer'd the hearts of our little compact. Brother Moore says, "I feel the most congenial esteem and regard for your brother Edwin, and through you, I offer him my hearty affection." I rejoice that you were all favored to be kept in health. The letter followed soon after I left America, which was kind in you.

I accompany this letter with my Diary, of which I have no copy, but which I have designed as an Epistle to you; from time to time feeling inclined to address you; or otherwise making minutes; and giving vent to my governing feelings at the moment of writing.

Passing opportunities to Calcutta, do not allow us time to write largely to our friends, is the reason I have written to so few of them. And I have little time for writing.

[106b] Ward's History of India,[130] of which there are some copies sent to Philadelphia, will afford you Interesting statements of the internal affairs of India. It will shew you that this is a Land of Superstition. But Superstition is not confined to India. It is a great pity that any addition of it should cross the ocean, to come hither. The arrival of a Bishop in Calcutta not long since,[131] with a *Canister of Holy Earth*, designed to consecrate therewith, the burial grounds of

[130] Ward, *Account of the Writings, Religion, and Manners of the Hindoos.*

[131] Thomas Fanshaw Middleton (1769–1822), the first bishop of Calcutta, arrived in 1814. His diocese included all the East India Company's territory.

the Company, is a *Superstition* as much in my estimation as any that can be found among the Heathen in India. At first, I considered it a mere quiz, or jest, but am assured it is a fact.

I have such a multitude to write to, that I feel quite oppressed. Some must take the will for the deed.

I read the 1 and 2nd chapters of John's Gospel this morning to a *Moonshee*, or Scribe, or keeper of accounts. I do not understand much of the Second chapter, as it is newly in hand. I lament Sister J's illness—give my love to her and to brother John[132]; to your dear Margaret and little ones.

Believe me ever affectionately
Your Sister Charlotte.

September 20th. 1816.
My dear little Nephews, Nieces and acquaintances,

I have thought of you so much today and this evening, owing to a particular incident, that I think in respect to you I should let you know that I recollect you all with much pleasure.

Today is my little son Josiah's Birth day, and as he is uniformly, one of the best boys I ever knew, I would have him honored on this day, so the *Khunsamah* or provider, made him a large plum Cake, finely frosted on the top, with sugar plums &cc. on it, as nice as you can get at Mrs. G's of Philadelphia.[133] I had the little table set in the

---

[132] Charlotte's siblings, Jane Atlee (wife of Rev. Elisha Rigg) and John Sayre Atlee.

[133] Mrs. G. was Elizabeth (Baker) Goodfellow (c. 1767–1851), who reputedly started America's first cooking school in Philadelphia. Thrice married and widowed, she was described by one of her students as "a very respectable, ladylike person, who, having been thrown on her own resources, opened a pastry cookery establishment, which soon became famous." Goodfellow supported herself and her family for more than fifty years through her baked goods, confectionary shop, and her cooking school. Her customers included many wealthy Philadelphia families, one of which was Stephen Girard, whose bank is mentioned in the July 29, 1816 journal entry. Daughters of Philadelphia's elite families were among Mrs. Goodfellow's cooking school students.

arbour between the bungalows, and the chinaware for children which I bought in Calcutta, and preserves, bread and butter, and tea, made quit a display. He was allowed to invite twelve boys in [106c] School, of his own age. I told him, that he was the master of the feast, and therefore must see his friends served before he helped himself. Now I dare say you will recollect a story in the *Child's Friend*, of a little boy, who acted quite the reverse. Well, Josiah behaved so sweetly, that we all admired him; and for that I gave him a double portion. He could not eat of it with pleasure, recollecting that there were other boys, but larger, who were not invited but whom he regarded: so darting from his place, he ran and gave it all to them. He had consented to me taking off the fine top of the Cake for his papa, which he handed to him when he came to take a peep at us. His papa gave him back the most of it, so that though he was generous, he lost none of his share, for that was the best part. His little guests unanimously wished him many returns of his birth day, and bowing, withdrew to the School house.

It is very pretty to see the little boys and girls skipping about the green—they are *all* dressed in clean white every day. The boys play

---

Elizabeth Goodfellow was said to have introduced the lemon pudding pie and is credited by food historian William Woys Weaver with inventing the lemon meringue pie. Customers eagerly sought her lemon pies as well as her coconut pies, Spanish buns, Queen cakes, jumbles, plum pudding, bread, and sponge cakes. She introduced the practice of creating recipes that listed the ingredients first, followed by the preparation process. Goodfellow's reputation was well established during her lifetime. While serving as a Paris correspondent for the *Public Ledger* newspaper in Philadelphia, William Henry Fry boasted the excellence of American cuisine by writing, "[A]n American supper is a novelty in this region of diluted syrups and cakes—the latter, by the way, are far inferior to those made by Philadelphia ladies, pupils of the classic Mrs. Goodfellow." Although she wrote no cookbook, Elizabeth Goodfellow's fame was perpetuated by students who featured her recipes in their own cookbooks. Levick, *Recollections of her early days,* 24; Reber, "Mrs. Goodfellow," *Researching Food History*; Diamond, *Mrs. Goodfellow*, 158; "Letter from Paris," *Philadelphia Public Ledger*, June 23, 1851, 1.

on one side of the arbour and down the long avenue; and the girls have the river side of the green and that around our house to play on. They have so much fruit allowed them, that they have no motive for intruding into the Garden; or if they walk there, they must not touch any thing.

Sometimes Mr. Rowe and I have chairs placed out on the green, and we get the little girls to join in singing. The boys, emulous of their own skill, will then place themselves among the trees, out of discovery, and respond to them. In this country, singing of hymns is a general thing amongst Christians. We cultivate it in them, because the natives are fond of singing, but they, from ignorance, sing bad songs.

My little William is never satisfied to go to bed until he has said his prayers and hymn. My three little Sons, stand before me, and repeat verse about, and period about, which takes no more time than to teach one, while all must be attentive. They join the little girls in being Catechized every Sabbath.

This education is very different from that which the poor heathen children all around us, receive. They are unconscious of the propriety of keeping the Sabbath holy. [106d] They have never heard of a Sabbath day. They play with dust in the streets and roads, piling it up in great heaps and then jump in it. Being naked, and having their bodies always oily, they come out in a sad figure, much like dogs. Some of the heathen children come to our School for natives, and some come to our Sabbath day worshiping of the true God; where they hear the Scriptures read and hymns sung, but they would not come if the School masters did not come and bring them, which they are obliged to do, or forfeit our employing them. I am sure, if you were to be let down amongst these people, you would first stare, then blush, and then cry.

You would be delighted with the little birds in my cage. I have more than thirty in one large wire cage. They are in size, between a wren and a humming bird, and some are spotted all over with little round spots of red, and white, and black, on a dark brown plumage. Some are quite a plain drab colour: these I conclude are little Friends or Quakers, as they never are seen to *sing*; while the others sing long tunes. One of them in particular, sings the entire first part of a tune to which I used to dance when I was young and did not love religion. It reminds me of days which I had to repent of. Rats and other things, often try to get at them; so little William has them tied to his bed side at night, to guard them. A few days ago, a number of them flew out of the cage, but being afraid of the crows which are always about the house, they soon came back and settled on the cage; so we let them in again.

You have heard of lizards—there is an innocent kind that keeps about our walls in the evenings.[134] They eat the insects that settle on the wall around where the lamps hang. Sometimes they jump upon my knee when I am quite still, to get a fly from my dress. They seem to charm it with their bright black eyes, and then extend their tongue out and dart at it.

I often wish I could send you a pair of Camelions,[135] [sic] but the recollection that they will have no live grasshoppers to eat [at] sea, deters me. It is said that they will eat but two a day. They have had the credit of living on air; [106e] but a person here tried the experiment, and in 2 weeks, the poor thing died. It is however quite true that they change colour—I cannot say that they do, to *whatever* color'd thing they are surrounded by—but I have seen one which when I first saw it, in its cage was a tawny colour, become so green all over, on being a little while in the branch of a tree that was put up in the room for it, that I could not distinguish it but by its form, from the leaves about it. When they have been alone, and a mate is brought near, they shew evident signs of joy &cc. changing to spots of all colours—but if they are irritated, they grow a slate colour, and look very badly. I have stood and seen all these changes, and then seen them settle to a livid pale ash colour. Their eyes are very curious—they stand a half inch out from their head, the pupil only being exposed or having no skin on it, and that is not so large as the pupil

---

134 Asian house geckos.

135 Chameleons.

of your eye; and they turn the balls every way and diverse ways, that is, adverse ways. They catch their food with their tongue, which they dart out at it, many inches. These are peculiarities which you would not learn from seeing one in the museum.

You would be pleased with the little horses, and the carriages to suit them, that fashionable children ride out with here. If children outlive eight years they stand a chance to live to grow up. Because so many young children die in teething and afterward, their parents send them to England. My little stepsons are very pale and delicate, but they are in general healthy—we take proper care to keep them out of the Sun, which often strikes persons, and they die of a fever on the brain in a few hours.

One plant from the flower-seeds my dear Mary Yardly[136] gave me from her garden, has grown. It seems to be a princess feather—I love to look at, for it whispers me of my lovely friend.

I hope dear Esther Atlee is a very good girl, and that Mary and her sisters, and Edwin and his brothers, are [106f] good and happy. They will give my love to dear little Augusta Dehaven, and Elizabeth Staughton.[137]

---

136 Mary Yardly (1788–1838) was a twenty-eight-year-old Quaker whom Charlotte may have met through her brother Edwin. In 1820 Mary married Giles Knight in Bucks, Pennsylvania.

137 Charlotte is referring to her nieces and nephews, who were Edwin Augustus and Margaret (Snyder) Atlee's children. The nieces were Esther Barton, Mary Patience Atlee, and their four sisters: Margaret Longstreth, Sarah Zane, Charlotte White, and Elizabeth Jane Atlee. The nephews were Edwin Pitt Atlee and his three brothers: Samuel Yorke, Thomas Scattergood, and Richard Jordan Atlee. "Little Augusta Dehaven" was likely Julia Augusta Dehaven (1809–1848), the daughter of Charlotte's cousin, Sarah Elizabeth Atlee, and her husband, Peter Dehaven. Elizabeth Ann Staughton (1807–1849) was the daughter of Dr. William and Maria (Martin) Hanson Staughton.

I hope the Lord will bless you all with new hearts. Then you will choose all those things that are good and profitable. Give my love to your elders and superiors, and believe me, your affectionate friend and relative,

Charlotte Hazen Rowe

[106 resumed] Dec. 22nd. 1816. Lord's Day.

This has been a trying morning with me. My cares are rather increased on Sunday mornings, in seeing that the young Ladies are all in proper order to attend worship. They, with the servants, are sometimes very unmanageable. This has quite discomposed me this morning, and I sat down to quiet my mind by meditation. The children born of native mothers, and of course reared thus far by them, are devoid of ideas beyond eating, sleeping, bathing, and dressing. They speak the vernacular tongue almost wholly, their English being quite a broken dialect. I have noticed with much surprise, many little fair misses, whose mothers have been English Ladies of fashion, speak nothing but the Hindostani, even to their parents: and fashionable women here, seldom think it worth while to study this language. They rest satisfied with picking up the common technical terms of commanding their servants &cc. [107] Thus trained by their mothers, they are brought to our school and the first that is to be done in them, is to unlearn them all they have learned, and lay a foundation for some thing better in their minds.

The present character of Schools in Calcutta, seeks chiefly to ornament their pupils externally, so as to make them attractive, to the many young officers constantly arriving. There is the Upper and the Lower orphan schools.[138] In one of these, the young Ladies have a ball day monthly, when young gentlemen are admitted, and many

[138] Class distinctions prevailing in Britain were replicated in India with the Eurasian children of military officers being sent to the Upper Orphan School and Eurasian children of non-commissioned officers or privates being sent to the Lower Orphan School.

matches are originated there. At another, the gentlemen are expected to call to see the Ladies, and they are called into the parlour, at least, such of them as are considered marriageable, and stand or sit in their presence, like dolls in a shop window for sale. A choice is made of some one, either on the first or second visit. I believe this to be quite true, as I know a married couple, who formed their friendship in this manner, and she acknowledges this regulation, to be a fact generally known.[139]

Now I wish to form the minds of my pupils, to adorn the domestic circle; but without any such lookout for a husband, as is described above. I have one young Lady with me who has been at one of those schools, and am more often vexed and disgusted with her, than with all the rest.

Through this morning's services, my mind has been unusually affected with the deplorable state of society at large in this country; and with the consideration that the young must grow up to become the same, unless snatched from among them, and trained up in a quite different manner.

My heart felt consoled at last, by a touch of divine love, viewing Christ as all-powerful to hear our prayers on their behalf, and to effect a gradual transformation, through the medium of pious instruction. As Mr. Rowe's audience this morning was chiefly of the schools and our families on the premises, he addressed his discourse to the young. O! that some heart may have been touched!

When I see the disrespect paid to the Sabbath by the generality of foreigners here, I am surprised—I think had they no Sabbaths in England, Scotland, & Ireland? [108] Or have they left their

---

[139] At the start, the Company encouraged marriage with local Indian women. As Eurasians increased in India, Britons increasingly chose brides from that community. The balls were held to secure marriage proposals for the young ladies. The girls, often as young as thirteen, could reject or accept the proposals. "Persons in want of wives frequently made their selection of an evening. Officers in the upper provinces sometimes travelled a distance of 500 miles to obtain a wife in this way." Anthony, *Britain's Betrayal in India*, 406.

consciences in their native country? For such as are building, let this people work on the Sabbath; and the Ladies keep their Seamsters or Dirzys at the needle. It is not enough in extenuation of their fault, to say that the natives do not ask rest on that day; nor that the natives have no Sabbath on that day. People professing themselves to be Christians,[140] should leave their servants without excuse from attending the means of grace, if themselves cannot call them in to join in them domestically. I am happy to say that there are a few in *this* polite world, who present an exception to the [rule].

Lord's Day. January 5th. 1817.

Have had my feelings much depressed today, by seeing this morning, over on the sand bed in the river, opposite our house, a party of Hindoos sitting near two heaps of prepared combustibles, and a man or woman lying wound up in a sheet, with its feet just touching the water; I could see a person every little while go down and take up a handful of wet sand, and then sit down by his head, and do something to it. No doubt it was to put the holy mud into his mouth and ears, dead or alive—by which means he was prepared for the next holy ordeal of being singed (called burned), and in the course of one hour, his blackened body was pushed into the river, to float off to the great deep, first to be pushed off as a nuisance from many a ghaut whither the tide has washed it.

The party then went home, as is their custom, to have a funeral feast. The *aged sick*, and *leprous* persons are generally taken alive, and drowned—sometimes with their own consent. Satan has stood lawgiver for this country. The spirit of the Lord seems to have fled from the human mind here. Wonder that his goodness clothes the land with bounty. It is because he is longsuffering and waiteth to be gracious.

---

[140] Charlotte was not alone in this judgment. Governor General Lord William Bentinck wrote in 1834, "We do not do as we would be done by. We profess but do not practice Christianity…." Carson, *East India Company and Religion*, 198.

Digah. Jany. 12th. 1817.

After having kept my school three months, and a vacation of one month expired today, I feel a cheerfulness in the idea of resuming it on the morrow. [109] The reformation which I conceit I see in the children leads me to hope my instructions are not in vain. Indeed strangers have remarked the alteration in them. If the Lord will but answer our prayers in our time, it seems to be all I can ask or desire. Their conduct today has been very interesting. Mr. Moore being absent, and Mr. Rowe having to preach at Dinapore this morning, it devolved on me to catechize them. They put frequent and pertinent questions on spiritual things.[141] Formerly they sat impatiently, endeavoring to excite each other's risibility.

At our last communion season, seven converted Hindoos partook with us. One of the larger girls of about eleven years old, seeing the emblems set, said, "I wish I could have bread and wine" on which one who sat beside her laughed at her, and told it to me: at this she seemed hurt, being misunderstood, and anxiously, said, "No, No, not for that." I asked her if it was that she wished to be good enough to take it? which she confirmed. I told her to pray to God to change her heart, and he would grant her desire. Today she is reading her little bible. May God bless her youthful inclinations to be good, and bring her into the full love of himself! One of the female servants has begun to learn the Lord's prayer by reading it. She learned the Alphabet of me, and she has persevered in learning to read. O! what delight would it afford me to see her so far advanced as to read and write her native tongue fluently, and above all, love the Scriptures. She would become just what I wish, a native teacher of native children.[142]

---

[141] Charlotte encouraged the children to ask questions, rather than simply learn the catechism through rote memorization.

[142] Charlotte recruited teachers for the girls' schools, starting with women she had taught.

January 23. [1817].

Welcome thou Godly tear, raised from dissolving ice that weighs upon my heart, while flames of conjugal and holy love combining, struggle around it. How shall I give place to both safely, and not love my God the least? Frail, overweening nature, seeks to be soothed by the fleshly covenant, almost forgetful of the privilege divine, of calling God our Spouse and head, who never changes. How shall I so rein my heart as at once to please my God, and him whom he hath made one with me. I thank my jealous heavenly [110] benefactor, that when he sees me deviate, he drops an embittering restorative into my draught: at once it pains and heals my soul. But when *he* calls to *prayer*, He reconciles the temporal with the spiritual covenant. If happy marriage were not sometimes clouded, it might quite steal off our thoughts from heaven. What delight that earth possesses can be compared with that the feeling heart encompasses, when equal love awakens a unison? 'Tis past imagination, *save to the pure and fine-toned* mind—With such, Domesticity is no pain, and peace, no Stranger.

Lord's Day. Feb. 9th. 1817.

Continue to be encouraged in my work. And see some symptoms of grace in the male natives who attend on hearing the Gospel by their brethren.

Feb. 16. [1817].

Mr. Rowe has just called to me to say that the 66th Regt. is off, that is, just set sail from their mooring at the sand bank in the river opposite us. There are perhaps, a hundred boats, that look like great covered baskets on the water—these are called country boats, in distinction to the budgerows and Pinnaces[143] in which the officers travel. The Regiments are not allowed to remain more than two

[143] Pinnaces: small boats with sails or oars.

years at a place, lest they should grow inactive. But this regiment is ordered to St. Helena. Two of our best girls are to accompany their parents; whose eyes sparkled with delight at seeing their improvement. During the few days that the Reg^{t}. rested here, a soldier was killed in fighting with another; his liver was frittered into three parts by the blow of this antagonist's fist. And an officer in a drunken fit, jumped overboard and was lost; and a man who was well one day, died the next, and was buried in the Sand. The poor convict who killed the man is in irons, waiting his trial in Calcutta. Brother Moore & Mr. Rowe went over to preach to the Regiment, last evening. There are several good men amongst them.

[111] [February] 26th. [1817].

There are three natives enquiring the way to Zion who attend daily at Hindostani worship, hearing the Scriptures read. It is a great drawback upon the admission of a great number in the Christian church, that the missionaries must find support for those who do turn from idolatry. But this consideration does not induce us to keep them back. If God has sent us here to make known the truth, he will order things for the extension of it. These people work at all trades in their own way. There are brass-founders, blacksmiths, Carpenters, White-smiths, Jewelers, Cabinet-makers, Tailors, Masons, Sawyers, Brick-makers, Bakers, Dairymen, &cc. and if the true religion was but tolerated by them, all difficulty of the above kind, would be done away. But those who forsake *their* religion, must forsake them also, or be murdered. They dare not, however molest them after they are owned by us, or by the missionaries, and place themselves under their protection: for all white men, are in their estimation, a part of the Company's Government, which they stand in great fear of. Yet they own that their own privileges are greater than when the Rajahs ruled. They taxed them heavier than the present Government does, and were less just to their complaints, being activated more by arbitrary power than by equal laws. The present Gov^{t}. is so lenient towards them, that if two men, one a native and the other an European, quarrell, [sic] the sentence is given against the European, rather than the native.

The bottom of our garden is walled up by a range of little cottages, or a long shed divided into apartments, where the native christians reside. Their doors are screened from the public road by a hedge of bamboos, allowing a sufficient area for a common yard. They have a porch built in the hedge, with a roof and a seat on each side, where the native brethren sit and read the Scriptures, so that travellers may be tempted to step in and rest themselves and hear the Gospel. They always keep a firkin of water and a cup for them to drink and refresh themselves.

In passing up from their cottages, through the garden, I counted 25 different kinds of fruit trees. The manner in which some of them grow is singular to my eyes.

[112] A fruit similar in appearance, and a little so in taste, to a small musk melon, grows round the trunk of the tree under a tuft of spreading leaves which form the branches: it is called the papeiah;[144] its inside is filled with round seeds like grains of pepper. The jackfruit grows like a loaf of brown bread, from the trunk of the tree, anywhere up or down it. I do not like the taste of either of those fruits.

It would be endless to describe everything. Suffice it to say that they make a principal part of the food for the lower classes when they are in season. A single Jackfruit will turn out a large dish full of sections, each of which is as large as a fig, and is a little flattened. When the fruit is first opened, it spreads forth an intolerable small, but when the sections are washed in salt and water, that effluvia is subdued, and they eat crisp, cool, and sweetish.

The pomegranite, [sic] on account of the mention made of it in the Bible, strikes me as something sacred. It is the most beautiful of all, resembling a wild rose tree. The blossom is the size and shape nearly of a morning glory. It is a much brighter Scarlet than the convolvolis [sic]. The fruit grows as large as the largest apple, the

---

[144] Papaya.

rind is very thick, and woody, is smooth and painted on the outside. The fruit or eatable part, consists of particles of [substance] resembling carnelians cut oblong, in imperfect squares. They become so from being closely stowed together and as if impatient of confinement. The moment the shell is broken they fall all about like precious stones. Put a handful of them in your mouth, and press them with your tongue, and you have a delicious wine. They become a small white seed from each gem.

Poppies are grown in large patches and fields, for the opium they produce. The opium is obtained by puncturing the calyx after the petal has left it. This is done at even, and in the morning the people scrape off the gum which has exuded during the night, dry it, and take it to the Governmental Opium House at Patna. It is under heavy restrictions, no one being allowed to raise it for his own private use. Every native almost smokes it and uses a little with his quid, or beetle-leaf.

Roses are grown in fields also for the making of rose-water [113] which is valued more as a wash, than for culinary purposes. Little children are done over with it after bathing, to cool their skin and make them lovely to approach. Yet without it, Indian European babes[145] are the nicest all the year, of any in the world. The neatness of those, form a striking contrast with the filthiness of the native infants, for they are *never* washed all over until they are old enough to bear bathing in the river. They substitute oil for water, and anoint them, and *rub* off the dirt with their hands. You will see native mothers sitting at their hut doors, doing this to their naked infants, and then they lay them on a little mat or cot in the Sun, to grow black and strong. Even their *faces* are never washed with water.

March 22nd. [1817]. Lord's day evening.

Ill today with a headache. My eyes shrink from the glare of door & windows—sitting in my darkened room, I listen to the sacred

[145] Eurasian infants.

psalmody from the lips of boys & girls. My dear partner making bass.

Though poorly, the change from the constant routine of Sabbath day duties, is a relief to my spirits—for on that day, I have no leisure, more than any other day. Well I often, while feeling my flesh wearing out, think it a happiness to be worn out in the cause of Souls, whether it be for Souls in black or white skins—all the Souls that get to heaven, will be white as the robes of Moses and Elias when they came down from heaven to meet Christ at his transfiguration. Glorious thought, when all distinctions shall be done away—earthly pride slain, and earthly connections absorbed in the love and admiration of Christ, who is to be *all* and in all.

I sometimes think, there never were people so often seen at prayer every day, as the missionaries. We have social prayer five times daily. Mr. Rowe & I together early. 2nd call our children, 3rd join family prayer at the mess-room where *all* breakfast. 4th the same at evening after supper. 5th by ourselves before retiring. Notwithstanding, *I* cannot live the life of a Christian openly, or in my own soul, unless I take five minutes [114] secret prayer alone, before I engage in the arduous duties of each day. It is then that *I* gather the manna that is to sustain me during the day, and I find it sweet to live by this daily gathering. Sometimes a crowd of occurrences seem to oblige me to forget it—then like Jeshron,[146] I grow strong in my own might and forget God: till he mercifully remind me of my remissness, by bringing upon me some soreness of heart, which again *drives* me back to the mercy seat so many times as to remind me of how negligent I have been, and then, like Peter, to atone for thrice denying him, by thrice confessing my need of his grace. I have much need to pray for strength to sustain me under my charge. I begin to go bowed down by care and some bodily weaknesses.

---

[146] Jeshurun: a poetic name for Israel found four times in Hebrew scripture: Deuteronomy 32:15, 33:4–5, 33:26, and Isaiah 44:2.

Last Wednesday, a native woman very poor, whose husband is enquiring the way to Zion, and has therefore taken refuge in our garden villa, came with her little girl to the schoolroom. I enquired of the child, if she wanted to learn (for now I can speak a few things in Hindostani). She nodded her head in assent. When her mother wanted to go, she huffed at her mother and kept sitting on the mat, (for mothers obey their children in this country). I told her that my children minded me, and that she must mind her mother. But the mother had to go a good way off, before the child would follow her, and then she slapped her mother, several times. Maternal patience is kept alive, under the declaration, that it will know better when it is older. Alas! thought I. 'Train up a *child* in the way it should go" while it is a child "and when it is old, it will not depart from it."[147] Solomon knew more of human nature than many *Christian* parents, of the present age. [What] a contrast does the conduct of this little girl form, to the behaviour of my sweet little step-sons! I have only to rear the fabric on a foundation well laid, that looks fair to be a sure one.

The next day, the child's father brought her, and desired me to instruct her in reading and work. I need not say how readily I complied, as it is the first hopeful encouragement I have met with in a girl, and seemed to me, to be an earnest of prayer. She learned that morning to pronounce five letters. [115] In the afternoon I put her to hemming, but she was very awkward. Let me describe the poor child's appearance—a dirty, greasy skin, a sore running eye, her head full of oil which smelt most repellingly. She had nothing on her body, but an unbleached, and dirty sheet, which from being brought over her greasy hair, had become very filthy. Her hair was long and blowsy.

A little notice makes such poor wretches very proud: and after they become insolent, they are not to be chastised else their parents will take them from school, and as they are not to be bourn with, and their example becomes pernicious, they are necessarily sent back

[147] Proverbs 22:6.

to their parents, who never chastise them as a duty, but as a gratification when they capriciously become angry with them; and then they nearly kill them. Sometimes they really do so. A father being offended with his daughter of about 12 years of age, took her behind his hut, and split her in two with his hatchet!

A few days ago, five native women came to see me—They were taken with my brother's portrait. They at first imagined that it was intended to be worshipped, as they had heard that the *Christians* at Patna, the Portuguese, had pictures hung round their Chapel, and paid adoration to them. This they thought was my domestic god. I assured them that it was only the likeness of a beloved brother whom I had left in America, and I pointed them to a smaller one, the likeness of another brother there. That as I might never see them on earth again, I had their likeness. The beautiful Scripture piece which I bought of Mrs. Otis,[148] next took much attention. The principle figure being that of Christ, they could hardly believe me sincere—but I took the bible and read to them in their own language, the 22nd Chapter of Matt. from 17 to 22nd verses, and endeavored to convince them, that the picture was designed to teach people to be just and honest, and to honour God by living uprightly. This cooled them down, like a settling lump of dough, for they do not love to hear of "sin, of righteousness, and the judgment to come."[149]

---

[148] Charlotte's portrait is unsigned. The American artist Bass Otis (1784–1861) painted the portraits of her brother and sister-in-law, Edwin Augustus and Margaret (Snyder) Atlee. "Mrs. Otis" may be Alice (Pierie) Otis. This would document personal contact between Charlotte and the wife of Bass Otis. Furthermore, Bass Otis painted a group portrait of his family which depicts his daughter Clarissa in a dress virtually identical to that found in Charlotte's portrait. Like some artists of his era, Bass Otis may sometimes have painted generic-clothed figures minus their heads, then later adding the head of the individual sitting for him. These details may be evidence that Bass Otis painted Charlotte's portrait.

[149] John 16:8–11.

[116] Lord's day. March 30th. 1817.

So that we are doing the Lord's work and are heartily engaged in it, 'tis no matter what part of the world we are in. My mind draws this reflection, from thinking much about Sister Judson this morning. And what she may conclude from my letters to her, having expressed in the first, a strong desire to unite with her in the toils of a missionary life, as she was the only American female in Rangoon.[150] But it was for the work's sake, amongst the benighted heathen, and the glory of God, that I desired it in the primary place. She will no doubt view it in the true light, since my work is not altered, but only my name & place of my labours. This field is indeed wide for cultivation, and I am a child in it. If a hundred such as I were engaged here, there would then be a lack. I endeavour to lose no time, by making my pupilship productive of instruction to those yet more ignorant; for my engaging a munsee to hear me read and to teach me to pronounce, though we cannot converse, has had the effect of interesting him in the Scriptures. He told me yesterday that he sits at home all Sunday, and reads the Scriptures. I asked him why he did so? He replied, "because God's words are good to read."

I proposed to the old man, to attend at eleven o'clock daily, to teach the three little boys to read Hindee, but he says he has no time at that hour, to come in, being engaged on the business of the station. Mr. Rowe has therefore allowed the other School Moonshee to attend here, and my three little boys, when they have done their exercises in my School (for their father will not now allow them to attend the boy's school) sit with him in one corner of the schoolroom, until 12 when I have him to teach me, until one o'clock. I learn to read the Persian character of him, and he condescends in turn, to learn to read the Nagree character of me. The Hindostani is printed in both, and all the guides to the acquirement of it are in

[150] Charlotte had been appointed to join Ann and Adoniram Judson in their work in Burma.

the Persian character, except Gilchrist's[151] works, which are in the English character, and it is quite a science to learn his nonsense, which must be unlearned to be understood by a native. Had he merely given directions *on* the language, nor attempted anything *in* the language by means of the English character, [he would have rendered a] service, as it is it is a disservice.

[117] I pray God, to make his word effectual to the conversion of these two poor benighted teachers. I have but little time left to work in. All the past is lost. O then may I be earnest for the extension of His Kingdom and the glory of his Name among the heathen. How little is it, that such a poor untaught creature as I can do for him here, since at the meridian of life I have to learn my duty to him. May my declining years magnify him!

They tell me, that if my mind is set on learning the language, it will take but little time. The want of a dictionary has put me to much trouble. For where I had by much pains found out the meaning of a word in the Gospel of John, rather than lose it by forgetting it, I made a blank book, and set every word gained, down in Alphabetical order, which has produced a very useful vocabulary of the book of St. John's Gospel. I have not only given the word and its meanings, but its *inflections* also. Hindee consonants contain inherent vowels—and an inflected word expresses person, number, gender, and case. Whenever I am able to make a new discovery in it, that is, to myself, I am as much delighted as a parent on hearing the first intelligent accents of her child. I regret having lost so many hours at home, which I might have improved in learning Latin, Hebrew, or French, either of which would have aided me in the acquirement of this language but especially the first. As young women cannot tell, nor their

---

[151] John Borthwick Gilchrist (1759–1841), a Scottish surgeon in India, was considered Britain's authority on the Hindustani language about which he wrote numerous books. Gilchrist advised Europeans to learn Hindustani from fellow European teachers *before* entering India. Charlotte critiqued this approach and advocated that Europeans learn from indigenous tutors *in India* who spoke Hindustani as their mother tongue.

parents either, what they may be called to in future life, they ought to keep *a something to require it* in view, and therefore employ that time, a part of it at least, in higher mental improvements, which is too readily, and often for want of more substantial employment, spent in fitting or altering dress, or making fancy trifles.

March 31st. [1817].

Last evening Mr. Rowe took me to Dinapore to see the new Chapel which has been raised by subscription among the Soldiers. The congregation had so much increased as to render the old one too small. The walls are built of *mud*—the roof is first thatched to keep out the heat, and over that earthen tile to keep out the rain. Messrs. Rowe and Moore presented it with a pulpit. The floor is beaten earth with a mat.[152]

[118] My heart was glad when I saw it all lighted up; and when I entered it, my heart melted in silent prayer to the God of mercies that many Souls might be born there. It felt to me, like a sanctified place.

As we were coming home, our horse was frightened by a throng of natives in the road having torches and tumtums (or drums). They were screaming an indecent song. The groom ran forward, and ordered them to disperse. They were presently all out of sight, scampering up the allies [sic] to get out of the way. It is quite amusing to witness the authority of a native Sahib or groom. What could people do without a *runner* in *this* country!

I have this evening finished taking the difficult words and their meanings of the book of St. John's Gospel. I have counted the leading words and there are 2200. 200 of which are those taken out of the Gospel. The rest are the *inflections* of them.

---

[152] This was the first rebuilding and enlargement of the "Grass Tabernacle" on the Dinapore cantonment. The chapel would later be enlarged a second time, the mud walls replaced by fired brick walls. The brick chapel still stands and is used to house an Indian Army press.

April 3rd. [1817].

Feel depressed under a salutary sense of my want of meekness, having been powerfully irritated this morning. I find I cannot, as my Lord has set me the example of in so many instances, resist the proud by meekness. I *said* naught but *felt* much.

With pleasure I contemplate the lofty palm tree, whose top looks like an opake [sic] Star on the azure curtain of night, amidst the numerous brilliants. It leads my thoughts upwards, as I sit or walk, so often alone of an evening, in front of our house. The palm tree, I conceive to have been viewed by the ancient Christians as a type of Christ. These are not the true palm—they are but a secondary species of it. There is a kind known in India, much larger than these which bears a blossom once in a Century. It may be said a *blossom*, because it sends forth a flower from the top of the trunk, much like a cabbage. I have not seen it. The palm tree was engraven on the doors of the Temple of Solomon, to shew that the "ancient of days" dwelt there.[153] Like the son of man, it *refuses to take deep or wide* root in the earth, its root being seen on trees that are washed by the river, to consist of a mere bunch of fibres like a split broom—"who shall declare his generation?"[154] [119] It shoots aloft above every other tree, erect and Sappy.

The Storms bow down its head, but they break not its trunk. At its towering Summit, are obtained, vessels full of beverage, which if taken and drunk fresh, as the manna was to be eaten fresh, is refreshing, but if stale, is pernicious. We carry our wants to the Divine Tree of Life, and receiving a fresh supply, have our prayers to be answered, in as much faith, as the poor Paresee[155] who takes up his empty vessels to exchange for the full ones. In the ascent to these draughts there are no resting places to stop and gaze from—he that

---

[153] 1 Kings 6:29–35.

[154] Isaiah 53:8.

[155] Charlotte is referring to Parsis in India engaged in toddy tapping and manufacture of liquor and sugar from palm trees. Guha, "More about the Parsi Seths," 117–32.

would attain, must yoke his feet, and clasping the object of faith and hope, hop and hop on, until he gain the summit—there he may rest. There is "healing in its leaves," a single leaf used as a fan, will cool one or many. They cast a deep but circumscribed shade, which travels like a shadow on a dial. The natives worship this tree also, for its qualities—not seeing through it, the Giver. Father, Preserver! enable me to live through each day in conformity with my petitions before Thee.

It is not of consequence to Mortals to be able to unravel the dealings of Providence, while in heaviness on account of them. Submission is our best Conciliator. What most becomes us, is ever to acknowledge *a need be* for every visitation. To those who desire to do his will, he gives the opportunity of trying their zeal and strength; thus proving to themselves the genuineness of their motives. O God! my mouth is shut here. I am a worthless wretch in *myself*; but thou canst make me fruitful—Do so for thy own name's Sake!

When Christ crucified is presented to my view, I feel like a very dog, nay worse, because defiled with sin; but when I see the prints of the Nails in his hands, I think my base nature a wound, together with his immaculate hand.

Letter to Dr. Atlee of Phil[a]. Digah. April 9th. 1817.
My dearest brother,

It is nearly a year since I arrived [120] in India. The present moment finds me contented, healthy, useful, and happy, speaking after the manner of men. Who has greater cause for gratitude? Yet I fear I am too insensible to the goodness of God towards me. I hope you do pray for me often. My mind often dwells on your beloved family—Why do I not hear from you. Only one letter since I left you, has reached me.

Perhaps I have overwhelmed you with my much writing. I do not expect as many *lines* in return; for *my* pen is often my only companion; I would it were always a *rational* one! I believe I have now no News to tell you, otherwise than my diary can give you if you receive it, except that we hear from Rangoon that Mr. Hough has printed a tract, which Mrs. Judson translated into the Burmese Language.

It is said that Government is more mild of late, and provisions plenty and cheap. Better things are now hoped from that quarter.

I send [a] set of pictures, painted on what Mr. Rowe calls Talk or tolk (pronounce the l). It is a preparation of rice. They were painted by the natives at Patna, and represent things very fairly. They are designed for your dear Esther,[156] if she is a lovely girl, if not they may be given to the best child.

The *hot winds* have commenced blowing a constant gale of dust. The thermometer stands at 83 today. We shut up the windows and doors at eight o'clock in the morning, when the heat becomes great; at nine the hot wind rises and blows a fiery blast all day until the going down of the Sun, when it subsides, and the doors and windows are again thrown open, and every [one] turns out of doors as soon as possible. The ground however, will be so hot for some time, that I cannot bear my feet with shoes on, to touch it. The grass *crumps* under our feet as we walk and the terrace has to be cooled with water before we can sit upon it, by the river. What I call the terrace is a brick-work raised platform, large enough to accommodate the family at tea. We have the air cooled in the house, by keeping thatched windows, wetted all day. The thatch is fitted almost into the frame without the glass.

[121] These thatched frames are called *Tutteen* (native) or Tatties, English. They are made of fibrous root called *cuscus*;[157] when [wet] it smells like violets. The air through these, and the air from a punkha, keep us quite as comfortable as *you* are in midsummer.

My Joshua is so deeply engaged in reading English newspapers,

---

[156] Charlotte's niece, Esther Barton Atlee, eldest daughter of Edwin Augustus and Margaret (Snyder) Atlee, was thirteen years old.

[157] Cuscus (also spelled khuskhus and referred to as vetiver): an aromatic grass made into mats.

that he cannot draw off his mind, to write to you by this hasty opportunity. You are already in his debt. We are all blessed with health at present. I conclude you have seen our good Captain, if God has favored his homeward voyage. I hope you will give my kind regards to him; and love to my relatives, and to Miss Moulder and Miss Whitehead.

I hope religion flourishes in your land, as it did a few months ago. This is a dreadful land on account of wickedness. The English *at large* are as bad as the natives. They seem to think God does not see them in India.[158] A sad example to the Heathen, who often cast their faults in their teeth. They do not know how to reconcile the term Christians with both army men and missionaries, and a man actually told me, that if we were Christians, he was afraid to embrace that religion, as the Soldiers made the natives ashamed. I was obliged to use all my logic on the subject, to convince him, that there were Christians by name who abused the character, while real christians were careful not to associate with them. These people have discernment, but natural conscience is quite obliterated in most of them. All nature seems to have gone out of the way here. Yet God bears with it, and gives his fruits in their season.

I hope the Lord prospers *you*. Let me know how Paul Cuffee[159] does at Sierra Leon [sic]. I remember taking tea with him and you at Joseph Clark's.[160] Give my love to them. My beloved unites with

---

[158] William Ward said that it had "become a jocose remark, that every European, on his way to India, always left his religion at the Cape of Good Hope." Ward, *Farewell Letters,* 161.

[159] Paul Cuffee (1759–1817) was born in Massachusetts to African and Wampanoag parents. He was a Quaker seaman, captain, ship owner, businessman, author, and colonizer who brought Black settlers to Sierra Leone and generally sailed with an all-Black crew.

[160] Several persons named Joseph Clark lived in Philadelphia in this period. Charlotte likely refers to the Euro-American Quaker teacher Joseph Clarke, a member of the Pennsylvania Abolition Society, who in 1787 became the first head of the Free African Society, the first mutual aid society of its kind in Philadelphia and probably the first in America.

me in best regards to sister and the dear children.

I remain your affect. Sister
Charlotte H. Rowe
Dr. E. A. Atlee
Philadelphia

[122] Diary [undated]

Have been a week ill in body, but received strength from God by daily Prayer, to fulfill my daily offices. At present more ill in mind than body. My faults weigh heavy on me. Lord, I desire rest from my faults, I desire to rest *in* them, but deliverance from them.

Oh! Let me not shame thy cause by them any more! Root them out from me, and give me to possess the meekness and forbearance and self abasement which my Lord Jesus ever more exhibited—then shall I be lovely, and not till then. Oh hear the prayer of the needy, gracious Lord!

[April] 25th. [1817].

In what a wretched state of Sin, does India lie! To bring up 40 boys and 20 girls in the sentiments of true religion, may give a different tone to the Society where they may mingle, when grown up. Our School increases daily. May God grant us strength to perform all our duties.

The complexions of the children which fill our School shew their parentage.[161] Their fathers glitter in military show, having a

[161] The English-language boarding school at the Digah Baptist mission was for mixed-race children of soldiers stationed at the Dinapore cantonment. Such children were first called "country born" or "Indo-Briton." At that time Britons working or resident in India were called "Anglo-Indian." By the mid-1700s Indo-Britons outnumbered Europeans in India, and their ethnicity bore no stigma. The East India Company considered them British citizens and recruited them for the Company's military and other workforce needs. By the early 1800s the term "Eurasian" began to supplant "Indo-Briton" and took on a derogatory connotation. After the end of Lord Moira's service as

stipulated household of servants allowed by government according to his rank in the army. Their mothers occupy one end of his house—are never seen but have a number of rooms, and servants allowed her.

A carriage is kept for her, which is enclosed all round with venetians, and drawn by a pair of hackney bullocks—and a rack carriage is kept for the *children*; who are admitted into company. They are genteelly educated at their father's expense—perhaps sent to England to complete their Education; while there, some of the mothers die, and some are removed to a distance on an annuity allowed by the father, who now being out of shackles, *marries* a fair lady, and lives as a man ought to live. By and by, the elder children are sent for, and are soon married off. There is a curious mixture of wrong and right in all this.

My Iah has desired leave of absence for a day, that she may go and have her daughter of nine years old, married to the son of another Iah, of eleven years old. [123] They made all the parade they could, placing the bridegroom on a little horse, and the bride in a close covered *dooly*,[162] carried by men; and together with all the relations and acquaintances they could muster, patrol the public ways at night, bearing torches, beating drums, blowing horns, singing &cc. It is common with those who can afford it, to decorate a cot bedstead with lamps and artificial flowers, and have it carried along with the procession. All this makes the Beeah-tamasha or marriage shew, essential to any degree of respectability in this country. The marriage is not *Sanctified*, unless the presiding Goddess Gunga,

---

governor general in 1823, the term "East Indian" began to be used. In 1830, John William Ricketts, a country-born Baptist, sailed to England and petitioned Parliament to redress the prejudicial policies directed at his ethnic community that had started under Lord Cornwallis (governor general from 1786–1783). In 1911 the viceroy Lord Hardinge approved the use of "Anglo-Indian" to identify the community which by then was regarded to be Indian rather than British. Anthony, *Britain's Betrayal in India*, 1–2, 17–21, 47.

[162] Dooly: a litter carried on men's shoulders.

passes a benediction on it, which is received by their going over the river to make merry.

When a new boat is launched, they have a frolic in it, before Dame Gunga, and filling it full of men and women as it can stow, make it go round and round in the middle of the river, while they beat drums and make merry.

Lord's Day. O Satan, thou art rich in sins and misery—but the day is coming on, when thou shalt gather up and take home all that is thine own. I have too much of thy dross diffused all through me, body and mind, but a day of separation will also come, and I shall be left purged of thy infections—but not till death—then thy triumph ends.

Went this evening to see the sick native sister. Had some conversation with her. Prayed God to restore her, and to make her useful. The native female Christians are of no use, except to make more pleasant wives to their husbands. We do not wish to make servants of them, but they should think we have sinister views in persuading them from idolatry and they are raised so much upon a level with ourselves, that they would think it an indignity offered them, to ask them to engage in anything. But they are yet, in the first stage of a religious life. They think it is enough that they have laid [124] aside idolatry.

I have but two requests to make of God, now at heart—the first, that he will cause my cup which is full of temporal blessings, to overflow with his grace, the better to govern my life and conduct, and sweeten my path to heaven—next, to pour out his grace upon the heathen, so that they may flock to hear the Gospel, and all unite in acclamations of praise to the true God.

O Lord Jesus! captivate my Soul and all my holy affections by the manifestation of thy charms. Let me behold thy beauties through the lattice of time, to stay my doubts until thou open the door and take me into thy presence.

[June] 6th. [1817].

The Lord manages for me, and graciously condescends to listen to and answer my petitions, even in governing my temporal affairs. We ought not to think any subject which concerns our individual peace or that of others, *too small* to bring before the Lord, for he is abundantly condescending, and will regard our lowest petitions, which concern the christian walk. We are finite beings, and must have finite requests to make—but God is as infinite in willingness to stoop to help us, as he is infinite in power to create a universe, or is infinite in all Godlike perfections.

Help me therefore, O Lord! to place full reliance on thee, and enable me by the indwelling of thy Spirit, to *live* my profession. O that I were indeed a temple of the Holy Ghost by his abiding in me! Then I should shew forth the Christian graces in all their forms. O that I might not weary in well doing, that I may work out the twilight of life in God's cause, and to his praise!

My spirit has of late thirsted for fresh supplies of His grace, to eat again of apples and drink of the flaggons of his table. O God! empty my heart of all the pride and vanity which have so long wholly occupied it; and fill it with thy meekness, thy forbearance, thy patience, thy love for my fellow beings, [125] and a never fainting desire to do thy will. Lay thy rein upon my irascible neck, and check my wayward spirit!

I never pluck a grape, but I cast a thought on some friend in America, whom I should like to have share with me in this delicious fruit, so abundant as we now have it. I have never viewed an Indian tree, without associating with it, the thought of my dear Brother and family, and some other relations or friends. My thoughts do not always fall on the same object, but they take turns in coming before me.

[June] 9th. [1817].

I do not always stop to date, when I seem inclined to scribble. I note down the changes of the weather for my own advantage. Of late we have a hurricane *daily*, blowing such clouds of sand and brick dust, that it keeps a bearer going round the house all day with a cloth in his hand, to wipe things. If he is prevented for a few hours, he has to push the dust off the table into something, and throw it out, before he can wipe it.

[June] 10th [1817].

When the heart is depressed under a sense of some trivial mistake, I find no peace, until I apply to Christ to grant me his peace afresh. Some would fly to exhilarations, but the searcher of hearts gives wisdom with relief, when he is resorted unto, to do it for us.

The rose that blossoms on the heath
 Is not so frail as I.
For *guiltlessly* it spreads its breath
 And fragrant, hails the sky.

[June] 18th. [1817].

This day completes the first year of my union with Mr. Rowe. May the Lord accept the praise of my heart for all the mercies of this year, and repeat them to us during the year to come! O! may he knit our minds together in holy conjugal affection, such as is pleasing in his sight. Now two years and one month of my life has been spent in wedlock, another month may find me a widow the second time.[163]

[June] 22nd. [1817].

One day the past week, a native girl eight years old, came with the

[163] Charlotte's first husband, Nathaniel Hazen White, died in Rutland, Massachusetts on Christmas Day 1804, one year and one month after they were wed.

little girl who first came to school. [126] She makes the third who has come. As she was as unseemly in her appearance as the other at first was, and not being willing to clothe her unless she was to remain a pupil, I sent for her father who was staying at the garden villa of native Christians, to know of him, his intentions. He said he wished her to continue at School—I asked him of what profession he was? He said, "I am a Bramin, but I have cast away my *jinnso* (string of beads) and my cast (jant); I have come from Juggernaut." I enquired how long he wished her to be at school? "Always, if you choose it." I told him to clothe her body. "We have no more clothes than what we have on." Where is her mother? "She died three years ago. I have no other child nor wife." I clothed her in his presence, at once. The father attends worship daily.

Visited the wife of our head native preacher, last evening—found her nearly recovered from her illness. Endeavour'd to make her understand, that as God had raised her from the borders of the grave, she ought to return to health with a resolution to serve his cause. That it was her duty to learn to read and sew, that she might teach others. I asked her husband why he had not taught her—He said, she would not learn—She said she could not. I assured her, it was not want of ability, but want of inclination which kept her from attempting it. I fear he is hypocritical for he said she would do nothing when well, but eat and smoke. But we had been informed that he had withheld her from it. Am glad that I can now hold a little conversation with them, without an interpreter. They spoke in very affectionate terms of the Mrs. Rowe and Mrs. Moore deceased.[164]

July 1st. [1817].

Have scarce any time to note anything in my diary of late. I have undertaken to try to construct a Spelling book for the use of our schools, as they have none, being obliged, like myself in my

[164] Elizabeth (Noyes) Rowe, Joshua Rowe's first wife, died on October 19, 1814. Eleanor Moore, William Moore's first wife, died in 1812.

novitiate, to jump from the alphabet, into the Testament.

[July] 5th. [1817]

The other day, I offered a native woman 3 rupees a month, to come and sit with the two native pupils and keep them busy, and learn to read herself—promising her double when she could undertake to teach. [127] This has set the native preacher at finding fault with *his wife* for not complying with my request, to try to learn. He even beat her, for which I told him, he was not a good man, and asked him, where he had learned in the Bible, that a man should beat his wife. He ought to love her as his own body, and he would not set to beating his own body. Mr. Rowe also reproved him. I then told him to make amends for it by sending his wife and all the women to me, on Wednesday afternoon and I would read to them, and teach them to read.

What a comfort it is to get under the grape arbour, in going over to brother Moore's to dine. It save[s] me 64 steps in the vertical Sun: half that number from each end of it to the houses, are as many as I can possibly endure without fainting, although I carry an umbrella. The sight of growing grapes is most refreshing. They fall through almost every lattice. One branch hangs ripening, which is at least one foot long. The thermometer stands now at 92 degrees.

Thirteen persons from the 24th Regiment at Dinapore, were baptized by Mr. Moore, a day or two ago—Mr. Rowe took the part on this occasion, of addressing the people. The baptistery is in our lawn beside the arbour. It is filled when required, from a well near it. The people sat on the green to hear. It was at night, and the moon was at the full. The whole scene was solemn and delightful. Such an accession to our little European church, is truly pleasing, in a country where sinners abound.[165]

The palm tree is now in its *fruit*; as well as yielding a larger portion of sap than at any other time. The fruit hangs from the bottom of the leaves where they grow out from the tree, like strings of onions in the market. They are large and have a wooden shell. The inside is a round pulp of a tough texture, and clear and white like cold starch; it is hollow, containing a large spoonful of clear, sweet water. The taste of the fruit is insipid. When first I saw it on a plate, I thought it was lumps of ice. [128] The Bakers use the sap all the year to raise their bread, and the army is supplied with arrack, from the sap when fermented. The natives love to get tipsy on it, as well as their examples, the Soldiers.

Letter. Digah. July 7th. 1817.
My dear brother,

If I were not to write to you when I have an opportunity, you might justly charge me with indifference. I send you my Diary, because it

[165] Charlotte and Joshua Rowe worked with two church congregations. Joshua preached in English for the congregation of Baptists and other Dissenters composed of soldiers, their families, and other English-speaking expatriates (the "little European church"). At first, members of that congregation had walked the mile from the Dinapore cantonment to worship in the Rowe's bungalow in Digah. In 1814 the soldiers received permission to build the "Grass Tabernacle" behind the barracks on the cantonment. When the soldiers returned to Dinapore following the 1814–18 Anglo-Nepalese War (a.k.a. "Gurkha War"), they replaced the chapel,which had bamboo walls and thatched roof, with a bungalow-style chapel with mud walls and a tiled roof. In 1821 that chapel would be replaced by a larger, more durable brick building that stands today. Charlotte oversaw the Hindi-speaking congregation at the Digah Baptist mission that met "at the native brethren's place" or in the Rowe's bungalow. Joshua Rowe, "Extract of a Letter from Mr. Rowe, Dinapore, to Mr. Lawson," April 1823, Unpublished papers, Angus Library and Archive.

contains the mention of things which I could neither recollect to write about, and which I should have no time for doing a second time. I do not know that you give it a welcome, but as you desired me to express myself freely to you, and having but little space for doing so when an opportunity tarries, you might think me reserved, if you heard no more from me, than my letters convey.

I believe I have not mentioned the recent accounts we have received, of an extensive awakening to religion among the natives of Benares[166] 200 miles above us. Brother Chamberlain's preaching there, and the distribution of tracts in the Hindee language, is said to be the instrumental cause.

We have to acknowledge the mercies of the Lord, to me and mine, as well as to all at this Station. No death or sickness has invaded it, since I came to it. Native inquirers increase in number, and they bring their daughters to me to be instructed in their own language and in needlework. So you see, those barriers which were for a long time held up to view as insurmountable, are by our patient perseverance in well doing, gradually giving way; but under God's overpowering influence.

I have not yet taken my afternoon "forget" of five or ten minutes; unless I do this, I shall be quite disqualified for my labours. I feel now as if I shall sink, unless I go to the couch and lie down. So do excuse me, and give many kisses to sister Margaret [129] and the dear children. To all whom I used to be familiar with, and to my dear cousins &cc. who if I may judge by receiving no letters from them, have forgotten me, or ceased to love me—must I include yourself too?

Ever thine,
C. H. Rowe

---

[166] In Hindu myth the ancient holy city of Benares on the Ganges is the eternal dwelling place of Lord Shiva who built the city for his consort Parvati. The city was simultaneously a sacred pilgrimage site for Hindus, Buddhists, Jains, Sikhs, and Muslims. The 1775 Treaty of Faizabad ceded Benares to the East India Company.

Continuation of the Journal. July 9. 1817.

A few curious thoughts by way of amusement, as I must be confined to my room today.

The *miseries* of India, or what a newlanded *American* feels to be such, (whom all the rest of the world take upon them to consider, a novitiate.) Viz. On entering within the Bar in the Bay of Bengal, met by a savage looking set of more than half-naked Bengallees in a canoe, sent from government to demand, your letters, address &cc. At the first sound on your ears of their police drum, you are startled with unpleasant feelings, but when they draw near, you are inclined to hide your face with shame and disgust, while your curiosity at beholding such never-beheld objects, pins your sight upon them. They chatter like ducks at a mud-puddle as if making *their* remarks about *your* address. They get their wish, turn about, and beat the drum and shout a roundelay by turns, till they are out of hearing.

Arrived in the Harbour of Calcutta, the stench from the strand which is a common Sewer throughout, intolerable if the breeze sets towards you. Should you chance to look over the ramparts of your vessel, you might see human forms and carcasses of beasts, brought up by the eddy.

In port, a set of Sharpers,[167] loaded with country goods, pour in upon you, and fill the cabin with things which they strive hard, in broken English, to persuade you to purchase, assuring you that you will need them and meet with none so cheap. They will almost pursue you into your state room, and would quite, if the customs of their country did not forbid men intruding [130] upon female apartments.

The next misery is to feel yourself jostled in a palanquin, in a reclining if not horizontal position, and to doubt whither the men are carrying you, unable to speak to them. Surprise at the mode of travelling upon the shoulders of four of your fellow men, and pity for their debasing employment, fill your heart, and mind, as you go

[167] Sharpers: swindlers.

onward. Your mind is agonized with hearing their grunts and the regular response with an affected sigh or moan; but before you reach the appointed door, you find out that they are only keeping time with their pace. This however, does not persuade you that your weight does not put them to some inconvenience, since you see streams of sweat channeling their naked backs.

Arrived at your abode, you are surrounded with male and female servants, the smell of oil and *pawn*[168] upon whom, makes you look around to see where the stable is so near the door—There is none indeed—Night comes, and you are shown to a bed—but not accustomed to brushing away the mosquitoes from the outside of the gauze curtains which are closely tucked up round the mattress you pull them out at the bottom, not knowing that there is a seam left unsewed, for you to open and bounce through—So when you get in, a dozen musical companions attend you and you pass the night between alternately being bitten, and dreading the next assault, which is as unremitting, as the return of the flies to the Sugar barrel in a grocery store in a hot day. For several days you have the "Scotch comfort" of allaying the irritations.

By the next night, what with experience and advice, you manage better—and lie down, weary and confident of rest—you may enjoy it, until everybody else has retired and then the Jackals finding no opposition from man, come into vacant places, and set up a howl which if you have never heard, you will imagine is the hysterical cry and laugh mingled, of a dozen females in frightful distress. You startle, and call, someone answers, "It is only the Jackals." And you lie down, hoping [131] now to sleep. You doze again—midnight now calls up her demons.—The drums and horns and many unhallowed voices, set up a sudden clang,—a light passes along; and you, wondering fly out of bed to see what next. A procession bearing flame bearers & torches, carry a bedstead hung all about with lamps—so much you clearly see amid a throng bearing it along. "Ha what is that?" "It is only a native marriage ceremony, go to sleep." Alas! I

---

[168] Pawn (also spelled paan, pan): betel quid chewing.

wish I could, and into bed you get again—but your forgot about the mosquitoes, which had made good improvement of your impudence in leaving your curtains untucked. "Well, I will not heed them, they are but mosquitoes," and *resolved*, you sleep. An hour passes, and now the crows and vultures commence their orgies, croaking and squealing like frogs and pigs, until broad day light tells you that to be risen is preferable.

Your honest unsuspecting habits *at home* leave you unsuspecting of the honesty of others. You had not locked up every thing which you do not carry about you and by this time, may things are missing. *Live and learn* is an old adage, now having meaning to you.

You expect that every servant will do everything or any thing. You call upon one by a *motion*, to hand you the candle—and are refused by a bow, while that one goes to call another, whose caste does not forbid of touching a candle stick, for that is used for *tallow*, and tallow is a particle of an ox or cow, which is *sacred*. For the same reason, if a drop of tallow fall on your table, the proper person must wipe it up. And so with regard to many other things you may chance to command or request done. You will now think, "I had rather do everything myself, and I will." So you set yourself about wiping off the dross, and dusting the chair you sit in, &cc. The consequence is, that you will see the servants scorning you, and they will not now come at your bidding—for they will not choose to serve one whom they now conceive had been a servant in his or her own country. Learning to shew to yourself the respect you wish to [132] command, you at last have every one to do according to custom.

You are now got home, and commenced housekeeping. Call the cook to take your command for dinner. You wish to have enough to eat, and therefore, give out what is a sufficiency—when it comes to table, you are surprised to see so little—The cook is called to answer. He tells you, that you did not give out rice enough (enough he means, for himself and family besides.)

Now think you, I will catch him—so you order a pudding next day, and will have the eggs broken & beat in your presence, for you know they will not eat what has been beaten with a *Christian spoon*.

He breaks the egg over the plate—but to your astonishment turns it into his hand to be strained through his black fingers!—Enough! Enough! Let him go, and do as he will—Tomorrow he shall have rice enough—it is cheap enough.

Evening comes—wearied with vexations, you order a light, that you may compose your mind with a book—It is brought and placed before you on the table—by the time you are interested in the first sentence, flap in your eye, comes an insect big or little, and now a troop of them flutter and buzz around the light, and at last thicken on the wick so as to bedim it wholly. "Well, I must now walk out, and have the lights lighted at the wall, and content myself with thinking, & gazing at whatever is around me." Tomorrow evening, I will ride.

Tomorrow evening comes—you ride out in some way, it is little matter what way. But as to air, it is all smoke; as to prospect, it is all obscured by dust, as to comfort, there is none but learning and yielding to the *customs of the country*, and in improving that time for pleasure in the open air, which the birds and beasts teach us is natural, early dawn. And at night sit under a punkha and get an associate to help you give a wing to time, so replete with discomforts.

[133] The comforts of an arrival in India, consist first, in thankfulness at sight of land, and beholding that land to exhibit something like primeval existence. When you met a man, he was not a savage in his behaviour towards you, as you expected at once, but shewed more civility than you would meet with under similar circumstances at home. It is certainly a consolation in a strange land, to meet with polite behaviour, how much soever duplicity with a design to defraud you secretly, there may be concealed under it. As yet, all this is out of sight.

In proportion as your blood becomes vitiated with bile, the mosquitoes will be fewer about you. The same divine presence is there, as every [where], and in your moments of sorrow, is as gracious to bless you. But His promise, that Christ shall have the heathen for his inheritance, cheers your heart, (if *you* love him more than all other comforts.)

To find Society—and some Christians, is an agreeable surprize. You had been told of privations, and difficulties—but as yet, you suffer few privations which are not supplaced by something as congenial for the time. And the difficulties are of quite a different nature from what you had apprehended.

The nights are seldom so warm as those in America in the warmest weather. When the Sun goes down there is some air which cools the house, though it may bring clouds of smoke with it. The means of grace are supplied by social worship, where there is no public place of worshipping God. A land of plenty; though it be not such as you have been accustomed to, it is enough for you.

July 16, 1817.

I am almost dissolved with perspiration, which brings out the prickly heat to such a degree, as to be quite a disease. It is so sore if I touch it, that I feel a sickness at heart from the pain. I often complain of it as an affliction. O may it serve to train me to [134] suffering and make me patient under it; my divine Physician can make it a contributing cause of my further sanctification. May he hide my moral deformities with the Robe of his righteousness, in which alone, I can ever stand in his presence; may he call me by the name of his Redeemed!

O Lord, if what I am engaged in be agreeable to thy will, grant thy blessing on it, to the use of others, and let not my daily labours be spent to *none* effect in the cause of the heathen.

[July] 17th. [1817].

Daily experience serves to shew me, that the holy Scriptures must have been in a land where customs were similar to these, as what I often observe, elucidates passage of Scripture which I have never before understood rightly. They wear Sandals, and always slip them off at the entrance of a house. Their bed is a mat the length of a man, or a cotton rug as large with sometimes a very small pillow. Cisterns are set for preserving clean water, several barrels, as it were, being set at a time. Leather bags or bottles are used for water, oil, and wine by the natives. They are in the habit of humbling themselves greatly to their superiors: even prostrating themselves on the earth before them.

[July] 18th. [1817].

Bless the Lord, O my Soul, for the Sweet feast granted me this Evening in prayer; and in reading the paraphrase on Solomon's Song in Watts' Hymns, who makes the church to say

> "Jesus, allure me by thy charms
> My Soul shall fly into thine arms.[169]
> Kindly he brought me to the place
> Where stands the bouquet of his grace
> He saw me faint, and o'er my head
> The banner of his love he spread."[170]

[July] 19th. [1817]. Sabbath day.

O Lord, my Soul giveth out in love; grant that it may be found love to Thee! [135] Empty me of all earthliness, and fill me with thy own perfections, that I may be meek, patient, long-suffering, thinking no evil, taking no offence, sympathizing with the distresses of others, loving in a due degree those with whom I am connected. O make me lovely in the eyes of my husband. Deliver me from my sinful and disgusting propensities. O Lord, I would be perfect in thy sight, but Alas! Alas how frail, how offensive I must appear to thee. O prepare me for that better sinless state, that happy abode, to which thou in tender mercy makest me to feel that I am approaching. Let my days be of thy numbering and let me be devoted in Soul, heart, and every member, to thy service and glory. Amen!

---

[169] Watts, "Hymn 66," *Hymns and Spiritual Songs*, 55.
[170] Watts, "Hymn 68," *Hymns and Spiritual Songs*, 57.

[July] 23rd. [1817]. The kid sacrificed by the Hindoos.

It is customary among the Hindoos, to make offerings to their goddess Gunga, the presiding female spirit of the River. Some people of the lowest caste called D'hoom, came to offer a kid. All of this caste, are extremely poor and could not well afford wholly to relinquish it; so when they threw it into the river, with some incantations, a party of them who had gone a little lower down, swam into the stream and recovered it. This *was* serving both *their* god, and mammon. It was truly a "pious fraud." The offering was quite as acceptable to the goddess, who is either pleased with greater atrocities committed on her bosom, or winks at them. This is the only caste who will eat bread from an European's hands. They eat the great rats which are caught in traps, and the fowls &c. which die, or are killed by shakes & weasels. The wife of one of them often presents herself before my window, making bare a part of her stomach, to indicate her want, saying affectingly, "very hungry" in Hindee.

[July] 24th. [1817].

My Moonsee is getting a little over his prejudices against females learning to read. Today, as I was teaching them, he came and stood by me, and said that if they were to write the characters, they would soon learn them. [136] They expressed their wish to do so; and I gave them each a *Tuchtee* or painted board the size of a slate, on which the Hindoos write in the schools, with a bamboo pen. It has afforded me much pleasure to see their application today. The young woman who engaged with me for three rupees a month, is still attentive. She has lately become the wife of the young native named Nanesook, of whom we entertain hopes.[171]

---

[171] Nainsook (also spelled Nyansookh) was a young Brahmin from Digah whom Charlotte hoped would profess Christian faith and become an effective evangelist. Her hope was not disappointed. After being with the Rowes for "a long time as an inquirer," Nainsook was baptized in 1819 by John Chamberlain. Mrs. Grant brought Nainsook with her to work as an evangelist at Agra. She then funded his work as a preacher with Chamberlain in Monghyr. Joshua

I have endeavored to shew the native Christians all the kindness I could, by giving them medicines, tea &c. when they are sick. They now come to me as regularly as to a physician, with all their complaints.

[July] 26. [1817].

The weather is extremely enervating. When there is no wind, it keeps us in a bath of perspiration and when there is, that wind is so damp as to soak us.

[July] 31st. [1817].

The bearer, every morning early, brings the great cage of little birds out of the little boys' room and places it before my bedroom window—There he sprinkles them with water, which sets them all busily to pluming and shaking themselves. After they get settled on their perches, some set up their tunes. They swell their little throats and warble opening their little mouths, as if to send up their praises to God. A note of one of them at such times, reminds me of my beloved, glorified mother. The note resembles that of a sweet Lark, which every morning early, perched itself on a large Locust tree in the corner of the yard near her window, and usually roused her from her slumbers. I recollect hearing her make some allusion to the duty of mortals, uniting with the early choristers, in giving praise to God—I was then in my seventh year—She died—and the Lark forsook the tree—Its kindred spirit had fled aloft, whither it loved to soar.

August 7th. 1817.

Today my Soul is sick on account of my sins. I feel that I am as full

---

Rowe, "Extract of a Letter from Mr. Rowe at Digah, to the Treasurer of the Baptist Board of Foreign Missions, dated May 14, 1818," *American Baptist Magazine and Missionary Intelligencer,* 107. See also Charlotte's undated letter to Edwin Atlee on page [212] in her hand-written journal and Journal, October 3, 1821.

of that heinous thing, as space is full of air. O Lord make me to feel [137] how vile I am! And that continually, that I may cease from disgracing my profession, and from grieving others, and wounding thy holy spirit and my own soul. O give me the mind which is in Christ, to *dwell in me*. Alas! I am altogether unclean. O purge me, Lord, from my vileness, and fill me with heavenly dispositions. Amen!

I feel that "Satan hath desired to have me that he may sift me as wheat."[172] He has torn my soul; he hath sorely shaken me. O that I were meek as a teachable child! O that this fountain of vain tho'ts my *heart*, were changed into a source of holiness dedicated wholly to the Lord, and not to self. A hardness of heart, and dearth of prayer, preceeds [sic] a famine in the soul. O that the spirit of the Lord would *never* leave me to myself, for then my spiritual adversary finds no antagonist. May the Lord save me, through the mercies of Christ, bestowed on sinners!

[August] 8th. [1817].

Yesterday, four of the native women, and my little native ward *Piarree* which means "beloved" came for the first time, to hear me read the scriptures to them. I read two chapters, often stopping to explain, and to answer their questions on it. Piarree is the child of the Bramin who committed his daughter to my instructions, her whole conducts gives me much pleasure. She has grown quite clearly—and has earned herself two coarse calico frocks, which she wears in change.

Who ever forsook God and prospered? "Or shall a man rob God?"[173] For this cause I am new in heaviness. I shortened my

[172] Luke 22:31.

[173] Malachi 3:8.

seasons of prayer, to get more time at my Hindostani, until my spirit has become impoverished and my temper susceptible of the incursions of the enemy of my soul. O Lord, take again, this desponding sensation from my heart. And settle on me that true sense of sin which will keep me humble, and faith therewith, to enable me to keep my soul beneath the droppings of the cross. Help me in mercy, to lean [138] on the arm of Him, who came to save sinners, of whom I am chief. O give me that spiritual eye of inward discernment, to see myself as thou seest me, full of faults!

[August] 10th. [1817].

O that my ways were pleasing in the sight of the Lord, that the thoughts and motions of my mind were acceptable! Leave me not O Lord, nor forsake me, for how shall I, whose whole nature is *sin*, please Thee! Evermore abide in me to teach me to will and to do, of thy own good pleasure. Let me glorify thee in my heart. Thou hast said, I "will bring back the wanderers." Thou pursuest after the strayed sheep and restorest it to the Fold!

August 14th. [1817].

This morning Lord Moira, the governor of India, passed up stream with his attendants. He was in a Pinnace. It had two masts, and an iron palisade round the deck. It was superbly ornamented at the head, with a gilt Elephant's head, and at the stern with the English coat of arms, from behind which, two large lions' heads looked forth. About these were [three] elegant figures in gilt intended to represent Minerva, Mars and Mercury. The Star of royal dignity at the extreme sides, all in gilt. His Lordship was not visible, being in his cabin, which had not the venetians raised. The boat appeared much like a small brig.

As there was a head wind, or none at all; it was drawn by men along the shore, going up the stream. A great number of budgerows, small pinnaces and behind them country boats followed in suit. On their way thus far, they have lost 44 boats, and 51 human lives in the storms. His Lordship is going up to quell the Mahrattas.[174] His pleasure or passage boat, preceeded in the train or van; it has a pavilion in the centre, and is altogether a very fine affair. The poor natives have hard work to get the boats along, by the strength of their limbs. They make a great deal of noise, which seems to keep up their spirits. Had there have been wind to fill their sails and bear them along, the fleet would have had a lively and beautiful appearance. Travelling [139] of this important nature, is generally performed at this season, in the height of the rains. When the wind is high, the waves rise as they do at sea, and become truly terrific to the inmates of these keelless vessels.

We have had several days without sunshine, and torrents after torrents of rain has [sic] fallen. The house and everything in it gets mouldy from one day to another. The chairs will have a blue mould on them every morning. We do but breathe without air enough either in or out of doors, to fill our depressed lungs.

[August] 17th. [1817].

Sabbath Day: I must minute this mornings meditations, lest I forget them, as I hope they will ere long be of good effect. On reclining to read and think before dressing for public worship, I opened to the sentence Hannah Moore's *Practical Piety*. "The modes of doing good in Society are various. We should sharpen our discernment to discover them, and our zeal to put them in practice."[175] It brought me to reflect on what further good I might do. My heart (as hearts are wont to do) acquitted me of doing *all most all* that I could in my private sphere: but my defects lie on the side of the natives, if indeed *defects* they are. I felt that I had it in my power to do them much more good, daily, [if] they would *come to me for it*. I excused myself

[174] This Anglo-Maratha War (1817–1818) was the third and last conflict between the East India Company and the Maratha Empire. Lord Moira (who became the Marquess of Hastings in 1817 and hence was titled Lord Hastings) led the invasion. The war gave the Company control of most of India.

[175] More, *Practical Piety*, 11:35.

to myself, by reason of the climate forbidding my going out to them at all times of day. But a secret half-born idea that, were I not occupied with our English school, I could *now* spend more time morning & evening with the native females, stole across my brain, and brought a sense of regret that it were not so, across my breast.

How many useful little arts, might I by this time, have taught the native women, if they would but become industrious. I am surprised at the indolence of the women, who if they loved employment as they love ornaments, might deck themselves with every desired bauble. If their husbands would deny them all but what they earned, they would be inspired with a *love* of industry. Female indolence so long established [140] by the custom of men denying them common capacity, is less conquerable than idolatry itself.

One poor ignorant creature, hearing "that God would grant to sinners their humble requests made in Christ's name" told me she prayed daily for fine clothes, a good house, and all good things. She thought her self really pious for doing this, and wondered she received none of these things more than usual. This gave me an opportunity to tell her that God had said, "Seek *first* the Kingdom of God and His Righteousness, and all things needful shall be added unto her."[176] I see in these poor creatures, the same disposition to desire and idolize riches, that I myself had when in a state of nature. And I have since been given to believe, that the disappointments and afflictions which God sent upon me in early life,[177] were to break the charm on those things.

August 23rd. 1817. Letter.

My ever dear Brother,

If not receiving letters from you, is any proof of your negligence,

---

[176] Matthew 6:33.

[177] These "disappointments and afflictions" included becoming orphaned at age eleven, the deaths of six of her ten siblings as well as her first husband and child, and the attempt by opponents to revoke her missionary appointment.

you certainly do not merit any from me.[178] I have sometimes dreamed of having tired you with my communications but I shall continue to let you hear from me, until I hear of something that will render it needless to write to you. Sometimes I imagine you to be sick, and unable to use your pen: or that other domestic trials engross your time and notice. Then I cheer up myself be [sic] thinking you may be so situated as not to hear of opportunities[179]—or perhaps you have sent letters by some vessels that have taken circuitous voyage, and in that case, accidents happening to the *Letter bag* of the vessel might cause their destruction. At any rate I hope I have some letters by the present declared arrival from New York. Avoid sending by way of England, as letters so sent come loaded with postage. When a communication costs us five rupees, we wish our friends to be better informed.

[141] I have nothing particular to inform you of, except that I have at length prevailed on one *woman* to come to learn to knit. She has consented to try to make up a plain garment for one of my scholars.

You may wish to know how I get on in the language. I labour hard at it early and late, and at intervals of school. I am yet, rather collecting materials for learning it, than getting deep into a knowledge of it—or rather, I know more about it, than I have acquired ability or facility in speaking it. It is so elliptical, reverse to our idiom, and difficult of utterance, that I am very awkward, often bringing more words to express a thought, than are necessary, which renders it only obscure. I have translated for the benefit of myself and children, such of Murray's simple stories in his first book for Children,[180] that I could adapt to these circumstances: and given

---

[178] Here Edwin Atlee inserts an asterisk, noting at the bottom of the page, "It is strange that three letters of mine long ago sent had not reached her. E. A. A."

[179] Opportunities to send mail on ships sailing to India.

[180] Lindley Murray (1745–1826), an American Quaker born in Harper Tavern, Pennsylvania. In 1783, following a successful legal career in New

spelling lessons after his plan, adapted to each story. I have thus, used our sons to writing Hindee, as well as Persian words as well as the Conjugation of verbs in both; a specimen of which I send you from under each of their hands, with their love to their Uncle, & Aunt and cousins, whom they never may see until they meet them in the world of spirits. They as well as myself, would be much pleased to receive some specimens of your children's improvements.

I have yet several interesting little girls boarding with us as pupils. They are fond of learning hymns and being questioned on their Catechism on Sabbath days. Their own questions in return, often detain me a long time beyond what I intended; they feel a good deal, as their quivering lip and suffused eye often testify.

As an instance of the pernicious sentiments of these natives the Hindoos I will relate an incident that happened yesterday with my teacher. I desired him to form for me a sentence bringing in the words *sick* and *aged*. So he wrote, "The sick and aged are to be despised." I shook my head at it, and told him [142] that *we* considered it the duty of all, to cherish, pity, and honour, the sick and the aged. He looked ashamed, as if convinced of the greater propriety of such conduct.

I wish land could be obtained and held in this country as it can in America on account of the Christianized natives. But no European can possess land in his own name. It is all rented of the natives, or of Government through them, I know not which. There is no title to land, given to a European. If it were, we should be able to settle our converts in the agricultural way. At Serampore, work is found for them in making paper and in printing, translating various languages, &cc. We can find no employment for them which they would not consider menial, except sending them out to preach and distribute tracts, few of them being capable to being School masters,

---

York, Murray retired, moved to England, and devoted himself to literary work. He wrote *The First Book for Children* (1804), numerous grammars, readers, spelling books, and exercise books that were published and used in schools in England and the United States.

not knowing how to read. We avoid employing them as Servants to the family, lest we should appear Self-interested in teaching them and were they to mingle with the other servants, they would have no peace. Excuse me troubling you with such details, but I believed you would like to know something of our concerns.

Our dear friends, Eustace Carey and wife, have been with us since the month of May, for their health, and that of their little William. They lost a fine little daughter, born after we left Calcutta.

Your portrait affords all the consolation I have in you of late—it sometimes seems to smile—and when conscience chides, it seems to frown. It does not change its true colours, and I trust the original is as little altered.

My dear Edwin, write me much, and in your own old style[181]—I may chance to get a little of you. Love to sister Margaret and all your children. Kiss little Charlotte for me. She seems not likely [143] to have any own cousins in India.[182] I hope you will give my love to my Cousins. No letter from them has yet reached. I have sent a box of *Talk pictures* for your dear Esther, and one for my former little pupil, M. Atlee.[183] Love to her father and to her. A third to A. Dehaven[184]—with my love to her parents. Send my affectionate remembrance to my two sisters[185] and brother John. To Joseph Clark,

---

[181] In the Quaker manner, using thee, thou and thy.

[182] Charlotte expected to bear no more children.

[183] Mary Wayne Atlee was the daughter of Charlotte's cousin, William Richardson Atlee, and his wife Margaretta "Polly" Wayne. Like Charlotte, whose mother died when Charlotte was eight, Mary's mother died in 1810 when Mary was eight. Mary was thirteen when Charlotte departed America. Her grandfather was "Mad Anthony Wayne," of Revolutionary War fame.

[184] Amelia DeHaven (1785–1858) was three years younger than Charlotte and had married Charlotte's cousin, Joseph Augustus Atlee, in 1809. Amelia was the daughter of Hugh and Sarah DeHaven, who lived in Philadelphia.

[185] Charlotte's two surviving sisters were Jane (Mrs. Elisha Rigg) and Sarah Ann (Mrs. Thomas Vickroy). Her four other sisters were deceased by 1817.

and his good partner.

So! Mr. Monroe is President of the United States. I hope the growth of religion there will quench the spirit of war, or rather send it from their borders—for I know that they disclaim war, unless it be defensive.

[August] 27th. [1817].

On Monday evening last, 6 soldiers of the 24th Regiment still at Dinapore, were baptized by Mr. Rowe, in our fount. Many more are expected to make an open profession of the religion of Christ, at the next full moon, for we are obliged to improve moonlight for it at this season, the Sun being intolerable. You will recollect that "the jailor" and such others as believed, "were baptized *in the night*.[186] The soldiers too, have no leave of absence from duty until after the exercises are over, on the Parade. It is these little gleanings which keep up our spirits, if by any means of our using, some may be saved from their sins.

I cannot say much now, concerning the progress of religion amongst the natives of late, or of the unexceptionableness, (as it expresses my idea) of those who have embraced the Christian faith. They are weak in mind, from habitual imbecility.

As I do not know that a Pomegranite [sic] has ever reached America, I will try to give you some notion of it, by sending a dried one opened. But it can only shew the shape and size, as the beautiful inside when fresh, is all discoloured by being dried. [144] It may be compared to a golden Casket of pearls—for the seeds lie in apartments lined with a thin membrane similar to an inside, yellow, cabbage leaf; and the Seeds are a transparent fluid tinged with crimson and pink. They are white in tone, but in all, they look like the stones so common here called Cornelians.

Love to Miss Whitehead and Sarah Moulder. The latter has suffered a deep affliction in the loss of her excellent brother

[186] Acts 16:33.

Joseph.[187]

Accept for yourself, my sincere love, and that of my dearest friend in India, my excellent husband.

Ever thine,
Charlotte H. Rowe

Sept. 5th. 1817. Journal resumed.

For many days my heart has been void—void of divine life—void of every amiable affection; and I still feel this guilty dearth of Soul! How can I serve God, being a mere machine, acted on by connecting springs, without the warmth of love in any of its parts? I have been conscious only of a faint desire to do good to the natives about me, and my efforts have been rewarded by their blindness and ingratitude and the frustration of a favorite plan, in which others were willing to join and to aid me, for their advantage.

But I take it from God, who sees farther into it than I do. I will bring it, or something in its stead, to pass more efficient of my hopes, and of his own designs than that would have been.

Sept. 7th. [1817]. Lord's Day.

The Lord has in mercy shewn me the reason of my late insensibility, and hath opened my heart in prayer this morning. My nature is frail, and Satan kindles at the fires of my flesh. If I lived as near the Lord as I have knowledge to do, his holy spirit in me would be stronger to resist evil without and within me.

[145] The Language is my hobby, my delight, the ever prevailing desire of my heart—everything else feels subordinate to it—everything else must give way in part, to it—and therefore *nothing* but inability to see into a book, can remain an obstacle in my way. To be able to do an equal portion at this daily is a gratification, and no gratification is so much valued by me, as to attain to some thing

---

[187] Joseph Moulder died unmarried in Philadelphia in 1816 at age thirty-six. "Departed this life…", *United States Gazette*, August 17, 1816, 4.

certain and fully comprehended by me. I am as eager after the study of it, a babe after its mother's breast—and to be denied it, causes me to moan in spirit. O that the Lord would give me power to be more useful to the heathen around me! O that he would send his all-subduing, all-convincing, all-sanctifying *Truth* into their hearts! For how can an old garment be made better by new pieces? How can they regard virtue, while their hearts are in the darkness of heathenism? Unless God shed his divine light *amongst* them our endeavours can do nothing effectually.

[September] 9th. [1817].

Since yesterday morning my heart has been troubled for having been too harsh with a little pupil boarder. She had been very naughty, and had aggravated her offence by adding falsehood to faults, a thing so common here, that we can come at the truth of nothing that we do not witness ourselves. I sometimes have to combat a confederation of falsehood: one aiming to defend another—and on the contrary, one aiming to convict another unjustly. Severity grieves me afterwards. But I now see the good effects of what was experienced, as those children came to me since, to have me teach them to pray on account of that particular sin. O may the Lord of my spirit, to whom I am accountable, impress my sinful heart with holy tenderness towards the children, and teach me *at all times* "to *will* and to *do* of his own good pleasure."[188] Then I shall not err. Thou O my Soul! art most endebted[189] to his mercy, of any creature—Bless thou the Lord!

[September] 12th. [1817].

The other evening, our neighbor N. was awakened from an early nap, by an affray between a very [146] large *Cobra Capella* (copper head) and a favorite turtleshell English Cat. The Snake had crept

[188] Philippians 2:13[.]

[189] Endebted: archaic spelling of indebted.

into his room through the lower venetians, and the Cat seeing it, attacked it. When Mr. N. first saw them, (for a light is always burning in bedrooms) the snake had wound itself round the body of the cat, but the cat maintained her part so as to receive no injury. He called aloud, for help, and the servants came in with spears and sticks. The snake then left the Cat, and took refuge under Mr. N.'s bed, which being very high, he had room to erect himself at least two feet, spreading his hood and making a noise like a gander when he is guarding his goslings, running out his tongue, and bidding defiance. At last they drove it under a case of drawers, where they succeeded in spearing it to death.

The snake is said to be of that kind, whose bite gives so much pain to the whole system, as to occasion a perspiration of blood. (This reminds me of the bloody sweat of our suffering Saviour, smarting under the sting of sin, taken for mortals. Satan the serpent bruised his heel, his fleshly part, but He bruised his head, when he rose from death and ascended up on high, to become his Judge.)

We are fearful, but not particularly from this circumstance, of stepping or feeling about our house at night without a light. How would anyone like to go into the next room without a light, and instead of a plate, take hold of a snake on the table—or on jumping into bed, be saluted by a Copper-head, as was really the Case, as one that [had] taken the place of Mr. Moore in Mrs. Moore's bed; but having a light in the room, the fiend was detected when she turned down the sheet. The natives catch them and extract the two teeth which convey the poison, and tame them, so as to make them erect themselves and shift about to the sound of a little instrument of music which they play to charm them. This I have seen done before our door. I have also seen the snake catchers play over the grass, and catch two immensely large snakes which had been seen there by the children. They take hold of them by the head when they first pull it out of [147] their hole, and immediately take the tail and let go the head, when the snake, hanging his whole length, is powerless. Thus they can snap them against a tree or put them in a bag. They do not like to kill them, lest they should destroy the spirit of some enemy of theirs, deceased, and now transmigrated into a snake, but they will allow them to be sunk in the Ganges in a bag, which was done with these.

[September] 14th [1817].

Sabbath evening—Eustace Carey preached for us in the Hall, (our hall being appropriated to a school-room on week days, and a worship room on Sabbath days, when the benches are set as forms and a carpet put down, and chairs brought in for strangers). Every one admires Mr. Carey. His style is affectionate and elevated. He looks so thin & weak, that it seems as if he preached to us from the borders of both the grave and of heaven—so solemn and yet so grand. I thought, if Christ be so good and so great, how can *I* approach him? His goodness made me in love with Him when first I knew him, and his Majesty excited my adoration. I feel a struggle between a strong desire to imitate Christ's *inimitable* perfections, and the sin of my nature, which lies heavy on my heart, and makes me feel how frail I am.

[September] 20th. [1817].

I thank my God for every token of his acceptance of me in the cause of the Heathen. Another of the wives of the native Christians, has come for a few days past, to learn to sew. She says she is not able to learn to read.

This morning before I rose, I thought I felt no friendship scarcely for the native Christians, seeing in them so much remaining of their former temper; but the thought of Peter denying Christ with Lies and swearing, pleaded loudly for these poor creatures. And yet no disciple loved his Lord more than Peter. I often think of Christ's Parable, of putting a piece of new cloth into an old garment.[190] It applies so well here.

Brother Moore lies very ill—and hundreds of natives are dying

[190] Matthew 9:16; Mark 2:21; Luke 5:36.

around us. May the Lord have mercy on us! in sparing the life of our colleague. Sickness has never entered my roof—nor has one died in our houses since I came here. Great have [148] been the mercies of God to our Station. The Cholera prevails more or less yearly amongst the natives. They eat so much fruit, and drink so much water after their meal of rice in the evening, that it carries them [from] us with a venom. They season their curry very high, which makes them thirsty.

Lord's day—My spirit enquires why I should be so easy with so little time spent in communion with God. My heart is not easy on account of its carnality, its forgetfulness of prayer; and disinclination for it. Christ is my Soul's Physician. I will seek my remedy in Him.

October 3rd. 1817.

Have been utterly disinclined for noting anything in my Diary for some time, owing I suppose to being indisposed bodily. I have felt no energy either in duty, study, or devotion of late. I think of nothing to remark else, but that Mr. Moore has recovered—and that our whole family consisting of about one hundred persons, are pretty well, considering the relaxing state of the weather. But if we see this month out, the next must be far more agreeable, equally free from sandy winds, and soaking rains. We have enjoyed the society of br. and sister Carey for several months.

Oct. 6. [1817]

Was so much overcome yesterday, by bodily weaknesses, that my mind quite sunk beneath my task of daily cares. I had been obliged to omit keeping my school in the afternoon, lengthening the morning's term to one o'clock. But Mr. Rowe did not much approve of it, therefore I resumed it again yesterday. I thought very hard of it, as he knew I had recently had cause for some repose, or recess from labours like those. I prayed to be made submissive to the Lord's will, to be willing to fill up my cup of sufferings as well as my measure of duties, with a satisfied mind.

I had been confined for some days, to my bed, and had taken a great deal of Laudanum to save my life, and consequently was weaker in mind as well as body. But men cannot feel with women. However, seeing me overcome with a weight on my spirits, he took pains to soothe and comfort me.

[149] I have had reason from today's experience to say that our God is a "God at hand" ever ready to help them that pray for His kind control; for I find my body has gained strength, my mind is supported, my school less harassing, all, as if he had descended to administer to me as an able Physician, and even to rule my house for me. O that I may realize his good hand thus, daily!

[October] 8th. [1817].

Heard from Sister Chamberlain. She mentions the burning of a widow down at the Ferry (Ghaut) near their house, and the horror with which the Sight of the flames filled her.

We are without company the first time for 7 months, our beloved inmates Mr. & Mrs. Carey having returned home to Calcutta. We however do not expect to finish this day without a fresh supply expecting some friends hourly. I feel better reconciled to Sister Carey's leaving us, because I am in better health. A few days passed when we could not see each other, for she had given birth to a lovely daughter,[191] and I at the same time disappointed of one, perhaps.[192]

Lord's day [October] 9th. [1817].

My heart has been prayerful this morning, going out in language like this "O that I "ripe" that the sickle might "be put in"!

Brother Moore seemed very tender concerning sin, last evening and this morning; and in addressing the family at stated worship, was very impressive towards the children. The prayers that have so

---

[191] Annie Yates Carey (1817–1824). Charlotte's journal corrects online genealogies that list Annie's birth as 1818.

[192] Charlotte alludes to having suffered a miscarriage.

long been put up for them, seem to an eye of flesh to have been lost; but Faith believes their answers are still in store, and will yet be granted. O that we could see some fruit of our spiritual labours amongst them! They are much reformed in outward things by dint of precept and watchfulness over them, but their hearts seem yet far from holiness.

O Lord, enable me to trust in thy grace, which thou canst make all-sufficient for me. Let me not murmur at my privation of what *I* may feel the desire to possess, since thy grace can supply strength to render it unnecessary, and thus occasion the loss to be unperceived. Oh that my stiff spirit could more cheerfully yield, and that [150] my mind were less ready at uncomfortable thoughts. I am often led captive by Satan, almost at his will, and if thou didst not "look after" me, I should utterly depart from thee.

Evening------How pleasant is the company of pious people, whose minds are *liberal* and well informed. Mr. Money,[193] a gentleman in the civil service is such an one, with whose society we are favored after Sabbath evening services, to take tea and pass an hour or two. Our neighbor Captain Alexander generally accompanies him, and seems to enter into his feelings on religious subjects. Mr. M. became serious through a word dropped by a nurse when his wife was extremely ill, and little hope was entertained of her life. She said, "I have heard that to read the form of prayers for the sick is good to restore them." They were Episcopalians by Education. Mr. M. got the Ch. prayer book, and kneeling down for the first time I believe, in a voluntary attempt of the kind, read them over. While thus engaged, his mind was struck with the necessity of spiritual prayer on his own behalf also. He let not go the impression that was made, and has become, from a gay man, a most humble pious man. His beloved partner, who was very gay also, recover'd so far as to go to England for her health, but has left off her vanities.

My beloved partner preached this evening in a manner and on a subject, peculiarly interesting.

---

[193] See Journal, July 29, 1816.

[October] 11th. [1817]. 12 o'clock.

Feel a severe pain in my breast. It seems like an affliction of both body and mind. I try to relieve myself by long breaths, and those breaths cut my vitals, and leave a sore weight behind. I feel incompetent, at last, to so much exertion of either body or mind as I have given myself unto. O Lord give me strength for my occupation. O give me those heavenly affections that will make me patient, long-suffering and cheerful! I long for cheerfulness. I need something to vary the scene from constantly straining my every nerve in my labours. I wish [I] had a sweet child of my own to enliven me. But the Lord's will be done.

[151] [October] 13th. [1817].

Today I have been favored with more tranquility. I rose under pleasant feelings of mind, and more vigour of frame; but by 10 o'clock the pain in my breast came on. It is attended with a weakness in my knees and a fluttering about my heart.

[October] 14th. [1817].

Am much better today, every way, and enabled to draw comfort from on high.

Company arrived from Agra. Mr. Carapete also.[194] He is on a preaching tour to Bombay by Turat, over land. He is an Armenian, and was of the Greek church, but he has embraced the religion of the bible, and is employed by the Baptist missionaries, to spread the Gospel.

It is now The *Mohurrum*,[195] a great Mahomedan festival. All the Mussulmauns in the district assemble at this place. They keep up

[194] Carapete was Carapiet Chater Aratoon, an Armenian convert working with the British Baptist missionaries.

[195] Muharram is the first month of the Islamic calendar and is the second holiest month after Ramadan.

their operations all night, every night for two weeks. They mourn for the decease of Mahomet, striking their bosoms, and calling so loud that heaven may hear, "Ulla Mahummed" until they become hoarse and their eyes look like balls of fire; some of them beat their chests until they swell up to a puff. They go in procession of thousands, having a band and barbarian music from graveyard to graveyard and village to village in the manner described. But they are preceeded [sic] by an artificial Pavilion called the Tajia or *throne of glory*, the seat of Mahomet. This is bourn on men's shoulders. # (here bring in the picture). Two men watch it with fly brushes made of peacock's feathers, to keep every insect from polluting it. These feathers are a badge of mourning for Mahomet, as they partake of a great deal of green, which is the colour worn in mourning by them. A branch of plantain also is carried, as a badge of mourning, and everyone has on *something* green, either a cap, a scarf, a belt, a coat, or pair of trowsers of that colour. They dig a grave, and sit and mourn round it. Then they go to the river and each one takes a handful of mud, and throws [it] into the hole until it is filled. Then they shout, and proclaim Mahomet is risen! [152] The crowd then disperses, exhausted with their long carousal.

This breaks up our Schools for a month at a time. I went down to the avenue gate to see the prosession &c. Two men, seeing us, commenced a single combat, in imitation of the two sons of Mahomet's daughter Fatima, whom they consider divine also—and who they say, decided a contest. But I am not versed in their history.[196] I hope some of them will listen to the Gospel, and be brought

---

[196] The mourning did not commemorate Muhammad's death but that of his grandson, Husayn ibn Ali. The cry "Ulla Mahummed" may have been a repetition of the lament by Husayn's sister that began with "O Muhammed!" The Tajia was not Muhammad's throne but a miniature replica of Husayn's tomb. The symbolic fight did not imitate a struggle between Husayn and his younger brother Hasan but commemorated the Battle of Karbala in which Husayn was killed. Islam does not teach that anyone is divine other than Allah or that Muhammad was raised from the grave. Since folk religions often incorporate non-orthodox actions and beliefs, Charlotte may have recorded

to confess him, who after he had fought a single combat with Death and Hell, ascended triumphant to the Realms of bliss, from whence *he* shall come to judge both *Mahomet*, "the quick and the dead."

The Musselmauns assume a deal of superiority over the native Hindoos, the original possessors of the country, as the Europeans do over both Mahometans and Hindoos. But the Hindoos are glad to get into milder hands; and both them and their former conquerors confess themselves happier under the Company's Gov^{t}. than they were under their own, of either reign—Both which were arbitrary.

[October] 15th. [1817].

Have been pleased with viewing two beautiful birds which came down upon the lawn to dig up worms. They are highly distinguished, as the native Rajahs, if able themselves, or if not, send a proxy on a certain day in every year, to behold this Bird, the sight of which secures them and their people prosperity throughout the year. # (here bring in the picture, taken by Sir Charles [D'oyly].)

So much for superstition—now how much for truth. This bird is as large as a wild pigeon, and much its shape. The predominant colour is a dark buff. Its wings, tail, and crest are striped with the brightest & purest navy blue, in gradual shades.[197] When its crest is down, it would measure five or six inches from the tip of the bill to the tip of the crest, which then looks another bill on the back of the head forming a straight line from tip to tip. But if any bird fly over where it is, it erects the crest to [153] to offer like a fully spread paper fan, having a beautiful blue edge. It raises it little or more according to the degree of danger it feels. They never come singly, but in pairs, sometimes three pair together. It is said by the natives that they have a watch-bird always attending them, a small black bird, which perches itself near, on the highest sprig, to keep a lookout for birds of prey, and on seeing one, gives the alarm, at which I have seen

---

things she had been told or may have misunderstood key elements of the Muharram observation.

[197] Likely the hoopoe bird.

them look up, erect their crest, and if the bird flies distant, resume their labour, but if near, take wing and be off. They come quite near the door in search of food.

[October] 16th. [1817].

I have seen my manifold sins of late, more than when I was in a torpid state of mind as well as body, and have bewailed them before the Lord.

[October] 18th. [1817].

There is too cool air through the hall for me to sit there this morning, while they lead worship with the Hindoos. Their voices, however dissonant and grating to my ear, give me pleasure, since they are raised to the true God Jehovah. They seem much like little children for their ignorance and simplicity. I am melted, when I hear them pray in their language "as the rain falls from heaven watering the earth, so, O gracious God, pour out thy Spirit upon us; as the earth, the thirsty earth drinks up the rain, so, O gracious God, prepare our dark and ignorant and sinful hearts to receive thy grace." I adore the goodness of God in so far fulfilling his promises to the Heathen. O may it please him to spread the knowledge of himself far and wide.

Lord's day. [October] 19th. [1817].

In my late illness I was roused to reflect on my wickedness in not hallowing the Sabbath as I ought to do, by opening upon the 20th verse of the 20th chapter of Ezekiel. "And hallow my Sabbaths, and they shall be a sign between me and you, that ye may know that I am the Lord your God." I have reason to bless God for his *truth*, for he hath said "I will not utterly forsake them."[198] So his holy Spirit follows us, and makes his word both reprove and comfort us.

[154] Truly there is no peace in a state separate from God.

[198] Hebrews 13:5.

There is no such consolation as feeling his good hand upon us to comfort us—and if we see his hand in our afflictions, it reconciles us to them—nay we prefer *having them with his hand*, than enjoying the ease of a secure state without his presence.

Note. The daughters of Shallum the Ruler of the half part of Jerusalem, assisted in repairing the wall of the city after the Captivity (Nehemiah 3rd.12) Ought not this example to inspire all pious females with a holy public spiritedness in all things relating to the building of *Christ's* Jerusalem?

The Lord made choice of Prophets instead of Rulers to rebuild the temple and city of Jerusalem, but "his good hand" being with them, turned the Spirit of heathen Kings and Governors towards the work of *their* God, and made them grant all their petitions for silver and gold, and herds and grain, and also permission for a part of the Captivity to return, and all those amongst the heathen, subjected to those Kings, who were disposed to do so, to join the Israelites in repairing the rifled temple and broken walls. Thus the Lord rules over the hearts of Principalities to this day, and make them aid the cause of religion, conducted by his ministers male and female, who labour *for* and *in* his cause. –

After the second Services. We had a small meeting, the family only, which was to me the best I had been in for a long time, because the love of God seemed alive in my heart. It was not long, however, before Satan set at me with my besetting sin in worship time, so as to render it difficult for me to preserve the suitable current of reflection. I rejoice in being again awakened to the inward warfare. I was delighted to see little Josiah find the hymn and bring it to me, and then find the chapter which Mr. Rowe read and follow him through with it. He was a little frazzled at the close, to find him go on with remarks that were not in the chapter, but he soon discovered the case. He is just turned eight years of age—late enough indeed to do so, but eighteen months ago he could not spell words of 3 letters, [155] nor could his next elder brother, proof sufficient to me, that beginning to learn to read at six years of age, is quite as advantageous as earlier. I have been wearied year after year with teaching children too young to read connected syllables. Their minds cannot grasp them. Very little ones should be put to schools where none but such are—and where their memories may be cultivated before their understandings can conceive much. The eldest of my stepsons behaved sweetly to me in my late indisposition: his father set him to attend me. It never seemed a toil to him [to] sit quietly beside me for half the day. And when I let him go out awhile, he would often come in, to see if I wished for anything, always ready and handy to do it.

The making a positive stand against the enemy of righteousness is the best way to foil him, trusting in God to help us. We must not expect to be let alone to go on unmolested in the Lord's work which may be set to our lot, but, being on the watch, must assume "our weapons" in the name of our Lord: allowing of neither delay nor frustration in the business assigned us. We must look unto him who divided the waters before Moses, threw down the walls of Jericho, and made the Sun stand still before Joshua; who caused the prison doors to fly open before Peter; and who left the guard to fall back senseless at the bursting of the tomb wherein was closed and sealed the everlasting Son of Righteousness, the Prince of Peace, and Ruler of the earth—even *he* who hath said, "Resist the devil and he *will* flee from thee" not he *shall* flee from thee, for Satan is a coward before the weakest child who holds up the sword of the word, with the hand of faith, against him. So strengthen us on the attempt He says, "My grace is sufficient for thee" and "Lo, I am with you" and then to remove all doubt, adds, "always, even unto the end of the world."[199]

October 20th. [1817].

A change in the weather indicates the setting in of the Indian winter. This day has been cool and cloudy. Surely the Lord will prosper our

---

199 2 Corinthians 12:9; Matthew 28:20.

attempts to bring about the improvement of the native females. To-day another woman came to learn to sew. This is Nainsook's mother. I asked her [156] how old she was_? she said she could not tell, but that she had had eight children. She seems humble and teachable as a little child. She cried out and shed tears at discovering that she could not see to thread a needle. I gave her a very large one, which she gets the younger ones to thread for her. She is blest in her son, who grows in grace and in the knowledge of our Lord Jesus Christ. He comes to read a chapter to me, daily, as Mr. Rowe is so much engaged he cannot sit to attend him.

Finding the care of both the English and Hindee school[200] at the same hours, to be very arduous. I proposed to my teacher the Moonsee, to teach the native females half the time, at an increase of salary. He consented to do so now, altho' when I first requested it to him, he felt very much offended.

Have obtained Mr. Rowe's consent to lengthen the term of the English School, and hold it but once a day. I now have all the time after dinner for Hindusthani—that is between studying and the Hindee School.

[October] 21st. [1817].

A conversation took place between my teacher and myself which gave me satisfaction. I adverted to the time when I desired him to take a part in the tuition of the native females, and though he did not reply angrily to me, he told a third person how much I had hurt his feelings by proposing to him, so derogatory an employment. He replied, "as your Servant, I am willing to do whatever you command me." I told him that it was a false prejudice that the men here, were under. That amongst other nations, very learned men undertook the education of females, and that we did not think any but learned and respectable men qualified to teach them. He replied with much

---

[200] The two schools at Digah were the English-language girls' school for Eurasian boarding students and the Hindi-language day school for local Indian girls.

feeling, "This is a very bad country," and immediately adverted to the Tyranny of the Rajahs before the English took the country, saying that the sufferings of the people were now much mitigated. I told him that they would yearly become more happy, if they would favour the instruction of females—That little girls must become mothers, ere long, and if they were taught to read, and read that children ought to be obedient and affectionate to their parents, and kind and obliging to their brothers [157] as well as to each other, that thus instructed themselves, they would make all around them happier, and would teach their own children to be amiable. How different would be the state of their families to what they now are, if that were the case. He was quite surprised to learn from me, that many schools for native females were already begun in the land.[201] He said that rank stood an obstacle in his country. That the people

[201] By 1817, when Charlotte made this entry, "many schools for native females" had indeed been started in Bengal and Bihar. Some appear to have been short-lived such as the private schooling in Calcutta run by Mrs. Hedges (1760), Mrs. Hodges (1780), Mrs. Pitts, Mrs. Savage (1789), Mrs. Durrel, Mrs. Copeland (1792), Mrs. Payne (1794), and in Dinapore by Mrs. Middleton (1799). A more institutional form of education was offered for girls and boys at the Free School (1742) and the Upper and Lower Orphan Schools (1783). Baptist missionaries started female education "on the modern and organized line" in 1803 when Mrs. Hannah (Sheppard) Marshman started the first girls' school and boarding house in Serampore. The same year Mrs. Martha (Blackmore) Pearce and Mrs. Frances Lawson ran a girls' school in Calcutta. By 1817 Mrs. Penny had ninety-four girls under her care at the Benevolent Institution in Calcutta. By 1817 the Baptist missionaries at Serampore had established 115 schools largely within thirty miles of Calcutta with more than ten thousand pupils under instruction. Some of those schools were coeducational or girls' schools. The Rowes and Moores had been providing education for girls from the start of their work in Digah. Most of their Baptist colleagues likewise opened schools when they began work in new locations away from Calcutta. Dutta, *British Women Missionaries in Bengal*, 32, 67; Laird, *Missionaries and Education in Bengal*, 67. Sarwar, "Christian Missionaries and Female Education in Bengal," 39. Carey, *Good Old Days,* 165–168, 171, 175.

were divided into two great distinctions (he meant, of Hindoos and Mahometans) and under each of these, were four or more divisions. That they were restrained to certain ways of getting their living. That he had 7 persons dependant on his salary, an uncle, two sisters, a wife and children. I advised him to send his sisters to my school to learn to be useful, but he urged that they were of the higher rank, and therefore were not permitted to appear from home. He granted, that it was false honour, which prevented them from doing good, even to themselves.

[October] 22nd. [1817].

The moonsee kindly did as he promised, and has undertaken the tuition of the native females in our veranda.

[October] 26th. [1817].

Brother Moore absent on the river, trying the benefit of the river air for his ague and fever. Mr. Rowe consequently has a good deal to attend to, and is much fatigued in the performance of double duty.

I find my eyes are so weak of late that I cannot read or write without pain, and see clouds and dots before me. The Scriptures again satisfy me, better than any other book. How much to be deplored, is a dereliction from divine things: but how much to be glorified by us, is our heavenly shepherd, who pursues us with his watchful care, until he make us feel that we have wandered, and then mercifully draws [us] back to his arms!

O Lord our God, strengthen those of us whom thou hast raised up from sickness, and restore the afflicted, and prepare us to do thy will in the work assigned us, with singleness of heart, and without desiring more than is allotted us of this world's goods. Bless and maintain this station where thou hast set up thy name, and cause it to prosper.

[158] [October] 27th. [1817].

Feel much pressed by my cares today, and irritable in my temper, accompanied with a tremour on my nerves: occasioned perhaps by the unfaithfulness of a servant. A new sort of servant has come to me today. She is the wife of an invalided soldier who is going to England. As she is almost a native by extraction, she cannot leave her country without a large sum of money being paid in pledge for her return to it.[202] This is done to prevent the native inhabitants being carried away. Slavery is not allowed by the company—and to prevent any kind of imposition, those Europeans who require their assistance on a voyage, are obliged to deposit two thousand rupees, in pledge for their return, before they can take a single one away. Many Portuguese women[203] are employed as children's maids on voyages, because they have no cast to prevent their eating anything which christians eat, for they are Roman Catholics.

Another native girl has been brought to school today. The child of old servants to the station, not christianized. If the new servant, who speaks English as well, can fit work, she will prove an assistance to me; then I shall get on well with both schools in operation under my view.

[October] 29th. [1817].

Yesterday a native girl of 14, and today a native woman came to school. The new hand sits with them all around her, fitting their work, and keeping them still.

My moonsee wrote me a note yesterday of which the following is a literal Transposition, word for word. Superscription—"Letter, her worshipfull excellence, Mrs. Charlotte Rowe's presence into,

---

[202] The Eurasian population had grown larger than the number of Europeans in India, and the majority of British soldiers in India married Eurasians. By Charlotte's time, Eurasians were experiencing increasing prejudice. As a result, the Company's objection to soldiers taking Indian wives with them as they returned to England now applied to Eurasian wives as well.

[203] The "Portuguese" women were Eurasian descendants of Portuguese men and Indian wives as distinguished from "Indo-Briton" descendants of British men and Indian wives. See Journal, April 25, 1817, entry and footnote.

arrive. Address—Holy honored Lady Charlotte Rowe to. Contents—Moonsee Ramdagal Singh's respected entreating her presence into, admission. My fortune such is, that this day my mother died thus; therefore, for this reason, I present not am, and fourteen days in, I this business for absent in engaged must be; but I two-one days in a person my substitute, Presence into, send will. First, thou Controller art; me upon kindness rest let. I misfortune from, Presence in, not can be, and more urge."

[159] Lord's day. Brother Moore returned from Mongire quite recovered; his family remain in the boat five miles distant, during today. Mrs. G. in her budgerow in company with her, coming to visit us. Mr. Chamberlain in trouble at Mongire, and it is found he will be obliged to leave it. He is so bold in preaching plain truth, that Government does not like it. For this reason he was ordered to leave Serdhana[204] some months ago.

Nov. 16. 1817.

Mr. Moore ill again. Brother Carapete returned. I have to be company for him. He says that the Greek, Roman, and Armenian churches are similar in their tenets, alike paying adoration and making prayers to departed saints. He asserts his firm belief in the alone Divinity of the Trinity. He was baptized at Serampore in the Hoogly together *with brother Judson.*[205]

The festival of the Mussulmauns still continues. I hear their

---

[204] Charles Milner Ricketts, private secretary to Governor General Lord Moira, had ordered John Chamberlain to leave Sirdhana in 1814 after receiving complaints about Chamberlain preaching in public at the Hurdwar fair. Ricketts feared that overt evangelization might cause public disorder. Chamberlain, *Memoirs of John Chamberlain*, 355.

[205] William Ward baptized Carapiet Chater Aratoon in the Hooghly River opposite the Mission House on September 26, 1812. Ward had baptized Adoniram and Ann Judson earlier on September 6, 1812, not in the river but in the Lall Bazaar Baptist Chapel. Wenger, *Story of the Lall Bazaar Baptist Church,* 83, 536.

yells and tumult as they parade along in solemn procession. Last night they awoke us by their incantations of *Hussa* and *Hosain* who fought the single combat in order to decide a victory. Br. Carapete is preaching at the garden cottages,[206] where many passing by go in to hear *what he has to say.*

It is striking to observe how averse a Hindoo is to being called a Hindoo after he has embraced Christianity. Having abjured the Hindoo faith he can ill bear being called a Hindoo in a mere national light.

I thank God, that I have been permitted to pass this day without pain of either body or mind. The application of a large piece of cotton wadding to my chest, has relieved the pain there.

I have often had it in mind to state what experience has informed me, is a needful outfit of apparel for a person coming to reside in this country. As many changes of *shirting muslin* [160] (not Irish linen) as will make one comfortable through a voyage of 16 weeks, 14 of which will be as warm as midsummer in America. Of course 2 changes will be required weekly, on the voyage. When you get to India, you must change daily at *the least*, and wait a whole week for clothes given out to be washed. Men must have as many changes of white jackets and panteloons and everything else to correspond. Women must have almost as many dresses—12 white gowns at least. 6 morning wrappers of white cambric muslin. A few ginghams—a silk or two: none of which ought to be put on at sea—lest they be discoloured. Five cotton hose, and some silk ones.

Men should have their trowsers to wear under their others. And both men and women, should be provided with a few pair of Musquitoe-trowsers to sleep in, made with feet, & very full, gathered into a foot, and to draw with a string at the waist. Ruffles about a

---

[206] The cottages for the indigenous Indian evangelists working with the Rowes and Moores stood along the roadside of the Baptist station in Digah. See Journal, February 26, 1817.

night gown, are intolerable to the neck in so warm a climate. A handsome, deep-faced bonnet of a light kind, and a green Calash[207]—but not to be opened at Sea.

They should prefer tin boxes, well painted, to their trunks. They keep out the insects the best. Well tann'd leather trunks lined with coarse calico, preserves clothes well, and last very well. They should be cleaned with oil to prevent their cracking from the influence of the hot winds. No feather beds are desirable here. Ladies should have easy corsets made of light materials, and enough of them to change often. Whatever not woolen, that is worn two days in the rains, becomes foetid in smell. Neatness and sweetness in person, is a quality so general here, that a deviation from it is conspicuous and disgusting. The natives only are lisenced [sic] to be unneat. European fashions prevail in dress amongst Europeans. *Fine & full*, forms the best dress.

[161] The months of December and January are as cool as September and October in America. But we feel it a good deal, owing to so long being by turns parched or melted with heat. Therefore, a suit of thicker attire, is desirable. Broadcloth for gentlemen and Bumbazeen[208] for ladies. Large and long shawls are worn in winter, abroad.

The mock-Camels hair, is so good an imitation as almost to deceive, and are very common.

It may be well to observe, as it is a fact that will not change, that Irish or any other linen made of flax, is much warmer than cotton shirting; that putting on a flaxen garment next the skin after bathing, feels like a wrapping of fire, while a cotton change is congenial. The heat from the body does not escape through linen—and in the rainy season when it becomes saturated with perspiration, it is very cold

---

[207] Calash: a silk hood or bonnet hooped to keep the fabric from disturbing a woman's coiffure. It drew its name from "caléché," the hood of a carriage that folds back.

[208] Bumbazeen: a twilled material made of silk and wool or cotton and wool.

and harsh to the tender skin.

I recommend the wearing of old shirting as far as possible on the voyage, to be torn up and used as dusters and then cast into the sea. I also recommend to voyagers, to retire to rest at night, in a garb sufficient to completely cover them from exposure, should any accident happen at Sea. All furs, beavers, and woolens, are liable to be destroyed the first year by insects. The best preservative against which, is wrapping them up as soon as not needed, in Russia linen,[209] and putting them in tin boxes, kept locked, and raised from the ground; for *ten fingered* vermin are as little to be trusted as white ants, moth, and rust.

Never take infants and young children to India, unless you are willing to lose them shortly after you get them there. But if they must be taken, make for then at least two dozen of dresses called Frock-piajamas [sic]– that is, frocks with trowsers sewed into the waist seam, and tucked and ruffled at the ankles. This with as many shirts with short sleeves, both for boys and girls, are all that is worn, except in the rains, when a fine flannel belt or banyan[210] is necessary next to the skin. A few Dimity[211] coats to wear and in the mornings early, and cotton-cord sun bonnets. [162] Children wear no stockings except in high dress &cc. Those are very cheap & plenty here.

[November] 18th. [1817].

Such a sick headache, that I can hardly do anything. I [grudge] every moment of indisposition that obstructs my progress in the Hindee, between schools. I find it difficult now to commit things to memory. Youth is the time for that: Then associated sounds dwell on the memory though not fully understood, and in riper years when Reason can apply them, return pregnant with improvement and

[209] Russian linen: hemp linen fabric mass produced in Russia.

[210] Banyan: a loose-fitted informal robe or gown.

[211] Dimity: a thin cotton fabric woven with a stripe or check of heavier yarn.

delight—then that which was committed to memory with weariness, brings a reward in newness and interest, bringing their "sheaves with them." I sometimes fear I shall do no other good in the language than to oblige my stepsons to learn it grammatically.

[November] 19th. [1817].

Heard that our friend Captain Picket, had a narrow escape from being murdered by a robber, while on his march in the present expedition against the Pindarees[212]—A set of ruffians who had plundered and burnt a village, seeing a Merchants Caravan of goods, and a palanquin not far behind it, supposed the owner was therein, and pierced the palanquin with his spear, which went between Mr. P.'s arm and side! How thickly set with dangers, are travelers over land in this country. The river course is as dangerous from natural causes.

Our recently formed excellent friend Mrs. Grant,[213] who is on a visit to us, has allowed her Lala or writing-master to inspect my little spelling book of the Hindostani. After examining a little way into it, he requested me to give it to him, as he said, he had never met with such a book, and he wanted it to help him teach Mrs. G's adopted daughters—He says that I am very wise and learned. I suppose he means, *for a woman to be*, comparing me with the women of his own country, not knowing those of other. The Hindoos are great flatterers.

[November] 21st. [1817].

Expecting brother Chamberlain's family. We hear that our Hindoo cloth merchant is very ill. We wonder that the Bramins suffer him to try his natural strength to [163] recover, before they drag him off

---

[212] The Pindaris were plunderers and foragers acting as non-formal military units. They existed first alongside the Mughal army, then the Maratha army, and then operated on their own. Governor General Francis Rawdon-Hastings' (Lord Moira's) campaign against the Pindaris during the Third Anglo-Maratha War (1817–1819) became known as the Pindari War.

[213] The full identity of Mrs. Grant from Agra is unknown to the author.

to join the citizens of that happy place, where murdered victims have grown gray in pleasure, centuries ago. His riches are a fine bait for such a fish.

The Temple of Juggernaut at Orissa is supported, for the sake of the Revenue it Brings to Government, from the Toll of the poor deluded pilgrims at the gate,[214] and by the "*permits*" allowed for the burning of Widows!

As Mahomet rose from his fictitious grave last night at 8 o'clock (as we have reason to conclude, from the shouts which we heard at a mile's distance) all is peace today, no drums, nor invocations are heard in the street.

When truth is conveyed by means of fables, some lesson may be culled; but when men found falsehood and delusion upon Truth, and act upon it with all their powers of mind and body, we wonder that human nature should be so void of an inate [sic] sense of Sense of Right. Alas! It proves how fallen we are, that we may so easily be led blindfold [sic] by the Prince of Lies.

When Mrs. G. talks to the natives through her moonsee, she tells them, that this was the favored country where Jesus Christ the Saviour of the world, was born. That these were the people whom he came to save, and that *we*, the English, were gentiles and descended from heathen forefathers, like them. That the difference which exists between us and them is owning to our having believed in Jesus Christ as God and Saviour. This, she says, pleases them by giving them any precedence, and induces them to listen to her. I must confess, I think this a most happy thought, and one which exhibits the humble desire of our self-made missionary friend, to do good to the Souls of these poor wretches. She is a worthy woman, for she has taken three daughters of a Sergant who on his dying bed gave them over to her care, without waiting her consent. She has placed them with us to be educated. She has opened a school which she supports with her own means, for the children of the native soldiers who have gone up to subdue the Pindarees. Mr. & Mrs.

[214] See Journal, July 30, 1816 and footnote on the pilgrim tax.

Chamberlain, with their little Mary Ann, accompanied her to see us.

[164] Lord's day—Have reason to bless God for better health, since the cool weather, as *we* call it, has commenced. I feel very little additional fatigue from having family visitors, as everybody brings their own servants with them. Their cook helps ours, and their waiters wait on them for all they want. They sleep in their boats when we have no rooms. The table is all we have to care about. Their company is therefore, a recreation to us, after long intervals of application.

Our friend Mrs. G. gives this account of herself—that her parents were Welsh, and belonging to the Established Church. That she lived until grey in the pleasures of society—those pleasures denominated innocent by unconverted minds, such as card-playing, balls, &cc. That when Mr. Chamberlain first went up to Agra, he found her so. He brought a note of introduction to her. What she relates as passing in her mind at the moment of introduction is extraordinary. The words, "Peace has come unto you and your house" took possession of her mind, and reiterated there whenever she thought of Brother Chamberlain. "Well," as she says, "it was not long before he *assaulted* her in his own rough way"—She was given to possess that candor of mind (though a stiff church woman) which made her patient to hear him, and *scrutinous* of what he said; for the *truth* of which, she repaired to the Scriptures when alone; and finding it founded in Truth, as she believed the bible to be true, she paid more regard to his reproofs and instructions, until she became a convert. Since that period, she has changed her manners, with all her house; and she now came up with him, to be baptized, in the presence of his brethren and sisters of the Baptist mission, and in her latter day, profess Christ in *His* appointed ways.

The boat people told us, that their Lady had provided herself with 20 Indian blankets to bestow upon such beggars as appeared in really suffering circumstances. That on a former passage, she had stripped herself of everything but what was barely necessary to take her along, that she might bestow what she could spare, on their wants.

[165] Brother Chamberlain relates a curious anecdote about Gen[l]. A. Br. C. says of himself, that he passed a place esteemed very sacred by the Natives on account of the goddess Luxmi dwelling there. The place forms a point in the river. While there, a native enquired of him why the English stole their gods? saying that a great man, Gen[l]. A. had put his Pinnace to shore there, having horse-men to attend on land, and solicited him to sell the goddess to him. She is a stone image, larger than life, and stands under a tree, deemed sacred by her presence. The man replied that he could not give up the goddess, she was much adored, and great multitudes of people resorted to worship at her shrine. The General then invited him into his boat; he went on board, and on entering the first room, saw many images arranged round it, and two Bramins making the offerings of fruit, rice, flowers, &cc. He made *his* bow to them and came out. When he returned on shore to the General, the request was made a second time, but was, as before denied it. During the night however, he sent his men and officers to take the goddess on board, and having stolen her, set off by night, and pursued his journey to Berhampore, where he has depositted [sic] them in his own house, and worships them, making daily sacrifices with his Bramins; for he has won over several Bramins to attend on him and them—that is as private Chaplains.[215] If he had not been an Idolater, I should have

---

[215] Using "Gen[1]. A." might have been Charlotte's way of reporting this story while maintaining the general's anonymity. "Gen[l]. A." may have been Major General Charles Stuart (1758–1828), an officer in the East India Company who in 1808 wrote *Vindication of the Hindoos* and *Vindication of the Hindoos; Part the Second* under the name "a Bengal Officer." Stuart asserted the moral excellence of Hinduism and decried efforts to lead Hindus to Christianity. His embrace of Hindu culture and religion earned him the nickname "Hindu Stuart." In the 1876 book *John Chamberlain: A Missionary Biography*, author Charles Bennett Lewis claimed that Stuart had stolen a statue from a temple at Baikunthpore in 1813 after the Brahmins had refused his offer to buy it. Lewis, a British Baptist missionary in India from 1847–1878, also mentioned Stuart's "travelling pantheon and establishment of ministering

believed that he was collecting them as an Antiquary, or to present to some academy of Arts or Curiosities, in Europe. A general may do so, but a missionary may not put his finger on them with impunity from Gov^t^. as the law of the Company is to protect all religious opinions. In this only, can the continued burning of widows and other Horrid rites, be accounted for.

Brother C. says, that when the widow was burned near his house, he tried to get to her but could not. She was walled in by a crowd of spectators who were Hindoos, while a ring of Bramins stood within them, with drawn swords, ready to *cut* off *her head*, if she should leave the pile, although it was impossible for her to escape, so laced down was she with bamboo poles held at each end over her [166] the ends of which were held and stood upon by the Bramins officiating. It is probable that they feared some interruption from so powerful and bold a preacher in their language, as Mr. C. under whose notice they perpetuated the rite. It is not probable however, that they would have dared to injure him had he have broken through the ranks, but they had a more satisfactory resort at hand, which would have been to complain to Gov^t^. of his interference, when, no doubt, he would have been ordered away, from Mongire, as he was from Sirdhana;[216] and perhaps sent to Botany Bay.

The query now arises, wherein consist the advantages of this tolerance? Perhaps, since the Gov^t^. cannot at once change their religion, they deem it better that they should continue under the restraints which their own religion imposes on them, until *Jehovah* take away the veil from their eyes. Magistrates (one or more of whom, is stationed within every district) have it in their power to prevent the *burning of widows* in general. Since no widow can be immolated without *a Permit* from the Magistrate, and the Law condemns murderers—A heedless Judge, or one loving bribes (for a request for a permit is always accompanied with one) leaves it to his

Brahmins." Lewis, *John Chamberlain*, 139, 141. Fisch, "A Solitary Vindicator of the Hindus," 35–57.

[216] See Journal October 29, 1817, entry and footnote.

Thana or native Deputy, to grant or refuse, who being either a Mussulmann that would rather a Hindoo should die than live; or a Hindoo whose profession is to make the sacrifice, *permission* is sure to be given. But a pious Judge (though he is rarely to be found), can prevent it according to Law, by sending word by a governmental officer, that *if* the devoted widow ascend the pile with fire in her own hand, and set fire to the pile herself, no one should prevent her doing so; but if she ascend without fire and another set fire to the pile, that person shall be seized and judged as a murderer. This has been done, to the honor of such a magistrate, though seldom indeed.

[167] December 6th 1817.

Have not taken up my diary for a long time, feeling poorly, and being much occupied. Last Monday Br. and Sister C. left us, for their own home 120 miles down the river—will probably reach there the third day; the wind and current in their favour. We had a comfortable visit from them. Mr. C. baptized Mrs. G. and a soldier of the 24th Regiment.[217] She will leave us on Monday next, to proceed up the river to Agra,[218] where she resides, a station about seven hundred miles higher up. She leaves her two eldest adopted daughters with me—one about 17, the other 18 years of age.

During this time I have had many trials of my faith and patience. I fear I have not acted nor felt under them, so as to hear creditably, the Scruting[219] of either. I have such a fearful, palpitating heart, ever agitated by the emotions of my mind, that I suffer much

[217] John Chamberlain conducted the baptism on the Digah mission grounds on November 25, 1817.

[218] During her return up the Ganges from Digah to Agra, Mrs. Grant distributed more than seven hundred Bibles and pamphlets. Chamberlain, *Memoirs of John Chamberlain*, 396.

[219] Scruting: here meaning to decipher the cause of her trials of faith and patience (archaic).

while pursuing my duty in so trying a situation. I am sure, *great grace* is *requisite* to enable me to adorn it. Feeling my delinquency in every needful perfection, drives me to the mercy seat for relief and help: and if I dwelt more in the presence of it, I should glide more smoothly down the perturbed current of time. My forward eye, often spies after the Haven of rest. Often when my body and spirits sink together, I derive some support from the recollection of what depend upon my stedfast [sic] progress—the comfort of my husband; the improvement of his dear little boys whom I hope to benefit; the welfare of this Station; the good I may do for others who may succeed me; the amelioration of the miseries of the heathen around me—and the hopes of my American friends respecting me. I am happier than I ever was before because nearer approximated to my leading object, the command of the language, and labours in it.

I account for feeling my task so heavy, by being set down in the midst of a full grown station, a heavy charge at once thrown upon me, in a land too, where I had to transact business through an interpreter, [168] one or other of my little sons always being at hand, to communicate for me. A land too, where all things are strange in custom and practice, to me: The feelings and [penchants] of our very lowest servants to be a matter of the first importance—But enough of this—

I prevailed tremblingly, on Br. Chamberlain to spend an hour in looking over my Spelling Book. [He] said it would be useful, and particularly so to the English learner, of Hindostani. This pleased me much, coming from him. I soon had some alloy cast into my pleasure. He noticed many Musselmanee words, and wished them excluded. I told my Moonsee of it. He said, "How can a man speak, Hindee alone? There is now, no such thing except amongst the oldest Bramins. The speech now is mixed with Persian, and other dialects" (corroborating what Dr. Carey had told me, though he knew nothing of that). The Mehometan invasion introduced the Persian—which being mingled with the rigid Hindee makes an easy dialect, and is spread all over India. Bengal is next neighbour,[220] and though Bengallee & Hindee both are said to have their origin in the Sanscrit, they differ oppositely, while they blend in some respects. The Portuguese also speak another language, and the English another. "Well," Brother C. said I must examine it myself when I should have learnt more about it; that "many daughters had done excellently but I had exceeded them all." With such a commendation to wind up the matter, I felt myself blush, and scarcely knew what to think of it, coming from so plain and blunt a brother.

[December] 7th. [1817].

Well. I cannot stop here with the Hindostani. I cannot keep my fingers from going on with something for the use of my native school, which has no other book to learn with, than the Gospel of John. They will need a simple grammar as well as a spelling book. I have therefore resolved to transpose part of Shakespear's grammar of the Hindee,[221] but printed in the Persian Character, and consequent [sic] beyond their use.

We had hoped by this time, to have added 2 or 3 native converts to our list, but on strict examination [169] into their private conduct, were informed that they were unfit subjects for baptism, that one had secreted stolen rice for the servants, in his hut; and the old man the gate-keeper, who gave up his gods to Mr. Rowe under pretence of becoming a christian, had let out persons from the garden with stolen fruit, for bribes; thus they are in a state of great delinquency.

---

[220] Hindi-speaking Bihar (where Digah, Dinapore, and Patna are located) lies north of Bengali-speaking Bengal (where Calcutta and Serampore are located).

[221] John Shakespear, author of *A Grammar of the Hindustani Language* (1813), was the first professor of Hindustani at the Military Seminary (later Military College) founded in 1809 by the East India Company at Addiscombe, Surrey, England. Hindustani instruction at the school was said to have suffered because it "was usually taught by someone who had never heard it spoken." Bourne, "The East India Company's Military Seminary," 206–222.

In fact, a Hindoo, though converted from the worship of Idols, can rarely become an honest man. It is said that they have no word in their language to express honesty, simply so. I have never found such a word: although they have that which expresses *thief* and *theft*. Old Brindabun or Vrindabund[222] as the natives say, who has been the most correct in his Christian walk, even unexceptionable as to the cardinal virtues, gives his testimony to the unfitness of those natives, for being received into the church.

[December] 12th. [1817].

This morning I was favored with enlargement in private prayer. I deplored my besetting sins before God. I fear I do not undergo my daily renewal of the inner man, to the image of its maker; as I ought to do daily—Oh that He would fill me with righteousness! in the present time, that I might glorify him here! Why, O my Soul, art thou so slow to learn wisdom? Oh that I could weep out my infirmities with my tears, so that they should be no more in me! I will come by the way of the *cross*, and taking the name of my Redeemer, present my case before the Mercy Seat. Have I not the promises of Christ, that I shall receive if I ask for *Wisdom*? O God! I am vile—I am foolish—give me understanding!

[December] 14th. [1817].

Lord's day—Received a very pleasing letter from my beloved Pastor, the Rev[d]. Wm. Batchelder of Haverhill, Mass. who baptized me in 1806. I derived great comfort under his preaching, during a visit at Haverhill amongst my first Husbands relations, in my early widowhood. How happy was I there in the Lord! Oh that the time of his love would return to me! All other loves sink low, when love to Christ [is] strongest, yet it serves as the regulator of natural affections, and sanctified them.

---

[222] Brindabun (also spelled Brindabund, Vrinda-bund, and Vrindavuna). See Journal, September 9, 1816, entry and footnote on Brindabun.

[170] A letter from brother Eustace Carey to Mr. Rowe, mentions the newly formed intentions of Messrs. Lawson, Carey, Yates, and Penny,[223] to form themselves into a Union distinct from, and disconnected with, the older brethren at Serampore, for missionary objects.

Brother Moore is again ill with the ague—talks of going to the north to breathe the mountain air.

No preaching at Digah today, as Mr. Rowe has to supply the pulpit at Dinapore. He addressed the family this afternoon, in a social way. It is a treat to me to have such a day sometimes, as it leaves me more time for reading. I do not find it profitable to *hear*, without reading also, and as I am situated, I can seldom omit hearing to indulge in reading. The head of a family must always be in her place at the head of everything good.

Since having attempted to analyse and parse a few sentences in the Hindostani, I find much more pleasure and ease in perusing the Scriptures in it. The proper construction of the Language strikes my notice forcibly, since. I am now inspiritted [sic] to "attempt great things" as Dr. Carey says and "attain great things."

Had my fifth examination of the English school yesterday. The Christmas holidays commenced—a Jubilee to me! O that I may be enabled to spend them for the good of the Lord's cause among the heathen. Everything done in this country towards the christian improvement of every class of society, is a benefit done to the heathen in as much as it reduces the current of evil example. I more desire solitude, that I may pursue my studies, than the promised company of a lady to spend next week with me.

The two poor shrivelled [sic] old women who present themselves before our door, with a multitude of male beggars, every Saturday, so made my heart ache at the thought that I had no cloth to bestow on such objects, that I burst into a flood of tears before the mercy-seat. Something is allowed for the native female pupils, to purchase coarse, unbleached cloth to clothe them—but I must not

---

[223] John Lawson, Eustace Carey, William Yates, and James Penny.

give that away to common beggars. The station allows 2 or 3 pice each, to be given to the common beggars every Saturday. The sight of so many crippled objects [171] so dejects my spirits, that now they are not to be allowed to come through the gate, but the moonsee is to stand there, and deal out the pice and two pounds of rice to each one there. About 30 come every Saturday. They would keep my mind always on the rack, were they indulged with receiving only one pice, as often as they might choose to come, one at a time, for they sit down before the door, and commence making such horrid, doleful noises as are enough to drive a nervous person into hysterics, until their heart become familiarized and hardened by them. I really pity those poor women who never beg, but go about their own concerns, shewing every mark of suffering from want.

[December] 28th. [1817].

The Lord has made me a prisoner this week, by the Erysipelas[224] in my face and neck. I had been to dine at Major A's with Rowe, and towards night felt a severe pain come on in my eyeballs, head and back. I returned home early, and found by my symptoms, that something unusual had seized me. I will try to unite with the many thousands who go forth to worship God today. Although I am shut-up, I hear the voice of sacred melody from our hall. I have had some deep feelings today, of love to Jesus and his blessed cause: not without having had a fight with the adversary of my Soul. I cried out to have my spirit renewed and released from the sins dwelling in this vile tenement.

Have had much pleasing conversation with Mrs. Murray,[225] a Christian sister, upon religious feelings, and the duty of Christians to do all in their power for the extension of Christ's cause everywhere. Her heart is all alive to doing good.

---

[224] Erysipelas: a skin infection.

[225] Mrs. Ann Murray was the wife of Sergeant Major Murray in His Majesty's Twenty-Fourth Regiment. She was baptized at Digah on February 19, 1815. "Hindoost'han," *Periodical Accounts*, 20.

1818. January 1st.

The New Year finds me a prisoner still. Found relief by steaming my face over a mug of sage tea, while my feet were in warm water, and drank some of the tea going to bed. Have followed Buchan's family Directory,[226] and found additional relief, from bathing my face [172] in warm water, and then muffling it up in flannel, to promote and keep up perspiration. The Lord is teaching me by this disappointment, that not my will, but His will is to be done by or in me. I had fondly fancied how much progress I should make in my favorite employment at the Language. I shall now pass the whole vacation without being able to do *any* thing in it—I do desire to feel my will swallowed up in the Lord's: and since it seems his pleasure to prolong my life, I pray for greater strength of body and mind to enable me to engage again in my School with cheerfulness. I have felt it an almost insupportable burden for some months past.

12 o'clock. O Lord my God, sanctify this dispensation to me; I am vile and foolish; O take away my foolishness, and make me what I ought to be! I cannot devise my speech before thee, O God; but do thou regard me in the desires of my heart in *this matter*. My happiness, and that of my husband and family are concerned in this petition—O Lord hear me and help me! Amen!

It is a week today since I was seized with the Erysipelas—What cause have I for thankfulness that I am not in the state to which this disease brings many to, on the 8th day—laid a corpse!

Knowing the nature of the complaint made me meditate much on death. I felt no fear, nor particular reluctance at the Idea of its approach. But as God has seen fit to continue me on earth, I desire and also pray to be so led and strengthened by his holy spirit, as to Glorify his name, and do good. O Lord, to this end, make me to know and eschew my secret faults.

---

[226] Buchan, "Of Erysipelas, or St. Anthony's Fire," 187–191.

Jany. 4th. 1818.

The Roses which were brought from the garden yesterday, and which I then imitated in Indian Ink, now lie by me, more fragrant than they were then. They are indeed withered, and drooping—Picture of human life after a course of virtue; beauty has fled, but the sweet influence of virtue, still is fresh. What avails the continuance or the loss of comeliness, without that spiritual fragrance which perfumes in old age. [173] O that God would enlighten my path with his ray of truth, to keep me in the strait and narrow path! How can corrupt mortality serve God thoroughly? I thank God for the decree of Truth, which will free a willing spirit from the incumbrance of sinful flesh, and base carnality. Well my feet, hands, eyes, ears, mouth, and heart moulder to dust, and reassume its origin. Could they enter heaven as they are, every pulse and motion would tell of sin practiced on earth. But oh, a spiritual body shall be prepared for us, suited to the purity of heaven.

I muffled myself up and went into the hall to hear Mr. Rowe preach—He was very appropriate and affecting, from 103 [Psalm] to the [5th] verse.

Was favored with a spirit of prayer this morning which was followed with a train of suitable reflections of benefit to my mind; but I cannot say I have passed this *day* in holy exercises of *heart*, alas! my wicked heart is ever prone to devise wicked things. Would to God! I could eschew my secret sins, and learn peace and true wisdom! O let me not cry unto thee in vain to heal my evils.

[January] 5th. [1818].

This evening I am to part with our estimable sister Murray, who has passed 2 weeks with us, and since my indisposition kept me in darkness, has contributed much to my comfort, as well as enjoyment. Thus, the time past of the longed for vacation which I had set apart in my mind for application in this Language, has been spent in sickness, company, and since I am better, in teaching some of my pupils to sketch flowers, and to paint on muslin in Durable Ink. My Soul enquires why the Lord hath thus over-ruled me! for when I can discern his good pleasure, I am reconciled. I only desire to see the sin which he means truly to reprove—that I may bring it victim of destruction before his Throne. O my many secret and *visible* sins! May God cleanse me from them, though it be as by fire. I hope I am at least brought to bear being found fault with better than before, and I hope to [174] gain still a willingness to recommence my school for English, seeing it is our support. O Lord, let all thy dealings with me prove for instruction in Righteousness, and lead me into the proper improvement of the present begun week!

I have often remarked that persons possessed of great virtues, are liable more than ordinary to commit small faults; because the perfections necessary to form such virtues, by being predominant in the mind at all times, are apt to be misapplied to inconsiderable objects.

Mrs. M. has left us—on looking into the state of my feelings, I find them much more cheerful than when she first came to see me, so needful is Society with one possessing similar feelings and sentiments.

[January] 6th. [1818].

Not quite so well today, taking medicine. My heart affected with the sense of my entire dependence on God my Creator, for health, and on Christ his Son for Salvation. O God, call me by *his* name; own me in *his* righteousness; be gracious to me for *his* sake, and hear my prayers because he hath taught us to pray and promised us, thy condescending mercy. Let me find true conjugal satisfaction with my husband, and bless him abundantly with the outpouring of thy spirit; keep him as the apple of thine eye, in all purity and devotedness to Thee!

11 o'olock. Mr. Rowe received a letter from Brother Chamber-

lain, in which he says, "Last Saturday I had the pleasure of accomplished desire, in baptizing the first Native Convert *here* (at Mongire) *Hingam Misser*;[227] he has been enabled to do valiantly. His wife, his children, his relations, his neighbours, all surrounded him on the morning before he left his house, and followed him even to our house, persuading him to lay aside his purpose: but he remained firm in mind, though by a long illness, much [175] feebled in body. Since his baptism he has not been to his house. The people look upon him as dead. The whole town is in consternation at the event, and all the children from Brother Page's School[228] are fled and gone. Brindabun says, that the birds fly away at the firing of a *fowling piece*; one is shot, and the rest are flown."

A letter from Mrs. Marshman to me, says "I have been very ill many times lately; on which account I am now on the River for a month; but I should certainly have been much better at home. The mortality amongst the natives has been so great, lately, that the shocking sights which are hourly to be seen on the banks of the river, are enough to make a person in good health, sick, and to deprive of the appetite which the river air excites. Could I have had the least conception of what I have had to see & to smell, I would not have come on the river; but my family were so urgent, that I was obliged to comply. I left all well at Serampore on the 3rd Dec. Brother Rowe would be so surprised to see Sister Ward and her daughter Hannah,

---

227 Hingham Misser was "a brahmin of very respectable family and connexions." Soon after John Chamberlain arrived in Monghyr in 1816, Misser visited him and requested a New Testament which he read privately and for his neighbors. In the margins he noted things he did not understand and then discussed them with Chamberlain. Almost a year later, he told his family and fellow villagers that he would follow Jesus. After his baptism, Misser worked as a preacher despite experiencing deep poverty and inducements of financial gain if he would return to Hinduism. He died of fever c. 1823. Carey, *Oriental Christian Biography*, 2:384.

228 See Journal, September 2, 1816, entry and footnote.

they are so much improved by their visit to England. I heard sometime ago, that Mr. Hough intended coming round from Rangoon to Serampore for a year, for the sake of printing the scriptures in the Burman Language."[229]

Night—can a Soul prosper without constant prayer? O God, do me good, for I am needy. I need to see my Soul's poverty. I need to be emptied of sin, and to be filled with divine graces.

[January] 8th. [1818].

Feel myself nearly well again. I desire a thankful heart. Was favoured this morning to taste of Covenant mercy.

[January] 9th. [1818].

Spent last evening with the Rev. Mr. Corrie & his Lady,[230] who are

---

[229] Hannah Marshman's news that George Hough wanted to relocate to Serampore came at a critical time in the Burma mission. Adoniram Judson had sailed to Chittagong on December 24, 1816 to recruit Burmese Christians for the work in Rangoon. Although ships could travel between Rangoon and Chittagong in less than two weeks, no word had been heard from Judson, and he was feared dead. In Judson's absence, officials interrogated Hough for several days threatening that they would "write with his heart's blood" if he failed to tell them about everything he was doing. Rumors circulated that all foreigners were to be banished from Burma. The harassment stopped only after Ann Judson made a bold appeal on Hough's behalf to the viceroy. Cholera then broke out, foreign ships began to leave, and the potential of war between Britain and Burma threatened the closure of the ports. In July 1817 the Houghs attempted to sail back to Calcutta with the printing press. Once again the available ship proved unseaworthy, the journey was aborted, and the Houghs were forced back to Rangoon. See Journal, September 9, 1816, entry and footnote. Anderson, *To The Golden Shore*, 204–213.

[230] Rev. Daniel Corrie, Chaplain at Chunar and Agra, married Elizabeth Myers (d. 1836) in Calcutta in 1812. Born in Calcutta, she had received formal education from an early age and knew French, Italian, and the elements of Hebrew and Syriac. Corrie went to England in 1814 to regain his health.

travelling to Benares. Mr. [176] C. is a clergyman in the Company's service in Calcutta. He differs much from the generality of Chaplains throughout this sphere, for possessing genuine piety, and being irreproachable in his moral conduct. He joins in no card parties—Neither does he take too deeply of the cup which his Master changed from water to wine. We are all much delighted with his company, which is new to me, though not so to my colleagues. He cheered us all by relating many things favorable to the universal spread of the gospel. We all met at Brother Moore's tea table. This morning he has sent all his domestics, to unite with our natives, in family worship. O how precious to my eyes, is the sight of even so few, gathered from amongst the worshippers of Idols. Grant O Lord, that the little Seed which thou hast caused to take root, may expand, spring forth, and become a Tree. O nourish it with the dew of heaven.

[January] 10th. [1818].

My hopes look with regard to my labours for the heathen. O Lord! if thou hast ordered my coming to India, I trust it is for the advantage of more than 3 or 4. I trust in thee, satisfy me with thy mercy. I commit myself to thy use; employ thou me—Let thy providence rest over my ways and my doings.

Night—Spent 6 hours in writing Hindostani today with my moonsee. Have worked today, as if I should have no more time to work at it more; and I have prized the moments as parting blessings, or treasures not to be recovered. Tomorrow my vacation expires. I purpose resuming my *task* and taking it as I can bear it; and not destroy my spirits by it any more. May I learn wisdom in meekness, and find the eternal word true, "as thy day is, so shall thy strength be."[231]

In 1817 he returned to India and was appointed chaplain at Benares. "Brief Account," Christmas 1821, 11; "Corrie, Daniel," India Office Records; Carey, *Oriental Christian Biography*, 2: 83.

[231] Deuteronomy 33:25.

[January] 14th. [1818].

Yesterday our valuable Sister Moore[232] died, a half hour after giving birth to a fine daughter! [177] Her husband was absent on the river, for his health, at the time. Today her lovely remains were committed to the silent grave, beside her little James whom she had buried two years before, in our garden, a part of which, has been set apart for a family burying ground. A number of friends from the 24th Regiment attended her funeral. Mr. Rowe, overwhelmed as he was, had to perform the solemn service. We are all in consternation; but our sorrows are not yet full, for when brother M. returns and finds his house empty, and a new born motherless babe, his heart will break. How dark and inscrutable are the ways of God! Had Br. M. been taken we should not have been surprised, as his health has been much shaken by disease. Sister M. had always enjoyed remarkable health. She expressed a presentiment, that she should never see her husband again in the flesh. The part Sister Moore took in the mission, was an important one, though altogether domestic. Her departure causes a double charge to devolve on me. We have to pray for grace & strength more than ever, to enable us to fulfill all our duties.

Deborah Biss, the eldest child, born in America, is drowned in sorrow. She is old enough to feel her mother's loss, but not of an age to fill her mother's place in domestic management.[233]

O Lord, thou hast sorely chastised us, and no doubt, for the hardness of our hearts—I feel it so. We implore thy grace, to shew

---

[232] Hannah (Biss) Moore. Hannah's first husband, John Biss, died in 1807. William Moore's first wife Eleanor died in 1812. Hannah Biss and William Moore married on February 5, 1813 and served together in Digah. Hannah died on January 13, 1818, leaving William Moore a widowed father with six children: a daughter from his first marriage, four children from Hannah's first marriage, and two children of Hannah and William Moore. "Death of Mrs. Moore," *Friend of India*, May 1818, 16–17.

[233] Deborah was thirteen years old, having arrived in India as an infant with her parents, John and Hannah Biss, in 1805.

us our sins, that we may repent and remove the obnoxious thing far from us.

Evening and morning, and evening and morning again, the two families and the two schools assemble at brother Moore's bungalow for family prayer, and as we lift our voices and hearts to God, in devout submission, the mournful tear steals down our cheeks, at seeing the vacant seat of our departed sister. How cordially knit together ought missionaries and friends to be, since a vacancy by death, leaves so painful a void amongst them!

[178] [January] 16th. [1818].

The thoughts of Sister Moore are ever in the mind of my dear partner and myself—we love her more, now that she is gone to blessedness. In proportion as we endeavor to penetrate into the conduct of God towards us, his wisdom exalts itself before us; we own his tenderness in chastisement towards ourselves, and with hearts full of commiseration for the deprivation of our Brother Moore and his children, prize the mercy shown to *us* in sparing us to each other. The stroke is terrific, falling so near us; while the chastisement of our iniquities, seems corrected in the persons of others. We seek to know our right way, and to receive grace to walk in it. May the Lord, thoroughly sanctify this dispensation of his hand *to us*: and graciously support our enfeebled and bereaved Colleague on his return home to his desolate family!

[January] 17th. [1818].

Last night I awoke in the night, and fell to meditating on the dealings of Providence with us all. It occurred forcibly to me, that my own recent illness was sent by unerring wisdom, to remove a root of bitterness, and restore serenity of mind to myself, and to enable me the better to console others under this stroke. God grant that the same canker worm may never again find its way into my breast. The Lord said to his disciples, "What I do, thou knowest not now, but thou shalt know hereafter"[234] teaching us a patient waiting on the wisdom and goodness of God.

[January] 18th. [1818]. Lord's Day.

Our afflicted brother returned this morning to his vacant house. How distressing is it, to behold him weep over the little stranger of his bosom, at the moment of her birth, made motherless! The ways of God are inscrutable. The servants appear to feel for him and the children.

In the midst of our trials, we have to receive an officer and his Lady whom a friend in the army has commended to our attentions—Poor Mr. Rowe seems ill able to do it, but the only public house in this country is, the principle that one good turn deserves another, which certainly is the best fare on the best terms.[235]

[January] 19th. [1818].

As my dear love had to preach three times yesterday, I was much pleased to see Br. Moore able to conduct [179] evening service. The reason I suppose is, that there is pleasure in the exercises of religion, which console him under his troubles—Where can sinners draw help and comfort, but from the Almighty hand?

Our two families were transplanted to *our* tea table this evening. The sight was affecting and pleasing, When the Lord wounds the righteous, he heals them by the grace he gives.

[January] 20th. [1818].

O that the Lord would not suffer the savor of his chastisements, to

---

[234] John 13:7.

[235] Bungalows, with their center halls, open sides, and verandas often filled the role of public houses. In addition to being their residence, the Rowes' bungalow in Digah was a place for teaching and housing English-language, Eurasian girl students, worship services, workspaces, adult instruction, and accommodation for both invited guests and travelling strangers. See Journal, September 10, 1816, entry and footnotes on bungalows.

pass from our hearts! I fear lest the ties in the flesh should intercept our love for the most high. O that we could be taught what he aims to teach us, *to hang on his arm*.

[January] 25th. [1818].

Sabbath evening. Have been much occupied with my school and other duties devolving on me, by the death of Sister Moore. I have rested in the tranquility of mind, which is in some measure restored, since the confusion of troubles some days ago. The expressions of my dear husband at the grave of sister M. often affect me. Viz, "Thirteen years ago, nine of us Missionaries embarked and landed together, in this country: out of the nine, 2 only remain! &cc." The conviction rushed upon my mind, that those two were himself and Mr. Moore. How awful was the apprehension to me, lest he should be the next called.[236]

My husband feels to me as one half of myself; how could I part with even a hand and a foot? much less a *side*, without all the vital springs of life being set a flowing! Yet the connection between us is nearer than that between the members of our bodies, for they are insensible of *loving* each other—if the hand be amputated, the foot will remain sound—but none would do their office, without the head: so, without the Lord, we can do nothing—he is the head of the man and the woman. O that *we* may derive all our guidance from Him, and remain united in Him.

[180] I ought not to neglect to notice the ease and satisfaction I feel in pursuing my duties of Instruction. I prize it as a great blessing: And pray God to continue my strength and spirits throughout the coming season. The two months of clear, cool weather which we have had, have invigorated my whole nature.

In worship time this evening, while thinking of sister Moore, I felt a strong desire to live serving the Lord's cause to my *last hour*, as

[236] Edwin Atlee added to the bottom of the page, "It proved indeed so in Oct. 1823."

she did. I have often prayed to be preserved from a long illness, on account of the time thus taken from actual service: forgetting that, should I not have magnified the Lord in his ways with my heart all my life past, I might require a lingering illness to train my heart to his praise, and thus be fitted here, to commence a state of glorifying, and glorification in heaven.

Lord's Day. Feb^{r}. 1st. 1818.

It was only Faith drew "virtue" out of Jesus, when the crowd pressed him; for among those thronged him, there was one strong believer, who *touched* the hem of his garment with the finger of Faith. Thus, faith is irresistible by the Giver of faith, for like two magnetic bodies, one of which has received its magnetic power, by impregnation from the other, simultaneously approach each other, transfusing the quality transfused—so the "*prepared*" receptacle of the human Soul, is attracted by the power which first communicated the virtue, and can now, no longer resist its touch. See Mark 5:30—Come then, if we *love* the Lord, he will own, bless, and reward that love, which first sprang from himself—for God is naught but Love, truly understood.

Brother Moore labouring under a relapse of his ague, and the infant poorly. Our station is truly in a mournful garb. How much gratitude do my dear husband and myself owe to God, for our health and activity, under such discouraging circumstances.

[February] 7th. [1818].

Hope it is with thankfulness that I realize myself and family brought to the close of [181] another week, in health and in the enjoyment of many comforts; and that I can lie down in peace, and say, "all is well." The "Snuffers of the Tabernacle were to be of pure gold." So we must consider afflictions that are sent from God, "to be of pure gold," to be highly prized, and used to make our "light in the world" burn brighter. The snuffers were sanctified to the use designed them—so let our afflictions be to us O most high!

I let one day pass this week, without private prayer. What was the consequence to me? Such inability of mind and body, that my task in the school became obnoxious to me. Prayer before engaging in my task, is the heavenly manna which sustains me for the day.

[February] 12th. [1818].

Much indisposed for three days, but not so as to give up my labours. My mental feelings not comfortable either. I can but just discern how *little* we see of things in their true light; and feel that, could we behold them with an immortal eye, we should never be moved by them as we are in common.

Through mercy, Br. M. is better again; and the little one become quite lively. There is great trouble in this country in rearing such children, whether they have a wet nurse or no. It is quite a formidable evil, to need a wet-nurse—The Bazar has no lack of such as would willingly leave their own children to starve & die, if they could but get to nurse yours—yet they will pretend that the sacrifice *they* make is great, to accommodate you. They must first sell their caste to you, that they may become so far assimilated with the English, as to eat their food, which however, must generally be cooked by a person of their own caste. Then they must have double the wages of any other servant; be supplied with a set of new brass vessels; several suits of clothes to be clean in; and last of all, have a considerable Sum given them when they leave, beside their wages, by which they may purchase back their rank, from the Bramins.

[182] Well, on such terms a nurse has been procured for Mrs. M.'s babe. She came in borrowed clothes. She had forgotten her own child in her new aggrandizement. The poor little creature was nearly starved to death at the dry breast of an old haggard looking woman, whose youngest sucking child, might be six years old, for sucklings can learn to abuse and scold their mothers, if they do not sit down to suckle them. When the old woman brought the child to see its mother, she took little notice of it, though it was grown very thin and miserable. She told the woman, very coolly, to wrap it up and take it away. Brother Moore, commiserating it, ordered it to be

taken to the wife of one of the native brethren, to see if she would nurse it. She took it, to oblige him, but her own child quarrell'd with it. It cried all that night—and from being much emaciated, and pulled about roughly, its arms were said to be out of joint. The old nurse was discharged, and the young woman who sews in the native school agreed to tend it during the day, if the native brother's wife would give it suck, when it would not eat anything else. I gave them a basin, soap, & a flannel to wash it clean daily—they replied that their custom was, never to wash their babies, but to oil and rub them, but I convinced her of how much more pleasant the child would be to take care of, from being clean. I suppose the mother was not glad that we took so much pains to prolong its life: as such deserted infants are generally first starved, then fed with opium until they die, inch by inch, for several days. Before they quite die, they take them over the river (as a sanctifying act) and fill their mouths with mud, and then shove them off, to be devoured by alligators.

There is a rich native merchant living at Patna, who was saved from dying after a stuffing at the river's brink, by a Physician who got intelligence [183] of it, and hasted to the spot; routed them away, and took up the man; cleansed him from the mud, emptied him of the water, and restored him to life and health again. This was an unlucky turn for those wretches, whose avarice was bent on his riches. In cases like these, they do not wait for the body to grow cold by death; but as soon as some struggles for life are over, they place them on a little rick, over a few faggots, and having singed the skin off, push the body into the river.

[February] 15th. [1818].

When I consider the state of a missionary who has children, my heart sinks, and my head grows dizzy. A maze of life presents itself through which I cannot penetrate.

Shall a man throw off his nature by coming to India as a missionary? Shall a parent repel the rising care for his own children? Look at him—see him zealously engaged (it was *at first* for Christ and the good of perishing souls; it is so still); his zeal would cause him to sweat drops that might furrow his cheek, were he in a cool climate; but under such a state of feeling, he gasps with the suffocating heat, or seems dissolving with humidity of the hot atmosphere—now his sigh or weary groan, is heard; he did not mean it should be, but what started it? Alas! his children crossed his mind—Poor puny plants in a truly hostile clime! What hope has he for them in temporal things? He has no fortune; he never had one; he never can have so much as to screen them from mendicity, should his labours cease. While *he labours*, together with himself, they enjoy a cheap maintenance. No provision made for them "*at home,*" (his native land) nor laid up at home, in his adopted land. He has no consolation but in the promises of God, that he will be a father to the fatherless. His faith keeps him. He has given himself to be a martyr, and his patrons have given him over to become one—he needs not to die at the stake to become so—He dies, and is one. Had the [184] sweet hope of friends to receive his orphans, and cherish them with the means before hand provided for them by his patrons, cheered his heart, he had died, but not a martyr—a self devoted servant to his latest hour, in the cause he *loves* above wealth or fame. I thank God I have no child;[237] for though I often feel as if I love my step-children as well as if they were my own, yet if I were left a widow with children of my own, a tie might strain a little tighter on my heart, and cause it to give way. I am glad they are Sons.

Mr. Rowe never throws anything in the way of my progress in the Hindostani. He comes past me as I sit either with or without my moonsee, casts an eye, and sometimes a smile, at seeing me surrounded with books, but never says a word, and goes about his own business. I intend putting my Spelling book in a form suitable for the press, shortly. I enjoy, in my pursuit, indefatigable perseverance, and proportionable satisfaction.

I have, after a year and half experience of the climate and

[237] Charlotte did not know that she was one month pregnant.

customs of the country, and of the dispositions of *my family* of 20 persons,[238] got them now into such subordination as to cause me comparatively, little trouble. For the first year, I had very little tranquility; but now, I have risen above some difficulties, and overcome others, so as to pass on, understanding and understood, as well in purpose as in speech.

Holy Lord God! on this *thy day*, create within our hearts earnest desires after grace, that we may experience spiritual comforts. Thou sustainest us: and thou art our strength and our eternal life. Impart of thine unto us, that we may abound in love to thee!

Evening. This I think, is what the Americans call Gen[l]. Washington's birth day, Feb. 22nd.[239] He was America's Temporal Saviour and Lawgiver—and is dead—But America own[s] a Spiritual Saviour & Lawgiver, who is Eternal. [185] Washington set this Saviour before him, and fought with His arm (for he retired yonder to pray behind a stump in the woods) and his holy arm gave him the Victory; in proportion of five against a hundred.

[February] 25th. [1818].

Half past ten at night. Mr. Rowe is busy writing the Society in England. I have been reclining on a sofa, thinking of my brother Edwin and others.

---

[238] Charlotte's "family of 20 persons" includes her husband, their children, and the Eurasian girls boarding with the family. Charlotte's Hindi-speaking pupils came from their own homes to the Rowes' bungalow for instruction as day students.

[239] George Washington was born on February 11, 1731 according to the Julian calendar then in use. When Britain and its colonies adopted the Georgian calendar in 1752, his birthday moved ahead by one year and eleven days to February 22, 1732.

[February] 26th. [1818].

Repeated arrivals from America are announced in the public print, but no letters arrive for me. I have received but ONE letter from my brother since I left him.[240]

March 8th. [1818].

Received letters last week from Calcutta inclosing the Missionary constitution of the 4 Junior Brethren at Calcutta. Viz. Lawson, E. Carey, Yates and Penny, together with their joint address to the Society in England.[241]

Received a letter this morning from Mr. Cauldwell[242] of New York. Not having heard from my friends in America for a very long time, made me conjecture that they had conceived some unfavorable impressions respecting me; and I had prepared my mind to meet the worst, though I could not trace how *I* had done anything to produce that effect. But the strain of Mr. C's letter, has banished all such conjectures from my mind, and restored my hopes of again hearing from them shortly. I ought to be thankful for having ever engaged the pen of any of them. And if I have not written to them as often as they might have expected, it is because I have so little time, ever to sit down to write in form of a letter; and when I do write, it is when my frame, already is pained with affliction—therefore I cannot feel precise enough to throw my expressions into so public a channel—my diary to my brother, I conceive he will dress up [186] by

---

[240] Edwin Atlee wrote at the bottom of the page-, "I before remarked, that I had sent 3 letters to my sister. I have since sent a 4th which I hope will reach her. E. A. A."

[241] The Calcutta Auxiliary Baptist Mission Society was formed as an auxiliary to the Baptist Mission Society in England and was independent of the missionaries in Serampore.

[242] John Cauldwell was the first treasurer of the Baptist Board of Foreign Missions and was serving as such when Charlotte was appointed as a missionary.

kind modifications, should he read a part to any friend. I can scarcely steal time for gaining that spiritual strength which is conveyed through private prayers daily. I often feel impell'd to write to my American friends to pray for me; but then I know they require so much *information* on various things that the task appalls me.

March 9th. [1818].

A friend going to Calcutta will convey this packet to some American Captain for me. No letter yet from my brother who writes. I am much pressed for time, and can only tell him that I live in hope of hearing from him and my other connections with whom I often dwell for hours.

Am happy in God's mercy, having better health than for some months past, and all well, except brother Moore, whose fever sometimes returns. The motherless infant [is] thriving at the breast of a native woman.

This Diary must speak for us, and for itself. With truest love to all my dear relations and enquiring friends, who stand like a host in view, too numerous to particularize.

I remain, with my dear hus-
band's regards, your affectionate
Sister
C. H. Rowe:
Digah near Patna, Hindostan.

Digah. May 1st. 1818.

Yesterday sent off a box for America containing an Idol that had been an object of worship; and some books. Major L. when on the excursion against the upper provinces, took it out of a temple, where it had been so lately adored, that the flowers were fresh that lay about its Shrine.

Sent my copy of the Hindee Spelling [Book] to Calcutta as a present to the *Calcutta Native School Book Society.* [187] Mr. Rowe wrote the letter which accompanied it. I did not add the little Grammar, because he had not had time to examine it. It remains to be proved whether they will print it. They have published encouragements to all who are desirous of aiding the cause of instruction in all branches of learning and morality, but refuse to print anything that treats particularly of *Christ*, lest it be a bar to learning. I do not conceive that this grows out of disregard to the Christian religion, but from knowing the aversion which the natives have to it, would rather be silent on it, and leave it to moral improvement to pave the way for its ready reception.[243] Missionaries take it upon themselves to teach Salvation by Jesus Christ. Between the two Societys [sic], perhaps the barrier may be made to fall, ere long.

2nd May. [1818].

The 9th native Female came as a pupil today. My prayer to God, and heart's desire is, that the number of those may be increased, who will be willing to learn *to read*; that through the reading of the Scriptures, which they can take home, but which they will not leave home to come and hear at the regular hours for Hindee prayers, the Truth may fasten on their hearts, and ultimately illumine their minds and convert them to Christ. O Lord, all the ends of the earth must know thee because thou hast said it. Thou must be the author and the

---

[243] The Calcutta School Book Society (CSBS) was organized in 1817 largely at the instigation of Lady Hastings (Loudoun), the wife of Governor General Lord Hastings (Moira). He was the first governor general to visit the Baptists at Serampore (1815). His wife started a school at the governor general's residence, Barrackpur Park, and quickly saw the need for printing schoolbooks in India in the local languages. Her husband became the CSBS's first patron and contributed personal funds to the cause. In 1821 the CSBS began receiving government grants. Government funding strengthened the stipulation that textbooks published by the CSBS should include no overtly Christian content. Laird, *Missionaries and Education,* 124–25, 143.

finisher of their Faith. Work thou in their own cause, O Lord, and bring every lip to confess Thee.

May 9th. [1818].

Have been laid mostly to my couch for 3 days. So true are the words of God, "in sorrow shalt thou conceive."[244] I desire to be reconciled to his will, for how can He err, who pitied a world in sin and death, desired its salvation, and whose Love for it, outweighed every fear and brought him to endure the flesh, and death itself for sinners.

The state of the air is noxious; owing to having no rain [188] for many months. A great number of deaths among the natives, and their manner of disposing of them, renders the air very foetid: add to this, the rubbish and sweepings of the stables which the natives burn to keep off the musquitoes [sic] from themselves and their cattle of an evening, fills the whole atmosphere with a thick, nauciating [sic] smoke, which pervades the air for miles around.

[May] 10th. [1818].

Last evening received my second letter from Br. Edwin; my first from Miss Moulder with a book; my first from Miss Randal; [and] Mary Yardly: my 3rd from Mrs. Elton; and a parcel from my good old friend Clark. I was much comforted by receiving these letters; and particularly pleased with the sight of the snuff-box, out of which I recollect taking a pinch of snuff, when I drank tea at Joseph's house with Paul Cuffee.[245]

My dear Edwin's letter was best of all. My thoughts lay folded up in it. The other letters, were too long in coming to the point of *information*. Apologies for "Procrastination" occupied too large a space on letters to cross the ocean 1700 miles. Yet they served as

---

244 Charlotte was almost four months pregnant.

245 See Journal, April 9, 1817 letter and footnotes on Cuffee and Clark.

kind remembrances, which was the cordial my weary-waiting spirits required. I am very sorry for dear Miss Moulder's loss, in the decease of her beloved brother. I can now no longer contemplate her, happily seated by their quiet table.

We do not conclude that our friends have not written to us before: we make every allowance for accidents at Sea. It is not good to have private letters cast into the Ship's letter bag. Many accidents happen to them, which might not, to letters committed to the care of private characters, open and left to them to seal, on putting them into the Post office in Calcutta.[246]

Am so much better today, as to hope I shall not forfeit my promised addition to the family: but am not able to sit at writing.

[189] (Under [May] 10th) Yesterday Ninesook, the young native convert, came to me to get medicine for a Poor Hindoo *Beggar* by profession; *a holy man*, self-abased, living upon alms (thro' shire [sic] laziness though, and pride, that he may be venerated for pretended sanctity.) Well, be that as it is—I was much pleased that the application was made, and that I happened to have Calomel and Salts, the medicine suitable for his case. It had to be mixed in his own brass lota[247] and the calomel mixed with dry sugar, or he would not have taken it. Applications for medicine are hourly, in time of the Cholera, every year more or less common among the natives.

---

[246] American businessmen trading with India noted that correspondence to or from their agents in Calcutta was often slow and uncertain. Historian Kenneth Wiggins Porter noted, "Sometimes a captain would agree to take letters but insist that they should be open, so that he might profit by any information contained therein; sometimes he would make no such specifications but the writers would nevertheless suspect him so strongly of an intention to use his teakettle for an unorthodox purpose that they would not dare intrust [sic] the missives to his care. Captains and supercargoes sometimes promptly accepted letters but were strangely tardy about delivering them." Other ways to ensure the mail's delivery were to hide letters in a bale of goods or to hand letters to a ship's officer, accompanied with a personal payment "to keep the papers from blowing overboard." Porter, *The Jacksons and the Lees*, 2:68.

[247] Lota: traditional Indian water jug.

Few however die of it, who make application early in the disease. Calomel and Laudanum, taken in brandy, is the common remedy. 16 grams Calomel, and from 40 to 60 of Laudanum in a half glass of brandy, for an adult. This is the dose prescribed by the army physicians here.

May 13. [1818].

I have felt very poorly today. If I should be obliged to lay by my pen forever I wish just to testify that my dear Edwin's letter to me, was like Gales of Circussia to an amaciated [sic] prisoner: that I love and rejoice in his prosperity, and earnestly desire the continuance of it—and of all God's favours to him—that I love all my connections and pray for their welfare. That if I die of this malady I wish to leave this testimony, Jesus Christ is my Redeemer and my Righteousness; that I have no desire to continue on earth unless it be to continue using my "talent" in His cause. That the prospect of life here, without the hope of being in some measure instrumental of enlightening the minds of the heathen, would be loathsome to me. I have regretted previous illnesses, chiefly because they appeared *to me* to interrupt my progress in so doing; but I afterwards reaped from them, the fruit of my Shepherd's chastening hand.—

Letter from Mr. Rowe to Dr. Atlee. Digah near Dinapore, May 25th. 1818.

My dear brother,

In a letter Charlotte has lately received from you, mention is made of your having written to me [190] many months ago, but I am sorry to say, that kind favour never came to hand. I know not whether, in point of Law, I am to consider you as having discharged the debt or not; but I suppose, that, in point of equity, I must view it in this light. I shall therefore set to work to bring you under a fresh obligation.

It appears that several letters, from you and other Philadelphia friends, to Charlotte, have also miscarried. That in which you include a letter from Mr. Page to his brother Captain Page, is one of the number. I regret this exceedingly, because I know how anxious he is to hear from his brother in America. In consequence of ill health, the Captain was under the necessity of retiring on the invalid Establishment, about two years ago, but since that he has obtained the appointment of Fort Adjutant at Mongire, a station which is about 120 miles below us. He is now gone to the Cape of Good Hope on leave of absence, for the benefit of his health, but it is expected that he will return shortly. His wife and children remain at Mongire. I believe him to be "an Israelite indeed, in whom there is no guile." He and his wife, joined our denomination about two years ago, and we have found them real helpers in the cause of our Redeemer. Immediately on his return, he will no doubt write to his Brother: and I hope the letter will not wait for an Epistle from him, e're he writes again. Could you ascertain by what ships these miscarried letters were sent. I should very much like to find out the source of all these calamities.

A week or two ago, I sent a Dissertation on the Chinese Language, and the first volume of Confucius, by Brother Marshman, to Calcutta to be forwarded to you. I know not what is become of the 2nd vol. of the above mentioned work. By these you will see to what a state of perfection we have brought the art of printing at the Mission Press, Serampore: and in addition to this, should they afford you any literary amusement, my object in sending them will be attained. By the same opportunity I also send you a few Pamphlets, among which you will find a part of the New Testament in Chinese, printed with the movable metal types, [191] and my eldest son has sent you a small map of the world on Mercator's Projection, to give your little ones an ocular demonstration of what he can perform at the age of twelve years.

My dear Charlotte has been very poorly for the last fortnight and she fears she will not be able to write to any of her beloved friends in America, by the ships now about to sail. If you should receive no letters from her by these ships, you must accept this as her apology. I fear this hot climate will be too much for her delicate constitution. The energies of her mind are more than enough for the strength of her body. She has made rapid and great acquirement in the Hindosthani Language, and her whole heart is set upon the Education of native females. Notwithstanding, her great application to the Language last year, and the year before, she did not feel the effect of heat so much as she does this season. I hope the great Physician will restore her health, and that every impediment will be removed that stands in the way of her fulfilling all the desires of her heart. We are endeavoring to get some assistance in our female boarding school; and I hope we shall soon either obtain the needful aid, or give it up all together. We persevere in this object principally as a means of support,[248] but after all, this is but a secondary consideration: the promulgation of Divine Truth among the heathen is the primary object we would ever keep in view. And should this hot climate so impair Charlotte's health as to render her unable to effect anything in this important work, and I should be able to obtain sufficient means, I shall think seriously about taking her to a colder climate to exert the energies of her mind for the Redeemer, there. This season, however is a very trying one; and I would fain hope that the setting in of the Rains, which we expect in the course of another month, will produce a great change in the state of her health. During the day, though we have our house rendered as cool as possible by watered Lattice. Fahrenheit's Thermometer[249] ranges from 88 to 92 degrees, and we shall have it higher than this before the hot winds are over. The Cholera Morbus has been very prevalent [192] in this

---

[248] Though appointed by the Baptist Missionary Society, Joshua Rowe did not receive a stated salary. As with many other early British Baptist missionaries, Joshua received some ministry funds from London but was expected to pay for the family's personal expenses by earning income from other work in India. The Rowes ran the English-language boarding school for Eurasian girls in their bungalow for that purpose, while a similar boarding school for Eurasian boys was run in the Moore's bungalow.

[249] The German physicist Daniel Gabriel Fahrenheit proposed his scale in 1724 and the Swedish astronomer Anders Celsius developed his in 1742. The British adopted Fahrenheit as their standard scale.

country, for the last twelve months, and we may truly say, that in the midst of life we are in death.

I am just returned from preaching in English to the Soldiers in his Majesty's 24th Foot, lying at Dinapore and hardly know whether I ought to be classed among solids or fluids; but taking it for granted that I have solidity enough to exercise a pen, I sit down to finish what I have above written.

You will no doubt think the Report which I have sent you relative to native schools, very interesting, but you must not suppose that this brings to light one half of what is doing in India in this department. *We* have seven Native schools belonging to this Station, and we hope to increase the number as soon as our pecuniary and other means will permit.[250] Indeed, if we can procure sufficient assistance to enable us to superintend them, we shall have little fear respecting the gold and silver that is necessary. The duties of our station are very heavy, and they are rendered still more so by the recent death of Sister Moore, and the prostrated indisposition of Brother Moore. We entertain a hope, that another brother and sister will join us ere long. Our brethren in Calcutta intend superintending ten Native Schools in that populous city and its suburbs and to increase the number if practicable. Brethren belonging to the Establishment and to the Independent denomination are also active in conducting Native Schools. Mr. May[251] of the latter denomination of Christians, has an allowance of about 800 rupees monthly from Government for this object. However, we meet with many who oppose the endeavours made to enlighten the minds of the natives, but we hope these prejudices are wearing away. When I look around and compare the present state of things in India with the state in which

[250] Unlike the English-language schools for which the Eurasian students' parents paid a fee, the free schools for local, Hindi-speaking students depended on ministry funds from the BMS and contributions largely from British expatriates in the area.

[251] Robert May arrived in India in 1812, sent by the London Missionary Society.

they were when I first came to this country, which was about 14 years ago, I am constrained to exclaim, "What hath God wrought?" It was a rare thing *then* to meet with one who feared God; *now* we meet with many who reverence His name.

[193] *Then* we were treated with suspicion wherever we went, now we can go to but few places without a hearty welcome. *Then* a very few could be found who would acknowledge the God of Israel, or come forward to support his cause; *now* we have a religious public.

Since the period of which I am speaking, a large chapel has been built in Calcutta by public subscription, an auxiliary Bible Society, a School-book Society, and two Missionary Societies with their branch Societies, have been formed in this part of India; and a considerable number of Missionary Stations, have been established in different parts of this and the adjacent Country. The Cast, Bramins &cc. are not held in such veneration as they were. What may we not expect, 14 years hence? Our Lord must have the Heathen for his inheritance.

Please to accept our warmest love, and present the same to your beloved Companion and family. I fear Charlotte's indisposition will end in another disappointment of our hopes.[252] You will hear from us again shortly.

I am, my dear brother
yours in the best bonds
Joshua Rowe

P.S. Since writing the above, your packet containing Capt. Page's letter has reached us, but my Epistle has not yet come to hand. I will forward the letter to Mrs. Page immediately.

Journal. June 6th. 1818.

Oh how my spirit longs to depart! to leave this fainting tenement, which is illy [sic] suited to answer the demands of the flesh. What

---

[252] I.e., another miscarriage.

remains for me to do, or why cannot I now leave these disgusting scenes, and join the redeemed, whose joys are all pure? O Lord, hear the cry of my Soul, and call my spirit hence, or prepare my body and mind to enter afresh on the active duties of life. My flesh and spirit cry out, being burdened, being disgusted with the things of time.

[194] [June] 7th. [1818].

We are authorized to pray for the best gifts. Grant me, O my God, *peace*, with the light of thy countenance, and entire submission to thy will. This is peace, this is the rest of the Soul. Make me content to live here on earth, if it be thy Will to prolong my probation: but O! rather prepare me to go hence, and let it be thy Will. Do all thy pleasure with me—*sanctify* me by afflictions. O let these present afflictions work out for me that which is lacking to fit me for thy presence! I long to depart—to change *time*, for the joys that dwell at thy feet. Seal up my time here, and commend me to eternity. Thou hast taken away my reproach and my fear; thou hast said "deliver from going down to the pit, I have found a Ransom."[253] Hell was my Inheritance; but Thy Son hath purchased me to a heavenly portion. He gave me his Spirit, in the washing of Regeneration. He sprinkled my guilty soul with "the blood of sprinkling" from his own veins. He dipped it in the gall and cast it on me, sweetening my whole nature. Hid me in his Righteousness, and gave me the welcome of a guest "having on the wedding garment" of his espousals. Thou wilt love me, for I shall be a fellow heir with the Redeemer. Thou wilt be an ineffable delight upon me, for thou smilest on thy "beloved Son." O behold me in the beloved.

[June] 9th. [1818].

The Lord sees fit to prolong my life, by restoring in some measure, my appetite and strength. If he have any thing more for me to do on earth, he will give me strength of mind and body requisite. He will

[253] Job 33:24.

not lay more upon me, than he will enable me to bear. I am exceedingly weary of this climate, and almost shrink from having anything more to do in it. But let me be thankful for present mercies, and rely on God for future.

[June] 12th. [1818].

Still gaining a little strength. Have been enabled to ride out 1½ mile, every other morning at 4 o'clock, which though it greatly fatigued me, served to do me good. Should the Lord crown my sufferings with a living child, and prolong my life to enjoy it, I may feel a stronger tie to the world; but my thoughts have dwelt of late, where

[195] "Their blooming joys shall ne'er decay
They never more shall leave their home,
Eternity shall pass away
And leave Eternity to come."

And my heart cried out all day and all night long;

"Oh! may I bear a joyful part
In that blest world of endless days!
Take, Saviour, take my willing heart,
Form it a Temple for thy praise."

The Lord of life, not having seen fit to answer my desires, my wishes are, to unite further with the lively authoress in saying,

"What e'er thou wilt, refuse to give;
But grant this one desire to me—
All to thy glory let me live,
And let me die to dwell *with thee*."

These beautiful lines are the fruit of the pen of that young Lady in England, whom Mr. Rowe, after becoming a widower, solicited through his influential friends there, to come out to India, and become his wife; but her health being delicate, her physician would not consent to it; and we have heard of her marriage, there.[254]

It was she, whom he expected either to meet or to hear from when he went down to Serampore, just before I arrived in India. Thus we see, that the Lord overrules human plans, by denying the *very gift* desired, and putting in its place one that He has allotted; the latter can be no less than a blessing, if the former were sought with prayer and regard to his holy will; and must become under his guidance, the *very gift* desired.

My dear Joshua contemplates taking a jaunt to Ara,[255] to consult with Mr. Waring who is high in the estimation of Government, on the subject of proposing him as a superintendant of native schools, for them. This benevolent gentleman entertained a wish that it might be the case. I hope he will succeed, as it would get him out of this toilsome mode of life. That gentleman's Colleague in office [196] is a member of the Calcutta School Book Society, and my Joshua thinks of taking the fruits of my labours to shew to him, as he is a candid man, and will, if they merit it, do something to bring them to light. My 2 years labour at the cost of so much feeling, will not I trust be unproductive of some good to the heathen.

I hope my dear brother will not expose my weakness at present, thought I do divulge so much to his discretion. I should not send the little fragment of my diary, but that my Joshua says I may as well, though I believe he never pries into it, and I never shew it to him.

I have yet to say—that should I not survive my lying in, my career in India, will have been short; but Harriet Newel's [sic] was shorter.[256] And as her memoir roused my desires to come here, so

---

[254] Sarah Wollingshead, a member of the Baptist church in Salisbury, England, where Joshua Rowe had been baptized by Rev. John Saffery.

[255] Ara (also spelled Arrah) was an ancient city located some twenty-four miles west of Dinapore that had been under British control since the Battle of Buxar in 1764.

[256] Harriet Newell died at age nineteen on November 30, 1812, five months after arriving in India.

my diary if made known in a prudent manner, might induce some others, better qualified that I, to come and labour in the Eastern Vineyard. It is a pleasant employment while health favours it—but sickness is harder to bear here, than in a western clime. The want of sufficient elastic air to fill the lungs, at one time—so much of it at another, impregnated with dust and suffocating heat; and at another so heavy, being filled with noxious fumes; and at another overpowering odors from flowering trees in the hedges and gardens; that this seems to constitute the most prevailing misery attendant on the climate. When the cool weather sets in, the beginning of November or December, the whole system both of animal nature, and mental spirits, is recussitated [sic], and lives again, for about *two months*.

It is 5 o'clock in the evening, and the thermometer stands at 92 in the setting room. I sit or lie, all day on a cane couch with nothing on it but myself and hard pillows; and this is placed so as to take the best air of the thatched window, which is kept wet all day on the outside, transmitting a portion of the external burning hurricane, cooled by means of the water.

[197] This has been an unusually trying season for the well and the sick. I have not been able to keep erect five minutes without faintness, for some weeks, and often feel when lying down, as if expiring; and sometimes a sheet of heat from the roof falls on me like an envelope of fire. Were it not for fruit, I think I must have starved. The Peaches, Grapes, Plums, Leechees, and fruits now ripe in our garden in *great* abundance, are my chief support and delight. Solid food is now beginning to be palatable, and it is recommended to me. I have my couch taken out of doors, after the Sun goes down, when the little Ladies of my school flock around me, and make themselves agreeable. A young Lady, boarding with brother Moore, takes my part in the school at present. I have not done anything for six weeks. The time has seemed an age, a century to me—So much of my life never before fell so wearisome on me. I cannot speak for the future, but hope the Rainy season will reinstate me. Our very *ease* is misery at this season; and there is nothing to be enjoy'd separate from something disagreeable, except fruit. Our sleep is interrupted by

musquitoes [sic] and fears of some venomous insects—our table is infested with noisome insects—and the rank smell of the attendant, who has it not in his power to put on a clean Suit daily, is very disagreeable, as he passes. The only moment of comfort is at dawn of day, when misery and treachery seem to slink from inspection.

I am fatigued—this must go off tomorrow.

Adieu!

Letter. Digah near Dinapore & Patna. July 10, 1818.

My dear brother,

The Lord has been better to us than our fears, in restoring me to some degree of strength of body, and to the hope of being in due time, relieved by realizing our first gift from the conjugal union.[257]

[198] My poor frame has been brought almost to the verge of the grave; which my mind was elated with the pleasing expectation of shortly quitting these terrestrial scenes, which had become almost insupportable to me. The kindest attentions of friends serving to counteract the depressing effects of a burning season, have done much toward reviving me. Within the 3 past days, my health has taken a favorable turn, and my spirits have derived new vigour. I think however, that I shall never again venture upon the same train of engagements, as before. They were complicated and unremitting, and quite too irksome thus combined, for so debilitating a climate as this.

The great mortality among the Natives almost all over Bengal and Hindostan, has no doubt a bad effect on the health of Europeans and trans Atlantic people; very few of whom comparatively have fallen by it. The mode of living among the natives is injurious—they sleep out of doors at night or in their little verandas; and go to sleep immediately after eating enormously and drinking a great quantity of water, and smoking. Were they so to divide their meals as to take

---

[257] Charlotte was now six months into her pregnancy.

an equal and moderate quantity of rice three times a day, warm, they would be more likely to elude the cholera. Leprosy and lameness are very common, from the same cause.

Should we obtain the help of another missionary and his wife, I shall resign the charge of the School in the house altogether; and if health permit, improve the remnant of my time for the good of Native females. Mr. Rowe intends soon to resign his boy's School wholly to Mr. Moore.

[July] 11th. [1818].

A storm which blew up in the night has served to cool the air. A packet of Pamphletts [sic] from dear America, serves to revive my Spirits, both causes combining, have rendered this the best day I have had for two months. My strength is fast returning, and I must say, I feel thankful for it. The glorious things stated of the Progress of Religion [199] in my native land, cheer our hearts, and invigorate our determinations to labour in this dark part of the Lord's Vineyard.

As I feel now a great barrenness of mind, I must beg my beloved Niece Esther,[258] to excuse my writing to her by this conveyance, promising to have ready, some pleasing accounts, of the manners of the natives by the next, should health permit. I thank her for her pretty letter, which deserves an attentive return. Give my love to her and Mary.[259] Tell them, that I expect to hear, that they are not a whit behind their brightest connections in point of virtue and

---

[258] Charlotte had two nieces named Esther. This niece was likely Edwin Augustus and Margaret (Snyder) Atlee's daughter, Esther Barton Atlee, who was then fourteen years old. The other niece was eighteen-year-old Esther Augusta Vickroy, daughter of Charlotte's sister, Sarah Ann Atlee (Mrs. Thomas F. Vickroy Sr.). The Vickroys, however, lived 200+ miles west of Philadelphia in St. Clair, Bedford County, Pennsylvania.

[259] Esther Barton Atlee's sister, Mary Patience Atlee, was then eleven years old, but Esther Augusta Vickroy's sister, Mary Jane Vickroy, was only two.

acquirements. My present weak state must also apologize for not writing to Eliza.[260] Tell her it gives me much satisfaction to hear she is so good and improving a girl. I hope the grace of God in her heart will stimulate her to every lovely attainment. Love to dear John, and Edwin. I shall be much pleased to receive their letters. I hope they will aspire to the highest Character of their ancestors, and like them, become the defenders and preservers of the lives and morals of their countrymen; seeking to have every action and thought savored with the sweet influence of holiness in their hearts.

The native women, on their betrothment or marriage set a token thereof on their foreheads, such as a spot of red paint below the parting of the hair, or a small oval piece of gilt tinsel: but Christians, on their espousal to their bridegroom, and virtuous women, put on the demeanor of holiness, with a happy expression of countenance as attractive, and more ornamental, and quite definitive of *their union* with the Redeemer of Souls. Hindoo mothers wear on their arm, enclosed in a locket of silver, and tied on with a string, a small part of the *umbilical cord*[261] of their first-born Son, and deem it a pledge of prosperity and a charm against demons: but Christian mothers bear on their hearts the insignia of the Eternal Son of Righteous[ness], in the earnest of heirship with him—for he has uttered, "everyone that doeth the will of my father which is in heaven, the same is my mother, and my sister, and my brethren."[262]

[200] If I were now in Calcutta, I should see several of my old American friends, and one related to me, by my former marriage, Richard Saltonstall,[263] of Haverhill, Mass. My remoteness from

[260] Likely referring to then sixteen-year-old Elizabeth ("Eliza"?) Amelia Atlee, since Charlotte then mentions eighteen-year-old John and thirteen-year-old Edwin. These siblings were children of Charlotte's brother, William Pitt Atlee, and his wife, Sarah (Light), in Lancaster, Pennsylvania.

[261] Edwin Atlee adds at the bottom of the page, "Here substitute a less common word in Latin."

[262] Matthew 12:50.

[263] Richard Saltonstall (1794–1834), a Baltimore merchant, died at sea sixteen years later. His mother, Anna White (Mrs. Nathaniel Saltonstall,

thence, cuts off many comforts. I am indeed, *alone*, for months together having no female Christian to come and be social. The agreeable acquaintances we form, are removed by Gov^{t}. from station to station with the army or otherwise. Mr. S. [Saltonstall] has made me some amends for not being able to see me, by writing, and giving me a most interesting account of his sister Mary's decease. She married Mr. Varnum,[264] who, you will recollect, was my attorney at Haverhill, in collecting some debts, due to the Estate of my former husband; The proceeds from which, accompanied me to Calcutta, as you will recollect, and are lodged in the House of Palmer & Co. to serve some future exigency.[265]

Your little pamplett [sic] is truly lovely. I shall be glad of Paul Cuffee's life. I admire the address of the young *Friend*. Love to J. Clark. But do not again send a heavy paper, nine-tenths filled with advertisements, 1600 miles: it were better to cut out the address.

My partner often asks questions about Sister Margaret when he looks at her profile.[266] He thinks it bears traits of a very mild countenance. We have not yet received *one letter* which you mention having forwarded; perhaps a circuitous voyage will bring it at last.

Give love to Sister and all my relations. Love to A. J. and her dear little brothers, who I hope, are doing well. Send my love to dear friends at Columbia.[267] Dear Edwin, accept the desired embraces of

---

M.D.), was a first cousin to Charlotte's first husband, Nathaniel Hazen White. Daniel Appleton White, *Descendants of William White*, 26.

264 John Varnum (1778–1836) was a lawyer in Haverhill from 1802–1811 before being elected to the Massachusetts State Senate. His wife, Mary Cooke Saltonstall, was Richard Saltonstall's sister. White, *Descendants of William White,* 24.

265 Palmer & Company had overextended its loans and went bankrupt in 1830, precipitating the bankruptcies of other great Calcutta trading houses.

266 Charlotte apparently had brought a portrait or silhouette of Margaret Atlee to India along with the paintings of Edwin Atlee, John Atlee, and William Staughton.

267 Charlotte's brother, John Sayre Atlee, and his wife, Elizabeth (Downs), lived in Columbia, Pennsylvania. Charlotte's sister, Jane Amelia

Your Sister
C. H. Rowe

May God continue to prosper you, Rear up your children for the service of Christ, and may his spirit convert them in early life!

[201] Digah, Octr. 16th 1818.

My dear Edwin,

I have this morning been favored with a few lines from Capt. A. now at Calcutta; but I fear he will sail before this can reach the vessel, which he says, has but a few days to tarry. I write just to say that I am in hourly expectation of a change in our circumstances, the happy result, or otherwise of which, cannot be foreknown.[268] My strength for the trial, is greater than I had reason formerly to expect. So the Lord is gracious to me. The weather is now all in my favour, being the beginning of our Autumn: the Thermometer fallen to 80 in a north room. I have been latterly, and shall be now particularly favored with agreeable female companions. Sister Chamberlain is so kind as to visit me at this time, and will continue several weeks with us. And Sister Murray comes in from Dinapore frequently, to pass the day with us. I have an excellent Physician, Dr. King:[269] and also a European woman engaged to attend me. I have an affectionate husband and delightful stepsons: and one of my Eldest young Ladies in our boarding School, keeps the School for me, by my sitting in the next room with the door open, to keep order. And we are favored with every common necessary to make us comfortable.

I have no way of sending you anything but this hasty letter. I trust you are still in the enjoyment of all your domestic comforts.

(Atlee) Rigg, moved with her children to live with John Atlee in Columbia in 1814 after the 1804 death of her husband, Rev. Elisha S. Rigg, in Queen Ann, Maryland.

[268] Charlotte soon gave birth to twin daughters.

[269] Dr. King was the senior civil surgeon at Patna.

Your likeness is so like you, that it keeps you all in my memory continually. No letters have come to hand since those acknowledged in July last. Write often. Give love to your dear family, and enquiring friends, if such there are.

Thy ever affectionate Sister
C. H. Rowe

Letter from Mr. Rowe to Dr. Atlee. [202] Digah, Dec^{m}. 23^{d}. 1818.

My dear brother Edwin,

Herewith you will receive brother Ward's Work on the Hindoos,[270] in two Vols. Quarto, by favour of Mr. Richard Burr,[271] which I beg you to accept as a token of affection from your Brother Joshua.

Charlotte and myself have written you, and you will find our letters in another parcel containing pamphlets &cc.

On the 30th of October last, my beloved Charlotte gave me a couple of lovely girls.[272] She and the children are exceedingly well. I just mention this in case you should receive this note, before our

---

[270] Ward, *A View of the History, Literature, and Mythology of the Hindoos.*

[271] The Boston East India merchant Henry Lee appears to have secured Richard Burr as a shipper or supercargo on the brig *Archer*, owned by his son, Joseph Lee, Jr., who in turn secured the Philadelphia firm of Perit & Cabot to charter the brig to secure goods in India. The *Archer* departed Boston for Calcutta in June 1818 under Capt. Abel Coffin. It sailed from Calcutta back to America on January 26, 1819, bearing a cargo of piece goods, sugar, indigo, cotton, twine, etc., arriving in Philadelphia on June 7, 1819 after 117 days at sea. Henry Lee had been owner of the brig *Caravan* on which Adoniram and Ann Judson had sailed to India in 1812. Porter, *The Jacksons and the Lees*, 2:121, 2:1330–31; "From our Correspondent," *New York Evening Post*, June 30, 1818, 2; "Evening Post Marine List," *New York Evening Post*, June 8, 1819, 2.

[272] The twin daughters were Charlotte Elizabeth Rowe (named for her mother) and Esther Anna Rowe (named for her maternal grandmother).

letters reach you.

Very sincerely yours
J. Rowe

My dear brother,

I have nothing particularly to say, but to request you to thank Joseph Clark for the pamphlets he was so very kind as to send us. The Soldiers as well as our friends, are refreshed by them. Such favours are *very* acceptable, as they afford Mr. R. and myself an opportunity of giving little testimonials of regard to the pious Soldiers and their wives.

My sweet babes are growing so strong and importunate, that I have concluded to yield to persuasions of the Ladies of our acquaintance in the army, and obtain a wet nurse to assist me in giving them their needful quantity of nourishment.

I get no time, or if time, no quiet moments *now* for writing; you and yours will not expect so much from me as formerly. What with the family, my twins, the school, and continual company of friends travelling on the river, I am wholly occupied; and am forced to break from all to get a half hour in the morning [203] to get a snuff of the open air in the fields, whither I am conveyed in a palanquin. This seems necessary to equip me for the engagements of the day.

Thus you see me again *stood up*, by a divine hand, to carry on the warfare with flesh and time, a little longer. Now, the thought of dying and leaving two such poor helpless babes, in a clime like this, and without female relatives to protect and cherish them, conveys a momentary pang to my heart. It was to me, at first, a mysterious providence which doubled the birth, and with it, my cares and affections. My mind at the first view of it, sunk, from the idea that my *missionary* efforts must suffer great if not a total interruption. But I now find that the relief obtained in attending infants, from the services of the native women, takes off much of the toil, though it rather augments the concern for the children. Since they are not to be much relied on, when not in view: which is very seldom the case with me.

Present my love to friends, and accept my dear, *dear* Edwin, a tear of love at this time.

C. H. Rowe

Diary resumed. Digah. April 9th. 1819. Sabbath.

Enjoyed today, what I have not for weeks, viz. opportunities of going to prayer, and that in a comfortable way, both of mind and body. Am excited thereto afresh by the receipt of a letter from Rev. Mr. Saffery of England[273] to Mr. Rowe, saying, that in consequence of the hints he gave concerning a Native female School here, 15 pounds Sterling have been subscribed to be transmitted to me yearly, for the purpose of the improvement of native females. Thus, by a little here, and a little from America, and a little from England, the Lord is preparing *means* for the object: and when he shall have brought things into a proper fitness for it, He, I doubt not, will unlock the hearts of the heathen also, [204] that parents shall become willing to send their daughters to be instructed, and women and girls become desirous of improvement. And now, O Lord! my Soul longs for the dawn of that day—O grant that it may be now breaking!

A school for native girls, has accordingly been opened, to which we give the name of the Female Society's School. The native instructress (as we hope she really will be ere long, but at present acts with a native master in it who teaches the reading &cc.) came to me yesterday, and informed me that since my last visit four boys have learned to read in the Testament; for whom I handed her, as many

[273] John Saffery was pastor of the Baptist church in Salisbury, England who baptized Joshua Rowe in 1800. Saffery was a "plain but powerful advocate of the mission from the pulpit" and served on the BMS Executive Committee. Cox, *History of the Baptist Missionary Society*, 1:287.

red silk caps, as rewards. I hope this will prove a stimulant, to induce others both to come to the school, and to remain at it. This school was opened specifically for girls; but there being so few willing to go to it, I concluded to divide the apartment by a matting partition, and allow of a few boys to come to the master, until the number of girls increases. The natives are divided in opinion respecting our motives—those who are so ignorant as not to know the printed character of their own language, say that the testament which they see in it, is *English*, and therefore conclude we mean to make the children first Christians and then slaves. Some Lads who know a little more about the business, tell their parents that they *will go* to the missionaries' school. Let their contending motives be what they may to detain them; the weather is too oppressive to allow of a regular attendance, no time being supportable out of doors, after seven o'clock in the morning.

July 2nd. 1819.

My dear Brother,

The same friend, Mrs. M. of whom I have often made mention in my letters, has offered to convey anything for us, to Calcutta; as she is going to the *Sand heads* for her health. We lament that the [205] liver Complaint has taken so deep hold of her. It carries off very many Europeans in this country. As we feel a particular interest in her, we are desirous for her recovery, for the spirit of *doing good* dwells richly in her.

Your translation has passed into the hands of Dr. King, a kind man indeed, he is. It can be of small use to me, as a family medicine book, since there are so many terms not translated into English.[274] It must have cost you much time, as the work is large, and I have no doubt that learned physicians will pronounce it good.

Our dear little girls, whom we call Charlotte Elizabeth and Esther Anna, have had two severe illnesses with teething. They are just

[274] Presumably not translated from Latin into English.

turned of eight months old; and have had two teeth nearly a month. They are lively *dolls*, for as yet they are extremely small. They have attempted to speak. The first word they ever uttered was *Booah* which means twin sister in Hindostani, and which they have learned by hearing their nurses speak it to them. This makes me feel a little jealous, for I had rather hear them speak, in English. I have therefore taken pains to sound the word sister, papa, and mamma, to them, that they may unconsciously acquire both Languages from their infancy—for the Hindostani they will most naturally learn earliest from their constant attendants. I do not intend that they shall be like most other European children in this country, unable to comprehend their parents unless they speak to them in the native language. Both that and correct English may be taught them, to their perfect comprehension through common conversation with them: for this reason, I never address them in the native language. Thus they say to the nurse dada, and to me papa, for father. To the nurse they say Myah, to me mama, for mother; but as yet they seem to be uttered wholly from nature as little lambs baa out the word *ma*. They are so small, that having the intelligence of children of their months, makes them appear striking. Our little sons improve in their education as well as can be expected in this drying climate. Joshua has completed a large map of the world, on [206] Mercator's plan, where on our moonsee has assisted him in writing the names of places, seas &cc. in the Persian Character, under Mr. Rowe's inspection. This is done, that the map may draw the notice of the more learned Hindoos and Mussulmans, neither of whom have any proper ideas of Geography. It will at last shew them that the world does not stand upon any animal's head.[275]

[275] William Ward recounted the ancient Hindu belief that the earth was at first covered by water. Vishnu then assumed the form of a boar and with his tusks drew the earth from the waters "and fixed it, according to shastrus, on the thousand heads of the serpent-god Ūnūntū; while others declare that it remains suspended in the air by the invisible hand of God." Ward, *A View of the History, Literature, and Mythology of the Hindoos*, 1:6.

We have attempted to draw in the native girls, by opening a School for the children [of] Portuguese & native parents, both equally dark, as well in truth as complections [sic]. Their mungrel [sic] religion will perhaps yield more readily to Truth than staunch Hindooism.

A Hindoo woman, pleased with hearing the boys repeat a poem of Mr. Chamberlain's translating, resolved to try to learn to read, that she might learn it: but her coming here, to a Christian's house to learn, and the act of *trying* so vexed her friends (enemies) that they declared she had "*lost cast*," and then refused *to eat* with her—a circumstance which renders them completely miserable, until by the usual ceremonies, oblations, ablutions, and offerings made to the conciliating *priest*, she be restored to *cast*. So she gave up her laudable resolution with her efforts to try to learn to read. These appalling circumstances however, do not deter me from using every expedient to effect the important object—an object apparently against all worldly hope of success—the Instruction of Hindoo females.

My health is better than it ever has been, setting aside the prickly heat, which with me, amounts to a disease as it is much hightened [sic] I find, by being a nurse. It is a most afflictive preservative of general health, in all who have it as I have. Some of the Soldiers suffer greatly with it, owing to their manner of living. A drink of water sends it out *on me*; how much more then must inebriety, in those who indulge in liquors. The chief support of a wet nurse in this country, is said to be English porter—a thing I cannot swallow a tablespoon of, without being set in complete flame. I therefore [207] have substituted chicken broth—every day at 11 o'clock having a good portion brought me; some of the same being reserved for my dinner: and at other times, cold weak tea. This I find much more palatable, nutritious, and attended with no disagreeable results, except that suffusion of heat on the skin which everyone suffers here, just after swallowing any liquid; it appears through the pores in a moment after. I am so changed to my own view in being *so much* of the matron, that I scarcely realize myself. Although my tender cares are increased, my cheerfulness is oftener excited by the infantine display of natural intellect evinced chiefly through the passions and gestures of the babes; who begin to do whatever they are taught.

It is now 10 o'clock at night—yet if I do not go out and take a few turns across the green, I shall not be able to sleep—a comfort I now realize very little of at a time.

[July] 3rd. [1819].

Mr. Rowe is at a loss for a varnish for his maps. The young Ladies are drawing some, which he would like to have them frame. I must either solicit from you, the directions for making a suitable varnish, or beg you to try and send us some. The English School duties, set lighter on me, than they did some time ago. I am obliged allways [sic] to have the babes present with me, which serves to amuse us all.

What with the changes which every season produces in our School, of old pupils leaving for England, and new ones coming, the number of borders keeps of late at about 12 in my department. The number of Lads keeps at about 20. Since sister Moore's death *the mess* has been brought to our bungalow, or rather since my inability to go to the other at meal times.

Mr. Rowe is about setting up other native schools, in different villages or clumps of huts. He is fond of retirement, study, and usefulness; is a man of a humble and upright walk; much respected when well known, but not emulous of being known, seldom taking pains to make himself so, where duty does not oblige him to it. Quiet himself, and enjoying quietness at home.

[208] The Rains have commenced, and the heat is mitigated. Digah looks beautifully now. I wish you and yours could sometimes trip to see us! Write me all about yourselves and my other relations. Give my love to brother John, and to sisters; and to cousins all. You will probably receive Mr. Rowe's miniature taken by a native Mussulmaun (pronounced by themselves moo-sul-maun) with his love.

Pray for me fervently, that the time already spent and yet to be spent in my Indian labours, be not fruitless. Pray also for my Soul's prosperity.

I love the Light when it beams upon my Soul; but now I am a Martha from necessity. I love my condition; (except the climate) it is that for which I was formed, since the feelings of years previous to my entering upon it, have reached their goal as bourne, here.

My ever dear brother, do thou and thine receive our united love; and our prayers for your welfare.

Charlotte H. Rowe

Diary. Digah. July 13th. 1819.

This is the 37th anniversary of my birth. What hath my Creator done for me the past year! O my Soul, approach thy maker with humble adoration. Lord, if I could behold thy glory, I feel that I should die of the splendour; but in as much as thou art invisible, thou art approachable. O that I could praise thee as I would and ought! But I will lift my supplications to thee, and implore forgiveness of my manifold sins; seek thy grace to enable me to live more to thy glory, and the honour of my christian profession. Endow me with that holiness, which if I possess, principalities and powers cannot sever me from thee; for in proportion as it is impossible for man to prevent the return of a ball thrown up into the air, so no power can intercept the access of a hallowed soul, to its God. O let my "life be hid with Christ in God!"

[209] Have felt a strong desire today, to become a mild and judicious mother and teacher. O may God cause me to glorify him in my ways better than I have done!

Gave my dear little boys each a book and a glass of wine as a birthday notice, in which they wished me, many returns of the day. May God grant their salutation, for their sake, and that of their twin sisters; whom it is my heart's desire to be past their 8th year, if consistent with God's will; when children quite out-grow their strength. At that age, they may be fit to send to school in America, among their relations.

Nov. 1st. [1819].

The first year of our dear Twins' birth was completed on the 30 Ult: the Day before yesterday. A holiday and feast to the school. As we cannot ascertain the birthdays of the scholars, we give them a treat on that of either of our own family, to vary the monotony of the scene here. About 18 little folks, and the two infants in their high chairs, surrounded our table. Here they are intitled [sic] to a few verses composed by their mother, who though she loves them tenderly, feels daily how brittle are their life-strings, which may be snapped in an hour, as so many other infants are, here. On which account, she does not dote on them, but looks on them as God's gift, or perhaps a loan, only for a little while. Never until they were nearly snatched away and seemed struck with death, did she know how much she really loved them—and being spared still, she has learned, not to rest in them for all her joys,

See on each hand an infant charmer rise,
Their mother's waiting breast attracts their eyes.
Eyes like the sky, bove parting clouds of snow,
And *look* the wish that only infants know.
Their forms, light, flexile, soft, sweet, fair, and free,
As zephers wafted from Cashmere's tree:
Like, as two lilies on the parent stem
Yet slightly diff'ring to the nearer ken.[276]
 Purest of joys to *me* dispensed were they
When first I heard them iterate "papa."
[210] Of wife, and mother join'd my Soul gave test,
and love connubial heightened in my breast.

———

[276] Charlotte and Esther were identical twins.

Letter. [undated]

My dear Edwin,

My beloved partner has some more Numbers of the *Friend of India*[277] for you. They will reveal much of the state of Missions in India. Our excellent brethren at Serampore, are very bold in attacking and exposing the horrible practice of the burning of widows, immediately under the eye of the Ruling powers. Some say that they are afraid to make a law against it. Others say that it brings in [too] good a revenue to Gov^{t}. to be dispensed with; and an intelligent Moosulmaun servant of ours has told me, that the practice could be done away, by a *word* from Gov^{t}. and that the Hindoos continued it, only because it has been the custom: and that *they* will never leave it off, until Government command them to do so.

I have lately received a letter from my first husband's sister, now Mrs. Marston[278] of Newbury-port, which gives me much pleasure. This is a welcome refreshment, after a dearth of letters during the months of May, June, July, August, and September, when there should, in the ordinary course of the elements have been rain, and letters too. But none from my brother! Some from Mr. Cauldwell and my friend Jane, who says in this, that she has written many times: This is the first received from her. I have heard, that a bad Captain, ordered her letters to me to be left "food for rats and mice." No doubt he was a hater of religious Missions and missionaries. So take a little notice, what sort of Captains you entrust letters with.

My partner desires his kind love to you and yours. He has not yet received your letter in question—will write largely when he does. We hope you have received Ward's work on the Hindoos, with Mr.

---

[277] *The Friend of India* began publication in May 1818 as a monthly journal of religion, literature, and news from Europe and America. The journal was printed at the Baptist Mission Press in Serampore.

[278] Nathaniel Hazen White's sister, Mary White, married Stephen Webster Marston, Esq., a lawyer in Newburyport, Massachusetts, in 1816. White, *Descendants of William White*, 32.

Marshman's on the Chinese language.[279]

[211] Mr. Rowe has set up two more native schools, supported by Mr. Waring. We have in all, male and female Eleven in operation; two of which are under my superintendence. These schools however, are very fluctuating. Sometimes, the frequency and duration of their festivals, leaves the schools almost empty; when it served needless to keep a native master under pay—they are sometimes set up and soon dropped on account of the discouragements thrown in the way by the natives; and after a while, those are again resumed. So we have, by any or all means, to get along with them. The school for Portuguese children was set up, on the strength of promised funds from Eng. which not having arrived, it will fall through, if not soon remitted.

The cause of the natives is much more promising, since the heads of Gov^{t}. have patronized the School-book Society. Lord Moira is its declared Patron, and other high personages have become, presidents, &cc. Proper knowledge must first be infused, ere the mind of a heathen can receive the true Religion, except by a miracle.

My poor, little Piarree (*beloved*) is dead! her father being a convert, and having business at Benares, took her with him, as he intended to remain some time with Brother Smith,[280] who is a Sub-

---

[279] Edwin Atlee wrote at the bottom of the page, "These came safely to hand, and in return I sent Hickenwelder's on aborigines of America. E. A. Atlee."

[280] William Smith was a Eurasian drummer in the native army. He had an Indian wife and spoke Hindustani as his mother tongue. John Peter was an Armenian's bearer before he was converted and became a Baptist missionary in Orissa. John Peter recommended Smith as a potential mission co-worker. In 1814 the Serampore missionaries secured Smith's discharge from the army. He worked first in Serampore, then with Joshua Rowe and William Moore in Digah before moving to Allahabad. In 1816 he began the Baptist work in Benares where he served for forty years. *Brief Narrative,* 84; Sherring, *History of Protestant Missions in India,* 184–85; Kennedy, *Life and Work in Benares and Kumaon,* 15–17, 21–22; S. Pearce Carey, *William Carey*, 266.

missionary, supported by the Serampore brethren. His wife was once a native but being converted to Christianity, has risen to respectability, and is much regarded by us. She keeps a school for any kind of pupils who wish to learn of her. Here little Piarree took the Cholera—a physician was sent for, who at once pronounced her case incurable. Her father than asked her what she thought of dying. She said "she felt no fear of death; it would only bring her into the company of her Saviour Jesus Christ." He asked her how she came to know Jesus Christ? She replied that she had learned to read of him, and she had heard him preached about, and she loved him more than any thing in this world. She longed to depart and go to Jesus. Thus died, the little naked, dirty, blowsy girl, brought to me a year ago. She had become clad by her own earnings at her needle, and kept herself neat [212] and she was uniformly a love child to me. She is my first fruits unto Christ, and glory be to his name! Dear little Piarree was about ten years of age when she died. Her pleasant image, as she used to appear when she would take her seat *lowly* beside me at worship time, will never be erased from my mind. I do feel, as if there is one Hindoo child in heaven.

I have condemned the practice of harbouring enquirers on a daily allowance. It has bad effects, but in the case of Piarree's father, it has been most satisfactory. Since he is a humble believer, and has been baptized and received into the Church, and by bringing his child into the way of hearing and learning the scriptures, Salvation came into her also.

Those who love religion as they should do, will rather "be doorkeepers in the house of the Lord, than to dwell in the tents of sin."[281] A short time ago, our beloved sister Grant, returned to Agra, and took with her, for the sake of promulgating the truth to the natives there, our young convert, Nainsook. She has been in the habit, whenever she put her boat to land of an evening, of making her Lala read to the people, which attracts many to hear on the bank of the river. She is now equipped with an attendant and interpreter, who

[281] Psalm 84:10.

loves the Word which he reads to them. She provides herself with tracts to distribute. Had brother Chamberlain never gone to Agra, it is probable this amiable fellow helper had remained as she was.

We have two other native Christians, one of whom was a native physician. The circumstances leading to his coming to Digah, have been published, I believe. They were very singular, a dream having induced him to seek the missionaries, never having heard of them. If I recollect the account, he had been on a penitential journey to some hallowed place, and had done every thing by way of penance and performances, to secure his soul's welfare, but found no peace of mind. In a dream, a figure clad in white (but that is not extraordinary where all wear white who wear anything) [213] bid him seek the *Sahabes* (gentlemen) who would tell him what to do. In waking, he resolved to do so, and travelled on until he came to the native Christians gateway into our Garden villa, as I call it: and there seeing a native reading, he desired him to read. It was the Gospel, and the words came to his Soul with wonder-working force—He found the pearl he was in search of, at the *Sahabes*, to whom he requested to be introduced. He has continued here, and having put on Christ Jesus, goes from village to village, carrying the good news of Salvation to his brethren. The name of the other, is Hurree Dass, or the *disciple* of the god *Hurree*, whom they so often invoke at their festivals, with "*Hurree bole.*" He was sitting reading in the gate-porch, when Roop[282] came, first. I often see several men sitting with him, to hear him read the Scriptures. Thus he opens the Gospel door, for he is gate-keeper at present.

When the mornings were long enough to admit of it, I used to take the babes out before breakfast, to sniff the unobstructed air of the fields; and when the weather is dry, I take them into the mango, orchards or groves. Sometimes we find there, the *light infantry* of our marches, a company of the Company's elephants; or an encampment of the presence and suite of a Native Raja; and when none of

---

[282] A possible reference to Roop Dass, the brother of Hurree Dass. The brothers became itinerant evangelists working with the Rowes at Digah.

these are there; the women spin ropes & twine from tree to tree, which they spin or twist by rubbing it down their knee with their right hand. I went up to one of these miserable looking objects, and in order to draw her into conversation, said, "This is hard work for women." She replied, "Kya kurre, gurreeb andme." "What can I do, I am poor." How much can you spin in a day? "Doe seer" (four pounds) or two seer. *&cc.*

Sep^{t}. 1819.

I look[ed] up the Life of Mahomet, one evening after tea, and endeavored to read and explain some parts of it, to the servants, the Khidmustgar[283] or waiter being a Mussulman.

[214] I read a deal, and that part which speaks of the great domestic Cock, which stands upon earth, and his head reaches into the third heavens. I asked them if there ever was such a fowl—"haa janna." *What do we know about it, or how can we tell.* I said, can any man in his senses believe such tales? "*Khoda sub suktahy.*" *God can do all things*. It seems impossible to shake their faith, in a religion favorable to all licentiousness. The book has since disappeared, and probably has made a fire to roast our dinner. The new moon being observed for the first time by one of them, an evening or two ago, she bows very low to it, uttering the words "Ulla-muhummed." My heart sinks to see such things in people who daily see the manner of christian worship, and do, from their seats in adjoining apartments, hear the word of God read, though they would not come in to be seen to hear it on any account.

I am obliged to close for the opportunity. I do not write as a thing of farther importance to you, than to amuse you and shew you that I love you. Give our love to all our friends, brother and sisters; to sister M., and her dear children.

---

[283] Khidmustgar: a male table-servant, usually Muslim. Usually spelled "khitmutgar."

Ever your truly affectionate Sister,
Charlotte.

Diary. Digah. Wednesday Decr. 8. 1819.

I have been much gratified today, with the improvement which several of the native boys have made in the space of a fortnight. Some who could read only in one character can now read three, in Hindee, viz. the written Kythe, the printed Kythe, and the Dav Nagree,[284] or common print. The master told me, that many men, both Hindoos & Mussulmans frequent his School, to hear him read the new tracts and the Gospels: that a Bramin came several times, and at last condescended to take away a Gospel of St. John to read by himself. Several others received pamphlets.

As cold weather has commenced, the School has increased to 41. The Lala or master, spoke of the inutility of worshipping [215] Juggernaut, he being a Hindoo. He confesses, that the books he reads, and the conversations he has with us, have done him much good. He said he thought the restriction of "touch not this or that" was very foolish; and that he thought God's laws alone were the true way to eternal life, and that nothing but they, were able to condemn the Soul. He comes every Saturday afternoon, to the bungalow, and brings about 20 boys, to be examined, and further instructed and he is very attentive himself to what he hears.

Mr. Rowe has given up the superintendence of this school, wholly to me. I was not a *little* pleased yesterday, to hear him ask my permission to teach native girls also, who have brothers at his school; saying that they could come and go, with their brothers, which would take off the shame of being seen in the road? I gladly gave consent. So their prejudices are crumbling away—they must ultimately fall. O God! hasten the day! I do think, that the ingathering of the native females, is nearer my heart at present, than the welfare

---

[284] Devanagari script.

of my babes and family.

This a wet and blustering night. There is generally one fall of rain in the winter here. The poor half-naked native is taken, unprovided for the inclemency of chilly weather—he shrugs himself up, with his clinging infant, in his coarse cotton sheet, while we lie covered with blankets, and are warmly sheltered: Why is this difference? Perhaps that we may shew forth God's religion, by our labours of love and compassion in his cause. Oh quicken us Lord, direct our views and assist our labours, and establish the work of our hands! Not so much are the natives to be relieved by charities, as by the Gospel, which will make them merciful to themselves—make them sober, industrious, and avoiding wicked, time-consuming festivals. They are the devastation of all moral intellect.

I have been favored with some days of comfortable feelings of mind, although my body seems not well. [216] I feel an irritability, which is extremely painful to myself, and which has an ill effect on others. Then a word of fit reproof, so timely from my dear husband, is like "apples of gold in pictures of silver."[285] It breaks the spell which Satan seemed to hold on me, brings me to reflection, and with a sin-convicted conscience and a sorrowing heart, I implore pardoning and strengthening grace. The *burden* and *heat* of the day, are sometimes too much for me, and I become like an animal, restive in his harness, from being gall'd to the flesh. O God! who holdest the reins of human nature, keep and guide me!

Mr. Rowe, has not only consented, but become anxious to have my Hindee Spelling book printed. It will suit this province if no where else, and we need it much, for the schools.

The Spelling book is completed, on Murray's plan of little stories appropriate to the spelling lessons; and it is packed up, to go to

---

[285] Proverbs 25:11.

the Calcutta School Book Society. I have spent the past week in getting it ready to go off. It had lain by a long time, in patient waiting to be smiled on.

Digah, May 28th. 1820.

It [has been] a long time since my Soul has conversed on paper. It has been restricted in two ways—by want of time to reflect, and want of reflection. O, the latter is the worst complaint it could make. The cares of the world, are the robbers of the Soul. Oh that I could bear Christ in my heart, through bustle and toil, as well as in placid retirement. Alas! the fault must be my own. *I* keep not hold of Christ. I give way to the sway of natural feeling and the tide of dependant cares, till they give [sic] drive me into the desert. I am "a reed shaken by the wind." I am a discordant wire, contracted or relaxed by every moral vicissitude. There is no health in my Soul.

If to enter an eternal bliss, depend on the holy rectitude of [217] *my own life*, I shall never, never see God! But Blessed, forever blessed be *His Name* for providing us a refuge against our own nature: forever glorified be his grace for *the way* of a sinner's Salvation in Christ Jesus. My Soul doth adore his Mercy for opening my mind to dwell more on the merits of a Saviour, than latterly. I will flee to Calvary; I will lay hold on his Cross as on "the horns of the altar." I will lave me in his blood; I will shield myself in his Righteousness, and thus will *I* come before the Most High, who cannot find iniquity in him, for in Him will I be found. I will be his purchase—an altogether depraved, undone, lost sinner; but sought out and redeemed by the surety, the ransom, which Himself hath provided for me. O Grace immeasurable! O condescension worthy of a God! Thou art *God*, and thus thou art explained. O draw me, that I may follow after Thee! Lead me, and let me not go, that I wander not from thee, which I am so prone to do, as the needle to the North. This day, let thy light shine into me, with the hearing of thy word!

[May] 30th. [1820].

Feel self-condemned, and ashamed on account of yesterday having given way to impatience with two servants, and having done as the heathen do, in elevating my voice when reproving them. I thank my Lord, who hath this day, thus far preserved me from it. Yesterday I omitted prayer before breakfast; and thus began my days work without fortifying my Soul in secret: therefore I was left to commit sin. If we walk not close to God, how can we proceed in a Godly manner, in our avocation, or enjoy any divine life. O may my children never have a precedent in me, henceforth, for clamourous behaviour. The servants ought not to vex us so, since we know that they are extremely ignorant, and ungrateful by nature. I ought to *bear*, until I can amend by mild government and tuition. They are far more dutiful to *me*, than I am, to my creator, *whom I have been taught to know*.

June 1st. 1820.

[218] The hot westerly winds have gone by, and the Easterly have taken their place, two weeks sooner than is usual in regular years. This would be altogether preferable, if the East winds were not pregnant with diseases, whereas, the west winds, turn them all adrift; but those will not blow again, until November. The mornings and evenings, are the only times for taking the external air; even then the air is pernicious. This is one of the miseries of India. Another is the sudden extinction of life, and the hurried interment of the dead, which is sometimes attended with very serious consequences. At Dinapore, two years ago, a case of that kind happened with a young officer. He was the joy of the mess, possessing very convivial qualifications. After a late dinner, at which unusual hilarity had prevailed, he made some strange expression, and suddenly afterwards, fell senseless on the floor. His companions alarmed, conveyed him to bed, and all medical assistance was immediately resorted to, but in vain, in the time allowed for it. At dawn of day, next morning, he was, conveyed to the silent grace, under military honours. The heat of the climate makes it necessary to inter a corpse before 24 hours

expire after the decease.

A monument was to be erected to his memory—and men were set to work the day following his burial, to dig the foundation of the grave, to lay the brickwork around the coffin, on the approach of which, they were horror struck, to find the lids cleft, and the arms and head of the poor man, exposed outside them! The earth having been saturated with rain, there was water in the grave, which was highly tinged with his blood. Some of the Soldiers who were members of the Baptist church, were immediately called, who were witnesses of the dismal fact. I enquired of a highly respectable man concerning the truth of it, who told me "that it was one of those unaccountable things which sometimes happens." Being then a Surgeon on the spot, he must have known.

What must have been the sensations of that unfortunate man, on awaking from his swoon, and finding [219] himself in the bowels of the earth, in his very coffin, distant from every ear, and his awful condition unsuspected by his friends! Just escaped the untimely Judgment, of the arbitor of all, and again to be turned back into the world of Spirits, without hope of Salvation, unless the Saviour had compassion on him, at the eleventh hour *in the grave*! Had he time to repent and seek mercy during his waking struggles with suffocation and death? Should not this be a warning to all such as yield to thoughtless mirth; and especially to such as venture, in their moments of extravant [sic] glee, to invoke the all-seeing eye?

True as the gnomon tells the hour
When Sun-beams strike the plate,
The truth-declaring gospel power
Reveals the sinners fate;
For in God's Sun-shine Eye, he stands
Stamp'd as the hour beneath the hands:
Yet God, to shew his glorious grace,
May save him, e'er he change his place:
Nor *minute* pass the finger's point,
T'wixt child of hell, and Blood-bought Saint.

And just as great a miracle
Must pass on all who with Him dwell.
Salvation is not born with man.
He to be blest is "*born again*"
How long *that* takes, let nature tell,
Nor dare to think, God does not *well.*

Though it may be so with a few, will any one presume repose such mercy passing upon him at *his last* breath, after a life spent in willful neglect of religion? Such presumption, would but render him a less liable subject of mercy. The Gospel does not say how long a time it takes to make a man a Christian, but it states that "in the twinkling of an eye" some shall be changed who are upon earth when Christ shall appear. Whether changed from a state of sin & condemnation, to a state of grace and favour with God, or changed from a mortal to an unmortal [sic] body, I shall not attempt to decide.

[220] Yet those who are changed from a state of nature to a state of grace, and spend a good part of this life in the latter, must feel no fears, but on the contrary, a secret rejoicing at the Idea of the coming of their Saviour, whether in person or in Spirit, to take them to eternal Rest. How profitable then to man's happiness in this life, is godliness! Why do the wicked hate it, so as to avoid its influence over them? even because they are dead in sin. Why then will they not, like the thief upon the cross, speak to the dying Saviour, "to remember" them, for whom has shed his blood in remission of *their* sins, on being like *that* thief's, *repented of.* The reply of the Saviour was prompt—"*This day* shalt thou be with me in paradise."—he is still and ever as free and as prompt, to reply to every sin-sick Soul.

This shews that God can love and change the heart of a gross sinner at the last extremity of life—yet have witnesses come from the dead to assure man that such have been the *frequent* tokens of his mercy.

Had this have been the method which God designed to act upon towards man, he had not seen fit to direct his Gospel to be preached, to bring all to repent. Or why would he invite the young to seek him if he would be as well pleased with the sacrifice of a black and filthy remnant of a man's life, as with the whole, pure web, of an unspotted life, dedicated to his service. What was the need of God's holy law being promulgated amongst men, if the whole of their lives was not to be governed by it. The path to eternal life which the bestower of it has pointed out, must be lost—"Repent and believe the Gospel—repent, for why will ye die," To the Soul that says "I repent" he says, "Return, ye ransomed sinner, home."

A few days ago, the wife of a Soldier at Dinapore was stung by a Snake, in her sleep. The pain awoke her. She roused her husband, who made search for it, and recollecting a hole in the wall by the bedside, put his hand there to feel for it, and was bitten also—remedies were applied to both—but the morning found his poor wife a corpse. He has recovered, from receiving less poison.

[221] Some nights ago, I was awoke [sic] by a pain on my right arm. I touched it, and found it swelled to appear the size of the palm of my hand. I rose to light a candle at the taper thus burning in the room, and while standing, noticed something dark, run down my night gown, to the floor. I followed its course with the light, and found it to be an immense Centipede, at least seven inches long. I roused Mr. Rowe, who putting on his slippers, tread upon it, and broke it into several pieces—each of which moved during most of the next day. One of my infants lay between me and my arm when it passed over my naked arm, but escaped being touched. It was the poison conveyed by its long *feelers* passing over the skin, which occasioned it to swell and burn. Had it have been disturbed, so as to cause it to bite with its forceps; or to have clung to the part with all its feet, the animal must have been picked joint from joint, ere it could be disengaged; and the consequences, if not fatal, would have been most painful. It ran up a silk Screen which stood so near the head of the bed, as to touch in some place or other, the gauze curtain, which being tucked under the mattress, the creature found its way into the bed. Bedsteds [sic] should have brass castors and caps,

at the feet, to prevent small reptiles and black ants from ascending. But snakes wind up the legs of chairs and tables, to sip the drink of infants, set for them at night. This however is not very frequent. It sometimes happens in the *rains* when the grass is high about the house.

In all these common fears, I see the goodness of God towards *us* in preserving us from sudden death by such means. The cholera mows down hundreds around us every year, yet *we* have never been touched by it.

Our little Charlotte has just recovered from the Ophthalmia, which is a dreadful complaint in this country. It leaves many quite blind; or subject to red and bad eyes for life. She was leeched on the eyelids [222] and temples—and a composition which the natives use, has wrought wonders for her. It is equal parts of opium, alum, and what they call russowot, which [is] a bitter gum, taken from a *cart yousy* [sic] of an ass, I have no English name for it. These they grind in a marble mortar with so much water as will make it a consistency thin enough to strain and squeeze through a piece of shire [sic] muslin; and is applied with the finger or, a hair pencil, round the lids of the eye, as near the eye lashes as possible, not to get within the eye-lid and is spread round for an inch or more wide. The comforting effect of this, is surprizing. Relief was also afforded her by frequently taking gentle hold of the upper eye-lashes, and letting the matter drop out from under the eye-lids; or press the lids back a little with the fingers, to let it escape.

Our dress at this season being very thin, I took a violent cold in my bones and on my chest, by walking out before the house a few evenings ago, when the wind blew fresh, after a day of rain. It was so mild, that the sensation was delightful, but it was a great contrast, to being shut up all day melting with heat and moisture. Squills[286] with pounded almonds, in warm water, have effected a cure. My voice was entirely locked up, for a week.

June 11th. [1820]

As I was going along the public way the last evening, in my palanquin, and reading the Gospel by Mark, in the Hindostani Language (Chap 8), that passage from vs 5 to 10th opened to my understanding; for I could never before discern the drift of it. It was also appropriate, seeing as I passed, a Sentry at his post, who bowed to me. The Centurion's answers struck me thus. "If I, who am a sinner, and a servant under a higher authority or officer, may say to those entrusted to my command, go, come, or do this, [223] and am obeyed; how much more wilt those O Lord! be obeyed by infernal powers, who are the Son of the living God: Therefore, *speak the word* and the evil spirit shall leave my son."[287] This reflection brought joy to my heart, and raised it to give glory to the Son of Man—O for new and renewed Light to Comprehend the Scriptures.

Neither did I ever before coming to this country realize the full meaning of the word so often mentioned in Scripture "the living God"—Here where we see gods in posts, and trees, and shrubs, and images formed with the fingers out of clay and baked in a kiln; or cut from wood; or moulded in brass, and copper, silver, and lead, the *Living God*, forms a transcendant [sic] contrast. These poor creatures see God in a bull, monkey, and other animals; and even tell *us* that we came from the gods. It is not strange then, that the people of Milite[288] should think Paul a being more than mortal, whom the viper did not hurt. So weak and debasing is idolatry, to the human

---

[286] Squill: a large bulbed plant of the lily family sometimes called a sea onion.

[287] Matthew 8:8.

[288] Acts 28:1–6.

mind; which *for the want of the Gospel*, are left to do these things—Christians of a wealthy land! will ye suffer it to be so?

Digah near Patna, June 29. 1820.

My dear brother,

We have nor heard of a useful sailing for America, for many months. The intercourse between the merchants here, and there, has suffered some interruption of late, and we have been led by the public papers to think America is afflicted by the miseries of other nations. We fear that a contest with the Spaniards, will involve the United States in difficulty. But I am no politician.

About a fortnight ago, Mr. Rowe received your agreeable letter, of 1½ year date, acknowledging the receipt of Confucious [sic].[289] No other letter has reached us, from you, in that time.

It gives us much pleasure to hear of your prosperity [224] in a professional respect. I hope your and our beloved Margaret's heart, will soon find rest. To stand clear of the world in a spiritual sense, and keep our heart at Rest in God! This is desirable with or without the former. May you and I, be enabled to do so! I trust we both feel an indifference to money, and the things of time, except as they are essential to aid us, in our vocations—To have enough to allow ourselves a little luxury in the way of mercy to others, is really desirable; and yet I feel such a distrust of my own heart, as to doubt whether, with the money, I should have the *feeling* to bestow it. He who knows our frame, knows best how to trust, and entrust us. Had we more money at our disposal, we might not be so willing to labour *hard* in the cause in which we have embarked, and which requires, not only our greatest efforts, but those of others, not a few. When we cast our mind's eye, over the lands we have left, and those we

---

[289] Joshua Rowe had sent Edwin Atlee a copy of Joshua Marshman's *The Works of Confucius; The Original Text, with a Translation. Vol. 1. To Which Is Prefixed a Dissertation on the Chinese Language and Character*, published in 1809 by the Mission Press in Serampore. See Journal, May 25, 1818.

have travelled, we feel an appalling solitude of motive; we long for the assistance and the society of others of similar views and feelings. It is good for us, as individuals, to keep our vile, wayward passions in subjection—this is the chief thing which concerns the *inner man*. If we succeed in this, we shall keep our hands clean also.

I have today been made to rejoice, in reading the account of the Missionary transactions at Tahiete [sic] in the South Seas.[290] How much joy would it give us to have the same things to relate of Hindostan!

I can state, perhaps, the beginning of such a day. The Serampore and Church Missionary brethren,[291] have been many years plowing the ground before us; and no doubt, a reward will yet succeed their labours. Difficulties stand in the way in this continent, which are not found elsewhere; but when they are made to give way, the downfall will be perceptible and glorious. We do not forget that Jesus *must have* the heathen for his inheritance, and therefore we feel as if we were doing the part allotted to us, in the work of making Him known amongst them.

[225] We hear of two native converts, one in Calcutta, and one who has been an enquirer with us,[292] who resolve to follow Christ at

---

[290] The London Missionary Society (LMS) initiated its work by purchasing the ship *Duff* and sending thirty missionaries and their families to the islands of the South Pacific in 1796. They arrived in Tahiti the following year. In 1801 the LMS sent additional workers.

[291] Missionaries of the Baptist Missionary Society and the Church Missionary Society.

[292] The inquirer was a man named Narion from Chandpore, a village about sixty miles north of Digah. Joshua Rowe wrote that Narion was initially "very anxious to be baptized, and appeared equally anxious to obtain a salary and to be employed as an Itinerant." Due to his eagerness for employment, the Rowes questioned the sincerity of Narion's professed faith. They advised him to return to his village, resume his work as a smith, and "do all in his power for the good of his neighbours." The Rowes pledged to send a co-worker later to Chandpore. Several days before Charlotte wrote this entry, two of Narion's relatives came to Digah. Joshua Rowe reported, "They say

their occupations, and risk the hatred of their brethren. It is said that ten of the relatives of the latter, agree with him. One of our itinerant brethren, has gone to their village to strengthen them. It is only necessary for a few to make a resolute stand, and the cause must grow.

Within the last six months, three schools for native females, have been opened; one under the care of the young Ladies in Sister Lawson's[293] School in Calcutta, one under the care of Sister Carey[294] of Cutwa; and one under my own charge, not immediately under my own roof, as my native female pupils have been heretofore. My school began with nine; but they are irregular in their attendance. I visit it every few days, hear their lessons and set them new ones; and fit some work for them. The young woman who teaches them in my absence, was taught to read by the master of one of our native boys' schools. Would you not, my dear brother, be pleased to see your Sister thus engaged in large mud hut? It is generally so blocked up by the spectators, male and female, whenever I visit it, that I can scarcely get light enough to see to teach the children. I sometimes hold interesting conversations with those who get inside the door. The native children possess very quick faculties. They always manifest pleasure at seeing me coming, and bustle to get to their places after coming out in a throng to salute me.

We have heard that the Digah Spelling book, was ordered to be printed; and we are in hope of soon receiving some copies. The same

---

Narion works at his trade, and reads and explains the Scriptures to some of his relatives and neighbours daily. From their account; there are ten of his family who have renounced idolatry, and are of one mind respecting the gospel. He is persecuted by many, and especially by those of his own cast; but he is determined to persevere. He wished to be baptized in his own village, that he may make a public profession before those who know him." Roop Dass was sent to visit Narion and to assess the state of things in Chandpore. Joshua Rowe to John Dyer, July 1, 1820, Unpublished papers, Angus Library and Archive.

[293] Frances Lawson, wife of John Lawson.

[294] Mary (Kinsley) Carey, wife of William Carey's son, William.

Author[295] has in part prepared a little Grammar in the Language for the Schools; but that lies dormant for want of time to set in due order.

[June] 30th. [1820].

I have been prevented from writing, by several stings received while asleep in bed; one of which being at the corner of my eye, has quite prevented my [226] seeing downwards. The flesh all around my eye, is blue black. There is a gnat, much smaller, and more insidious and venomous than a musquito, [sic] and can seldom be got out from under curtains, when once there, unless by taking them off, and shaking them out of doors. I have seen one of these fly from under my wrist-band; and the sting it left swelled to the full size of half a duck's egg the long way.

The only thing which affords relief, is the application of the fine *Lime paste*, which the native women chew with their beetle leaf, or *pawn*. This is one of the *mitigable* miseries of India, which patience wears away—The sting of the Arch-enemy, in the heart of every man, will yet I trust, meet an Antidote in the Captain of Salvation.

Has the really worshipped Idol which I sent to Dr. Staughton, ever preached to the Infidels in Phil[a]? No one is an infidel and not an Idolator, if it be but of his own diabolical opinions, of which he must in secret as rationally doubt, as a heathen does the power of the Idols to save or to condemn him. O! that Rulers were every where Christians. How careful would men become as to their sentiments openly. Much corruption of the mass of mankind would be saved; and the mind of all, left freer to embrace Christianity. How my spirit laments for such things, I cannot express.

Dear Edwin, excuse incoherency; for I write at intervals when my noisy little girls will allow me to do so between school hours. With the assistance of goats' milk for their breakfast and supper, I

---

[295] Charlotte is referring to herself and the Hindi grammar she has prepared.

nursed them both at my own breast until they could run alone, which was at 16 months old. I could not keep the wet-nurse, for her unfaithfulness to the child.

I am so thin, and disfigured with prickly heat & stings, you would not know me. My health has been indifferent the last two months. I have not animation enough to make any greater progress in the native Language, though my inclinations turn altogether that way. When I read or [227] write a good deal in it, I can speak it pretty well.

Our dear little boys are very healthy in general but have a bleached countenance, as most have in this climate. The babes have got on so as to *live* through all the trials of their early age, to the astonishment of our European Ladies, few of whom, raise their children.

My dear partner has enjoyed excellent health, hitherto. He desires his love, and says he will write you shortly.

I wish the Society would send a pious pair to join us in the Mission[296]—I wish to be relieved now of this burden of an English School, which stands so much in my way as a Missionary to the natives.

Digah looks beautifully now, that every thing is so green, and the Ganges rising above all the barren Sand-beds, which in a dry sunny day, shone so as to dazzle the sight in looking over the river. This river is never so clear as to let one see to the bottom, even where

---

[296] William Moore contemplated moving from Digah to engage in private business. Joshua Rowe wrote to Carey and Marshman concerning Moore's plan: "Brother Moore, I suppose, has informed you of his intention to remove to Monghir. He proposes keeping a school for little children taking in boarders, breeding cattle, sowing oats, trading in castor oil and grain &c. &c. For this purpose he has negotiated for Captain Griffin's Estate, and intends taking his brother-in-law, and his son-in-law into partnership. If he acquires more than is necessary for the support of his family, it is his intention to apply it to missionary work." Joshua Rowe to John Dyer, July 1, 1820; Joshua Rowe to Carey, Marshman & Co., January 10, 1821, Unpublished papers, Angus Library and Archive.

the water is shallow. The mixture of earth, sand, and fragments which it sweeps along in the rains renders it tremendous.

As I have nothing more to write of a particular nature, and our conveyance to Calcutta, appears in no haste, I will contribute to your amusement at least, by giving the sequel to the Pomegranate, instead of the reality, which I had procured of the finest imaginable in [hope] of being able to send two of them to you; but the season of the year being too damp, caused them to wilt, rather dry; and one of them rolling from the table, split by the fall, and spilt its juice, partly on the floor, but being laid upon a plate, it filled the whole round of the plate in a purple ring. Our garden presents some of the trees, which exhibit buds, blossoms, young fruit and ripe, at the same moment. I have had some young shrubs of them, transplanted from the Garden into a circular flower garden before my bow-room door—interspersed with the myrtle hedge: and I have discovered that transplanting has had the effect of both [228] multiplying the number of blossoms, and of doubling the leaves or petals in each flower to the greatest fullness I ever beheld in any flower. They appear like the brightest *Scarlet* rose-bushes. The simple flower is no more double than the convolvulus, and is much the size of a small morning-glory. The tree bears no fruit after it acquires this state, nor does it grow large.

Address to the Pomegranate tree.

1. Thou mystical shrub! Whose bell-shapen flower
Divine Wisdom decreed, Aron's [sic] Robe should adorn,[297]
Say, why wast thou chosen, or what was thy power
To prefigure the Saviour foretold to be born?
2. Were thy blossoms so glowing, arranged to appear
As the mouths of the prophets, foreshewing that love
Which the Gospel announces so free in our ear;
Or the Angels proclaiming "good will" from above?
3. When I look on thy thorn-pointed spray, and red bud,

[297] Exodus 28:1–2, 28:31–35.

My mind is induced some resemblance to trace
With the thorn-piercing wreath, stain'd with innocent blood
That encompass'd the brow of the Author of Grace!
4. Thy fruit hangs so pendant, in form like a heart,
And full ripen'd exudes crimson dew on the ground,
That it brings to my view, in Gethsemane, apart,
The agonized Jesus when Deity frown'd.
5. Thy smooth painted rind, when it met with a stroke
Effus'd such a flood as to startle the eye—
Oh! was it not so when his swollen heart broke,
Struck by Justice relentless, for Sinners to die!
6. Thy fruit, both refreshment and healing afford,—
Lucid gems that dissolve to delectable wine:
Thus shewing how precious the heart of my Lord,
When it melted, atoning of guilt—even mine!
7. As the feverish palate owns grateful the taste
Of its mingled astringence with acid and sweet,
So my sin-mourning Soul on the Antitype placed
Feels her conscience restored and her comfort replete.
8. As the *Rose* on the *Mountains of Sharon* so fair;
The *Beloved* amongst the *well-favor'd* of men,
Sweet Pomegranate! thou in the Gard'ner's pasture
[229] Art the brightest, most beautiful shrub to be seen,
9. For thy blossoms all others out-lustre in dye,
And successively budding, ne'er wholly decay
So the Love of *Emmanuel*, all Love doth out-vie,
And shall glow in the Christian as time turns her grey.
10. Holy awe fill'd my Soul, and my frame felt a shake,
As these sacred comparisons flow'd from my pen;
They have served my reposing devotion to wake—
May it never—oh never, be languid again!

Note, the two Pomegranates above alluded to weighed together 32 ounces: one weighed 14. The other 18 ounces.

The eatable part, which consists of small flat white seeds,

covered with Lymph slightly tinged with purple, crimson, or pink, confined in a transparent cuticle, assume the appearance of cut stones, from being closely packed together in their cells or compartments, and when the rind is broken apart, they fall loosely all about, and retain their form, until pressed either by the fingers, or the tongue.

I desire you to give my love to all my old friends. Tell my Nephew Xavier,[298] that I thank him for his letter. It evinces a good understanding that deserves more cultivation. I had thought much about him and his brothers,[299] before his letter came. Such a letter from each of them would be gratifying to me. Thy Mary's[300] gift of the Sampler, is like a flower garden in my School. The little Misses are constantly transplanting choice flowers from it. She could not have made me so acceptable present in any other thing. I hope thy children are all improving like her. With kindest love to them all, and to Sister Margaret, brother John, Sisters Jane and Sarah[301]

I remain thy ever affectionate

Sister
Ch. H. Rowe.

---

[298] Francis Xavier James was the twenty-one-year-old son of Charlotte's sister, Mary Rachel Atlee, the wife of Edward Victor James.

[299] The brothers of Francis Xavier James were nineteen-year-old Jesse James and sixteen-year-old William Atlee James.

[300] Mary Patience Atlee, fourteen-year-old daughter of Edwin Augustus and Margaret (Snyder) Atlee.

[301] Charlotte's letter to her brother, Edwin Augustus Atlee, ends with greetings to his wife, "Sister" Margaret, and to Charlotte's siblings John Sayre Atlee, Jane Amelia Atlee (wife of Rev. Elisha S. Rigg), and Sarah Ann Atlee (wife of Thomas Vickroy). Charlotte's six other siblings were deceased by 1820.

July 6. [1820].

I have just succeeded in cutting a golden singlet from my little ones' heads, to send you. They have been very poorly with cutting two upper teeth.

[230] Digah. Sept. 26. 1820.

I write to my dear Edwin now, chiefly to enclose a letter which our esteemed friend Captain Page has left for that purpose, hoping that through you, it will safely reach his brother, near you. His Lady[302] is now at Dinapore for change of air, with a sickly infant. We often see each other. She is a good woman.

I am in expectation of parting with Mr. Rowe for three months—this will be trying, as we never have been separated a whole day. He goes to Calcutta on Missionary business, and though the voyage is but 4 or 5 hundred miles by water, the returning takes up much time, and is very difficult and dangerous.[303] There is but one alternative in the mode of travelling in this country, and that is, riding *Dawk*, which is in a post palanquin, the bearers being provided by officers under Gov^{t}. This mode is greatly more expeditious, but quite as expensive: it allows no rest, but what you may take *racked* on men's shoulders. It takes as many hands to convey an individual to or from Calcutta either way, as to man a vessel for a voyage to Europe.

Mr. Rowe will probably see Mr. & Mrs. Judson, Mr. & Mrs. Coleman, and Mrs. Wheelock in Calcutta.[304] Mrs. J. has come

---

[302] Jane (Morgan) Page.

[303] Richard Lloyd, the first to hold the post of Hooghly surveyor that was created in the 1830s, drew new charts of the Hooghly. Lloyd confirmed that it was "one of the most challenging and dangerous rivers on record." Ivermee, *Hooghly*, 162.

[304] Adoniram and Ann (Haseltine) Judson, James and Elizabeth (Hubbard) Coleman, and Eliza (Newman) Wheelock, widow of Edward Wheelock. In 1817 the Baptist Board of Foreign Missions in America had sent the Colemans and Wheelocks to join the Judsons in Burma. Their ship

round for her health. My voyage companion Mrs. Hough, is keeping Mrs. Marshman's School, during her absence in England for her health. I heartily regret being at so great a distance from Serampore, as I am never able to participate in the pleasing varieties afforded by the frequent landing of friends. My children are too troublesome and delicate either to take abroad, or leave to the care of natives. Their brothers are very fond of them, and take much delight in drawing them round the room in their little carriage, one or the other playing the Harlequin to the infants which make all laugh heartily. They have a free space round a ten feet table which is always open.

[Crossed out sentence:] I am writing to you before our brother Moore has accepted the invitation given by the [indecipherable] church [231] at Mongire, to supply the place of br. Chamberlain, deceased.[End of crossed out sentence.]

I have lately enjoyed the assistance in School hours, of a young Lady recently from England, who was so unfortunate as to have lost her Aunt who wrote for her to come, before she arrived. She has been boarding at brother Moore's since her Uncle gave up housekeeping.

Jaffur Shah, a native Landholder, has lately been to make us a visit. On his first being introduced to me, he bowed three times very low, to me, and taking a fine, white pocket handkerchief which was

---

Independence arrived Calcutta in May 1818. Wheelock had suffered extreme seasickness, and the heat of Bengal continued to weaken him. His illness continued in Burma. He and his wife departed Rangoon on August 8, 1819, hoping that time at sea and the ability to consult physicians in Bengal would bring healing. While onboard the ship on August 16 he became very depressed and feverish. He attempted suicide twice but was prevented by his wife. The third time he succeeded. "In the delirium of a moment he plunged himself into the sea, while the vessel was proceeding with such velocity as to preclude the possibility of saving him from a watery grave. So sudden was his disappearance, that Mrs. Wheelock scarcely missed him from her side before the dreadful deed was accomplished." He was twenty-three years old. "Retrospect of Missions," 225–229.

still nicely in the ironed folds, from his pocket, he laid it on his hand, and laid a gold mohur[305] upon it, and approached me, handing it to me. He designed I should take up and accept the gold rupee, worth 16 rupees. I hesitated, but Mr. Rowe told me, that I *must touch it*, if I did not wish to take it. I did so, and he bowed and took a seat. Such profound respect, I had never before witnessed. He has several times visited us since that; and sometimes comes with a Suit of thirty or forty persons, very few of whom, are admitted into the house with himself. I shewed him the manuscript which I had in hand; he praised it as marvelous, but that is a thing of course with the Asiatics. Joshua is making a large map of the world which he designs to present to him. There is no such thing as yet brought within a Hindoo or Mussulman's comprehension, that we know of. He looks with some complacency on the little school of Hindoo females, but has never opened his hand on it. As he is the most consequential native near us, he might do much good by his patronage of native instruction, if he had a heart inclined for it.

Our English school for young Ladies, has decreased so much, as to render it necessary for us to apply to the Society for aid. I shall be very much pleased when I may have to relinquish it altogether. It is a great task to form the minds of India children, grown wise in the sins and superstitions of their native mothers: and even [232] such as have European mothers,[306] are so deeply imbued with similar ideas, that the task is the same, to new-modle [sic] either.

---

[305] Mohur: a gold coin that was the highest unit of currency minted in India by the Mughal Empire. It was later minted by the East India Company and by several princely Indian states.

[306] For many years the East India Company encouraged its employees to marry local women and prohibited British women to travel to India, even if accompanying their fathers, husbands, or brothers. The pupils in the Rowes' English-language boarding school had therefore almost exclusively been Eurasians. More British women arrived in India after the Company changed its regulations to prefer European wives to Indians and Eurasians. This brought to the Rowes the occasional pupil whose parents were both European. Anthony, *Britain's Betrayal in India*, 16.

It is late at night, and the Equinoxial Storm blows and I am melting, [being] shut close on every side.

With love to all my relatives,

Accept my warmest affection

Thy sister

To Dr. E. A. Atlee. C. H. Rowe

Digah, Oct 21. 1820.

I received dear Edwin's letter by his friend Dr. Burrows, two days ago. I thank him for it. It is a rare thing as I have not had one for two years before. One to Mr. Rowe 18 months old came some time ago. I fear that the book which you sent him,[307] and the tracts, will meet the fate that most of your letters have.

I truly lament F. W.'s death, in the way it happened.[308] It is a retributive stroke upon his father, whom I have often heard contend

---

[307] Edwin Atlee wrote at the bottom of the page:, "Hickewelder's History of the Aborigines of America. E. A. A."

[308] F. W. was Charlotte's nephew, Francis Bowes White. When Charlotte became an orphan at age eleven in 1793, she moved into the Rutland, Massachusetts home of her oldest sister, Elizabeth Amelia (Atlee) White, and her husband, Maj. Moses White, a family with four children. Francis was the second of six more children born to the Whites during Charlotte's adolescence. Francis White became a lieutenant in the Marine Corps where he met Lieut. William Bolton Finch, who had moved from England to the U.S. and joined the Navy. A conflict arose between White and Finch in 1815 when both were in the Mediterranean as officers on the *USS Independence* and Finch reprimanded White in the presence of the crew. Furthermore, Finch flogged two marines without White's knowledge or consent. White also charged Finch with ungentlemanly conduct and with telling a fellow officer that White was ignorant of his duty. Four years later White demanded satisfaction by duel. On September 25, 1819 the two men met on Noddles Island in Boston Harbor (land later incorporated into east Boston). Standing between two elm trees, Finch shot White in the breast, killing him instantly. White was twenty-four. Finch later changed his name to William Compton Bolton, became a naval commodore, and died in 1849 at Genoa, Italy.

in favour of duelling. He was a fine looking officer, and but for false sentiments, might have lived longer. There can be no hope, of eternal happiness for one who dies under such opinions. His pious mother was taken away in fit time to escape such a heart-rending trial.[309]

Give my noble minded Nephew J. L. Atlee,[310] much praise from me; and charge him in my name, never to dishonour his father's house, the birth-place of his Uncles and Aunts, and especially the worthies, from whom he is but the second step, since to dishonor them, must bring disgrace upon his own reputation, and hinder the reward of his talents, now so promising.

I rejoice in the pleasing account of your son Edwin[311] and hope he may reach India in safety if he should attempt the voyage. I hope he will take a Dawk palankeen and arrive here as soon as possible, which he may do in five days from Calcutta, for about 150 rupees.

---

[233] The promised little gold watch, will I trust, ere long be safely conveyed to my little Namesake.[312] She is now old enough to claim it, and to take care that others do not wear it out. She must let it lie by until she is of an age to wear it. But tell her from me, that unless she be a true lady in her deportment, as well in private as in public, it will appear ill-placed. To become a real Lady, she must give her attention habitually to all that is improving to the heart, and amiable in her daily behaviour. A Lady is one who is humble and affable towards every body. Indeed, a christian deportment in any

---

[309] Francis B. White's mother, Elizabeth Amelia (Atlee) White, had died in 1808, eleven years before the duel.

[310] John Light Atlee, twenty-year-old son of Charlotte's brother, William Pitt, and Sarah (Light) Atlee.

[311] Edwin Pitt Atlee, twenty-one-year-old son of Charlotte's brother, Edwin Augustus, and Margaret (Snyder) Atlee.

[312] Charlotte's namesake, five-year-old niece Charlotte White Atlee, was born in Philadelphia to Edwin Augustus and Margaret (Snyder) Atlee on March 17, 1815, nine months before Charlotte departed for India on the ship *Benjamin Rush*.

one, must at the same time be that of a Lady. I would not infer, that to be a Lady, in the common acceptation of the word, is to be a Christian; for a gay dress, superficial accomplishments, and a haughty air, constitute not a Lady, but a pimp. To find a real Lady, I would follow a female through the paternal home—I would trace her steps from the chamber to the kitchen, and listen attentively to all she says in the chamber, the parlour, and the kitchen, before I should pronounce upon her. If she be active, neat, and industrious; dutiful, kind and pious, she is *a Lady*.

I would not now desire my niece to come to this inauspicious climate for young persons. My own two poor and puny little girls, suffer so much illness, that I am never free from the deepest anxiety: add to this, the difficulty of keeping their minds uncorrupted by the pernicious ideas of the natives. My twins will be two years old in a few days.

My own health is tolerable; but I have become an old woman. Much care, toil, study, and night-watching, have served to alter me very much; but I am wonderfully sustained, to go on still. I seldom enjoy a half hour's tranquility, such as feasts the Soul—perfect stillness, with holy communion with God. My mind has no time to unbend, until the hours when nature requires exemption as well from thought as from labour, after every one else is asleep. *Sleep* [234] in the true sense of it, seldom fall[s] on my eyelids. I have left my pen several times since I commenced writing this.

My heartiest grief as yet, and what I have felt of late more especially, is the opposition shewn by the male natives, to native female instruction, and the little interest in it, exhibited by Europeans about here, as yet. The idea too generally prevails, that they are better in a state of ignorance. Truly, they cannot so well discern their abjectness. Mrs. Murray was the first, and Mrs. Waring the second Lady, who has favored my views, by affording a little pecuniary assistance towards them.

A Bramin at Moinpoora, who has been for a long time on friendly habits of intercourse with us, offers to allow us the use of a vacant place, where the natives meet to hold consultations; where he says, we may not only have a girls' school, but that he will send his two little daughters. A fine lad, a son of his, has been under our tuition some time; and when I go to visit his family, he hangs on my shoulder, and reads the Gospel fluently to his parents. I cannot say whether he ever does it, or is allowed to do it at other times. The place where I have had to go to visit his school, was over a place that was overflowed in the rains, and through a cattle yard in one end of which, was the mud hut, where I examined my native pupils, the surrounding air being noxious to inhale—yet I have my regular days for going there, all the year, glad to find any corner where I may carry on the work of Christian instruction to the natives.[313]

One very hot season, I had to go there at four o'clock in the morning, in order to get home alive. One morning the Bramin's family urged me to take breakfast. I consented, to let them see that I had no prejudices against eating amongst them. They said they could give me an egg, and some milk; I had some biscuits with me, for *bread* they do not use, nor any thing baked in that way, on account of the expensiveness of it, to them. The little boy who was my pupil, thinking I should relish my biscuit and milk better if it were sweetened, ran off and [235] bought a little brown sugar in a paper, and keeping possession of it, helped me with his fingers; keeping them in the sugar read[y] to help me again. I was much amused by the act, as well as gratified with his spontaneous hospitality, but I dare not let it be seen that I was treated any other way than I had been accustomed to, lest I should offend their feelings. I ate my

---

[313] Charlotte described this coeducational "Liverpool School" at Moinpoora as a mud hut with two inlet-like doorways that was "small and so dark and close that it is quite disgustful." In dry weather, the yard was crowded with feeding cattle that filled the hut with suffocating animal fumes. On two visits following the rains, the condition was even worse. The yard overflowed with muddy water, forcing men to wade waist deep to carry her to the hut's door where she "ascended with difficulty, having no dry place for my foot." Thirty-five boys and ten girls awaited her inside the hut. On a third visit she was unable to get to the school at all because of the slime remaining after the floods. Trulson, *Charlotte Atlee White Rowe*, 135–6.

breakfast out of one of their brass cups, all the family gazing at me. I however discovered, that for me to eat in their vessels did not defile them for future use—whereas, *offering* them food in one of our vessels would nearly break their cast and they would turn from it with dread of defilement.

The Bramin had recently buried his father—his mother being with them, I enquired why she had not been burned with her husband's corpse, as he was a respectable man? He answered me, that "all do not choose to burn." The fact is, that none choose to be burned, but the sons and uncles insist upon it. He had learned better, it is probable, from his intercourse with us.

We sent you a packet a little time since, and one copy of my Hindee Spelling book. It was printed for boards. The Society presented me with 150 copies; a reward I scarcely expected.

When ever I see my children in health, so as to set my hands at liberty, my mind turns on some work for the natives; thus I am enabled to effect a *little* in the way of my proper undertaking.

Brother Chamberlain has just got through translating the Scriptures into Brij-Bhaka, which is a variation of Hindee, suited to a particular Province.[314]

The Church Missionaries[315] have published many excellent things in Hindosthani. Abdool Messuh, a Mussulman, converted by the preaching of Henry Martyn,[316] has been very useful to them, in correcting translations, and I believe he has transposed some

---

[314] Brij Bhaka (also known as Braj Basha or Bruj): a western dialect of Hindi spoken in Agra and elsewhere southeast of Delhi. John Chamberlain had lived in Agra from 1811–1812.

[315] William Wilberforce, John Venn, John Newton, and others in England formed the Society for Missions to Africa and the East in 1799 as an independent voluntary society within the Church of England. It was renamed the Church Missionary Society in 1812 and began work in India in 1813.

[316] Henry Martyn (1781–1812), an evangelical Anglican, accepted commission as a chaplain with the East India Company and gave prominent focus to Bible translation.

hymns.[317]

You would find the Memoir of Henry Martyn, a most spiritual work.[318]

I should be glad to receive from you, a child's book of short and easy stories, that I may translate them, [236] but scarcely any English story will do here, without some modification adapted to this country, which I should make.

We have lately had a wedding. Deborah Biss was married to Mr. Beeby,[319] and went to Calcutta to settle, not a long time since. Another marriage is shortly to take place between brother Moore and a young Lady of our School. This has been a bustling month with us, having had the company of the families of two of our

---

317 Abdool Messuh (also spelled Messeeh, Musseeh, and Abdul Masih), whose original name was Sheikh Salih, was born in Delhi. He met Henry Martyn in Cawnpore, heard his preaching and eventually secured lodging on his premises. After Martyn completed his Hindustani translation of the New Testament, he gave it to Sheikh Salih to bind. Reading it in secret, Sheikh Salih become a follower of Jesus. Martyn was unsure whether Sheikh Salih's profession of faith was sincere so refused to baptize him but brought him to Calcutta and recommended him to the care of David Brown, pastor of the Mission Church in Calcutta. After observing him for five months, Brown baptized Sheikh Salih in 1811 and named him Abdool Musseeh—(meaning "servant of Christ"). From 1812 to c.1820 Abdool worked as a catechist under the Church Missionary Society. During those years he wrote commentaries on the New Testament books of Matthew, Romans, and Hebrews. The Church Missionary Society asked Bishop Middleton to admit him as a candidate for ordination. Middleton didn't consider himself authorized to ordain ministers so recommended Abdool for ordination by the Lutheran missionaries serving with the Society for Promoting Christian Knowledge. Following his ordination, the Lutherans set him apart for missionary service. Carey, *Oriental Christian Biography*, 1:455–466.

318 John Sargent's *Memoir of the Rev. Henry Martyn* was first published in London shortly after Martyn's death in Tokat, Türkiye. It was republished in London in 1819 followed by many succeeding editions.

319 Deborah Cauldwell Biss married Englishman William Thomas Beeby on October 7, 1820. He was a businessman. Upon his death in 1842 he was buried in the Scotch and Dissenters Burial Ground, Calcutta.

brethren, most of the month.

I must now conclude, offering my best love to each of your dear family, and to enquiring friends.

My dear partner offers you all his best affections. His health is very good, except now and then, a little bile has to be removed.

Pray for us, my dear brother, when you find access at the divine Mercy Seat; and may you draw fresh supplies of Grace with every temporal blessing, *thence*.

Your affectionate Sister
Charlotte H Rowe

March 27th. 1820.

I feel myself to be the Lord's servant and that it behoves me to use all my endeavours to promote the advancement of His Kingdom. Oh! for Grace to enable me to honour my profession, and glorify Christ and his Gospel in Life and death!

In the effects of some of our attempts, I think I see the dawning of the wished-for day, and the truth of the promises, as well as the first Rewards of faith.

August 13, 1820. Sabbath.

While dressing for the hour of public worship in the hall, I felt rather solicitous to appear a little tarty, as I was told, Major G. would attend, and would wait for an introduction to me after service.

This attention to my appearance on account of a fellow mortal, led me to reflections which ended in prayer: [237] that I might be as suitably anxious to appear acceptably to the All-seeing God, by having on the Robe of Jesus Christ's imputed Righteousness, ere I ventured into His August presence, for the known purpose of worshipping Him: and that He would send his Spirit into my heart, to unite my thoughts in Himself, and draw them off from every object that would intervene between me and Him, whom I *have seen* in his works, his Providence, and in his Grace to my Soul, by revealing to it, the plan of Redemption, and making me to feel an interest in it, and an earnest of it.

Mr. Rowe delivered an impressive Sermon, from "Now is the accepted time."[320]

By the pious people in the Regiment at Dinapore Mr. Rowe is called "the little great man" being rather below the common hight [sic], and of a plain & humble aspect. When he preaches, the depth and impressiveness of his matter, conveyed in simple yet correct language, gives him weight and magnitude.

August 27th. [1820].

Where is my brother to comfort me? I can neither see him nor hear from him. He would pour into my distressed Soul, the Wine of spiritual strengthening. But O Thou! who stickest closer than a brother—Thou who *art* my *brother*, Immanuel! Son of Man! stand not afar off. Teach me to bear, and thus purify me for the day of my union with immortality and Light!

[August] 29th. [1820].

Am laying hold on every work of Education, which will be likely to assist me in the proper management of Children. I often feel impatient and surprised at the little sense and discretion of the elder ones in my school. O that I could divest myself of this detestable passion. I am constantly expecting more from them than they perform [238] forgetting the old saying that we must not look for old heads on young shoulders. I must pray more about it, to Him, who alone can affect the heart, and endow the human mind with amiable qualities. My cares are now extended, in the watchfulness necessary over the opening minds of the infants. O God, grant me assistance in forming their minds *aright*. Condescend to guide me, when I look up to Thee, and breathe the speechless desire for help. Especially when the suddenness of gusts of passion in them preclude more. Incline me at all times to lead them in right paths. O that Thou wouldst

---

[320] 2 Corinthians 6:2.

form their minds to love Thy ways, and to give no lasting place to evil in their own hearts! Oh that *Thou* wouldst help me to train them and their brothers for Thy Service! Could my pen have reached my heart, it would have written this petition with its warmest blood.

Infants are lovely plants, sown on earth to be cultured for heaven; heavenly spirits in fleshly moulds, to be formed by the skill of parents and teachers. How great is their responsibility—how shall *I* mould aright, those committed to my care? not by my alone experience and wisdom and virtue—O for Grace and wisdom from on high! else I shall not frame them to the image with which they must be impressed, to bear any resemblance to the holy Law of God. Spirits are they, endowed with infinite powers, not of holiness like God, but of duration like Him; for he has pronounced them immortal. Such, are committed with this divine mandate, to me, "feed my Lambs"—Be thou their teacher and their guide. O how holy ought I to be, in all the imitable perfections of the Deity! that they should bear the impress I am to give them, into the Presence of their creator and my Judge! Then, will their moral beauty assimilate them with heavenly beings (for spiritual forms assume the character of their minds) or will their moral *deformity* repel the heavenly tact? Awful consideration! May it ever influence my [239] conduct towards them.

Already, scarce two years old, I have seen in my infant daughters, the force of example, either good or bad. Already discerned the bent nature gives, to evil rather than good: but I have as certainly seen the pleasing effects of judicious principles gently instilled into their minds, counteracting, if not overcoming that peculiar bent, which if left to take its full bias, w^{d}. soon distort every feature of both mind and countenance, in them. I perceive the wisdom of the apostle's warning "provoke not your children to wrath, lest they be discouraged."[321] How feeling, how just is the caution! Let me then avoid untimely, misapplied, and too harsh reprimand—I have seen in them, the magic power of gentle *address*, exercised in moments of

[321] Ephesians 6:4.

querulousness. Blessed power that turneth away wrath and foileth the Tempter. "A soft answer turneth away wrath."[322]

Parents and teachers should avoid being absorbed in themselves, so as to disregard the applications of children for a thing, or an answer. In the first place we should make it a point to answer them promptly and mildly, in order to prevent a repetition of the request; in the second, we should teach them *to wait*, and not speak more than twice, but still wait for their patient standing by us, if we have been absent or engaged, will arrest our attention, and then they will be satisfied. Their requests are not often wholly futile; but on hearing them we shall find something in them of as much interest and might in their tender little minds, as things of great moment, are with us. Since they are but little men & women, and ourselves but "children of a larger growth." It is just to them, to allow them every opportunity of having their minds enlarged by the replies elicited from us by their importunities.

I am no advocate for the fashion of the darker age, of keeping children forever from the parlour circle where their parents and friends hold free conversation. Their minds will be very narrow in riper years, if banished to the nursery, to spend their evening in that [240] routine of wrangling which takes up the chief topic there, when left so much to themselves, and to inferiour authority. From the eldest to the youngest, according to their gradations in age, they should *be taken by the hand* (in the common acceptation of the term) by their parents. They should [be] *inducted*, as their minds appear capable, in every thing proper to be known or talked of among their little selves. This ought to be done, in order both to prevent improper subjects from laying themselves open to them, and to raise their conceptions of things. What is proper to unfold to them, and where it is proper to lead them, a *Christian* can easily decide: and here I leave the subject.

---

[322] Proverbs 15:1.

December 5th. 1820.

Let me not suffer this day to pass without noting down the special favours of the Lord unto me, his sinful creature. As I sat with the Pundit this morning, I was surprized by seeing the Lala of the Lyme School coming in with an air of confidence, and beckoning behind him saying "aiyo, aiyo" come, come, and in a moment, five little native girls came directly before me and made their salam and bow, very profoundly (for females do not bend the knee in salutations, here. They *bow*, to some purpose). I asked him who these were? He said they were scholars of his, whose parents had forbidden them to go to the *Guorosine*[323] or native *Priestess* or *teacher*. He at once reminded me, of this being the answer to my prayers. I thought it very especial too.

One of the number, wrote the ten first letters of the native alphabet on paper with a quill, for me as she stood. She had never touched either before, as the palm leaf split at its folds, or a dried and pressed plantain leaf which forms a wide sheet, is what they use in the schools, and write on them with a pen made of a seed. They had been with him only part of the week. I encouraged them by telling them, that if they could read books and write letters to each other, they would become superior to the casts higher than their own, which pleased them very much: for none of [241] those who deem themselves *respectable*, will be seen walking in the street. The master also encouraged them by many arguments. He reminded me of my saying to him a few days previous, "What good news have you to bring me about native girls?" "Now," said he, "have I not brought you your desire? I have sought without ceasing for these."

Just before sunset, a man handed me a scrap of paper, on which there were the names of eleven girls written, who had, within a few days, joined another of the boys' schools. This intelligence was an additional cause of surprise, and as I was just going out to take a sniff of fresh air, in an Tonjon (or kind of chair carried like a palankeen)

[323] Guorosine (also goorooine): a female teacher.

I went along meditating on the goodness and faithfulness of God, who had respect to my petitions and I could scarcely refrain from a burst of tears of thankfulness, in the face of numbers of gay gentlemen and Ladies whom I met in gigs and on horse-back.

Now, I trust, I shall have actual Labour among the heathen females. I am glad that I now have matter for answering the letter from the Female Society in England, promoting the Instruction of East India females. Hitherto disappointment and shame withheld me from it.

January 8th. 1821.

Having got through my Monday morning's fatigue, and set down to my desk to pursue my other calling, as well as watch by the side of my sleeping little ones while their nurses go home to eat their meal, not yet having found opportunity to retire, my heart felt much tried, and my soul longed for communion with God. Here as I sit, trying to compose my thoughts to meditation and prayer, as feeling arose, the agitation I felt, subsided, and I was favored with a moment of prayer and praise unmolested by the adversary. At that time, I was excited to adore the grace of God to my Soul, and to see through the passage of Scripture, saying "he giveth Grace for grace."[324] He draweth us by his grace, and for the improvement we make of the portion [242] we possess of it, he bestows more grace upon us.

O! the glory of the goodness of our heavenly father, towards his poor, sinful, undeserving children! I fall far below those of his Saints, who have done good in the earth, and I see that I merit not the least of his favours; but that if he were to deal justly with me, *out of Christ*, I should be forever banished from his delectable presence.

Lord's Day evening. Feb. 4th. 1821.

Attended the common ordinances of Worship three times, once at Dinapore and twice at Digah, and fourthly with my dear partner at

[324] John 1:16.

the bed-side: but I find no such satisfaction in divine service, as I enjoy in a few moments of prayer, alone. My Soul testifies that I have never tasted pleasure like that—none other can compare with it. The first love of a youthful heart, in mutual fondness with its beloved object, falls far short of the love of the Soul to God, in moments of nearness to Him. Still these joys are but tainted springs compared with draughts of heavenly delight, flowing from his immediate presence. There the Saviour sits, "The Wonderful, the Counsellor, the Prince of Peace, the Mighty God!"[325]

Oh how imperfectly able are we in this mortality, to speak his praise! How cheering to the Soul, is the thought, that all inability to render worthy praise will drop with *this* mass, this polluted, dregging mass of flesh and sin! Blessed be God, for the denunciation of *Death* to *sinners:* for so long as I am in the flesh I shall be subject to sin: but I have the all transcending hope of admittance into sinless *Rest*, thro' the *atoning* Blood of Jesus Christ. He hath pledged his Righteousness for a Rainment to those who love him, and his truth is *Alpha* and *Omega*.

Sweet are the tears exuded by holy love and adoration to God and His Christ. O that I could always preserve their pacific influence on my Soul! but characteristic of my mortal nature in sin, "I go from the lov'd place of prayer (or praise) and leave its sweet enjoyment there."

[243] Let me note the mercies of God to us at this time. All in health, and in possession of every faculty of body and mind. Our dear children favoured with such health as to enable us to rest at night, which is what I have not been able to say, since the infants were born. We are great debtors to Mercy—may it please the Lord to pardon my past murmurings on account of broken rest, and a double charge; and now give me to see his distinguishing goodness in the gift. I behold their sweet countenances fraught with infantile utterance; their opening minds awaken delight in us; and their activity encourages the hope, that they may be spared to inherit "a

---

[325] Isaiah 9:6.

Name and a Place" among *the Lord's people*. May the Moulder of our frame, and the Renewer of the heart, shed his Light into the mind of each of our fine, dear children, and enable them to "behold Light in his Light." Amen!

Note, the following scrap being misplaced, is copied also out of place. It should have preceeded [sic] the last two.

Dec. 6th 1820.

Having taken a little recreation with my partner in the fields now covered with promising crops in full verdure, my mind feels relief from study and toil, and my heart inclined to retrace the mercies of the Lord to me, particularly in the restoration of my infants, to health after having been given over by surrounding beholders. Eighteen months ago, my little Charlotte fell suddenly ill, and appeared convulsive. She was seven months old I think, and was still at my breast. I afterwards attributed her illness to my having indulged in green peas, of which I am extravagantly fond. I found that whenever I ate them, she was seized with violent pain a few hours after. Of course, I denied myself that pleasure esteeming it a small thing on my part. Her eyes when so ill, stared senselessly, apparently in death. My neighbours came to see us in our affliction, and brother Moore took [244] feeling part in it; for [he] went immediately to bring the Military Physician from Dinapore. Being left alone with the child on my lap, the servants came into the room, one of whom, appeared to sympathize with me; feeling mounted to his dark face, which quite overcame me. I raised the babe to my face, to hid my struggles in its bosom, and thus prayed to the Lord of Life, ever present. "Oh! alpowerful [sic] God! who createst this child, Thou hast power to restore her. But perhaps thy allwise [sic] Will is adverse to my desires and my hopes. I dare not pray for her restoration to me, for thou mayest have designed to take her to thine own bosom. I pray 'Thy will be done' but I implore thy *mercies* mingled with thy Judgments. I dare not ask the continuance of her life here; I scarce can desire her life on Earth, for I know my ill desert of such a favour—I know the world—I distrust my ability to rear her to *Thee* alone. But if it may not displease thee O my God! direct, mercifully direct the use of such medicines as thou will bless to her restoration. Without Thee we can do nothing. Thou hast provided antidotes against human maladies. In vain do Physicians prescribe them, if Thou bless not.

O let not thy presence depart from us: and whatsoever thy will be concerning us, graciously reconcile us to it, and sanctify restoring grace or bereaving chastisement. Amen! The Lord heard, blessed, and the child recovered.

October 3rd. 1821.

I have not sat down *to answer* a letter of my dear Brothers. That pleasure has long been withheld me. The only letter I have had from him for nearly three years, was received nearly a year ago, and it was 1½ year old then.

I have lately received a short letter from Dr. Staughton, of a year's date. I had not seen an American paper or pamphlet, for three years, until Mr. Adlington[326] passed up, the other day, and brought a parcel of the *Missionary Herald*,[327] of which he gave me a few numbers.

[245] I have experienced a great deal of satisfaction from reading therein of the Missions to the American Indians. The work is ready at their hands, as many of the Indians speak English, and they are near home. May they have much joy in success. Their trusting, ardently desiring spirits have not to *wait* as those who are engaged in missions to the East, for some fruit of their toil. *Their* prayers are

---

[326] Rev. John Adlington, missionary of the Church Missionary Society, came to India in 1817. He married Sarah Clarke at Digah on February 18, 1822. They subsequently served in Chunar. Stock, *History of the Church Missionary Society*, 1:185.

[327] The magazine of the American Board of Commissioners for Foreign Missions.

like evening dews, which open the blossoms in the morning: *ours* like seed sown out of season, that must endure the drying heats, and withering winds before the moisture from on high condescend upon it—and then it rises, a puny, hopeless thing. We dress and prune it, but its fruit will remain acrid. Where missions have existed for a series of years, the fruits begin to appear fresh and desirable. There has not been a native baptized at Digah, of Digah fruits, for two years past. Some that own their spiritual birth here, are doing what good they can, elsewhere. A young man named *Nainsook*, who grew up here, is preacher to the natives at Monghire. He is supported by a widow Lady there, our beloved Mrs. Grant. His wife, who learned to sew in my first native female school, is about to become a teacher of little girls of her own nation, under the superintendence of Mrs. Grant. This Lady is a member of the Society of Ladies, formed at Digah in 1817 for the Instruction of native females. It consists of 12 members as yet; and the half of these are engaged in the actual duties of their alliance, at their respective homes, many miles distant. I have to say, that the members of this Society being better able to render their personal services in the cause than their money, its funds are very low; but the same effects result, that could, if they were much larger, and expended on so many assistants. Were it not for 150 rupees from Mrs. Waring now gone to England, the School at Dinapore would want support.

The religious in this part of the world are few and generally poor, of course their [246] subscriptions are low. The irreligious are numerous and very cold, as to feeling for the poor natives. Indeed they do as yet, esteem every effort to reform the heathen, as ridiculous; and the enlightening of their minds, impossible, and as we hold very little intercourse with such people, we are too little known among them, to have any influence over their purses. The Regiments are so often changed at Dinapore, that we should be continually forming new acquaintances, if we sought to form many out of our own circle. They fancy the society of such Methodistical folks as we are, about as little as we fancy theirs. Even the Evangelical Episcopalians are dubb'd *methodistical.* Beyond the circle of old friends who have resided near here ever since I came, we have very few associates. There is a brotherhood of pious Soldiers at Dinapore now amongst whom, are several worthy and intelligent men, whom we esteem. Mr. Rowe preaches to them regularly on Sabbath days, and Wednesday evenings. They were privileged to have a hut set apart for their use, as a closet for private prayer for the soldiers. This was built by them with the permission from the officers to do so.

A few days ago, a concourse of people for a *Suttee* which means the *act of Righteousness or Truth*, or in our comprehension, *the burning of a widow* on the funeral pile of her dead husband, whose ashes are to be mingled with his! A great act of fidelity, to adorn her children to misery and poverty. O how is the human mind perverted to "believe a lie" to be Truth. The scene took place, or preparation for the effectuation of it, in a mango orchard nearly opposite out garden. As they cannot perform it without Permission from the Magistrate, that being in this instance denied them, the poor deluded widow, was obliged to give it up. She threw herself on the earth, bemoaning the dishonor to which she was subjected, while her two little children jumped about clapping their hands, at being told [247] that their mother was not to die. The pile was left to be taken possession of wholly by the corpse; the usual incantations were preformed around it by the priests, and fire set to it. The crowd soon dispersed, and the widow affected so much mortification at the disappointment of being with her husband in paradise, and on account of the shame she suffered, that she fell down several times on her way back to her home. Does not this indicate that the horrid practice might be done away by the union of sentiment on the subject, at the head of Government? Our noble magistrate dared to be singular in being disinterested and merciful. There has not been a Suttee at Dinapore for the last 7 years. Many thousands have been perpetrated around the seat of Government in that time.

During the last six months, three places of worship have been built at Dinapore. One by the Roman Catholics (which is already beginning to melt down), one by the Methodists, a very small society in the 59th Reg^{t}., and that erected sometime since by the Baptists is rebuilt with *burnt bricks*. The latter will contain 300 persons sitting at ease.[328] Mr. Rowe generally has a good congregation, made up chiefly of the Soldiers & their wives. It is very seldom that I can attend there, as the boarding school requires my Catechetical superintendence at home: But when I go, I find it good to be there. There are about 40 white communicants in our church. Amongst them, there are a few women who subscribe a trifle monthly towards native female instruction. Their subscriptions for the last six months amounted to $15, or 30 rupees, enough to pay a native teacher six months. This assistance is to be withdrawn next January, as the 59th Regiment is ordered to remove higher up.

We are alone at Digah, Brother Moore having married[329] and removed to Mongire. He accepted the invitation of the little church there, to supply the pulpit for them, Brother Chamberlain having died [248] soon after he set sail to go to England for his health. His amiable widow carries on the native schools, still. An equal division of the proceeds of our English Schools, proved too limited for our support, both families having increased, and the number of pupils diminished. He hopes to improve his condition by opening a school at Mongire; which will leave us with only the girls' School, as Mr. Rowe wished him to take all the boys with him. I should be very happy to be relieved of a European School, for of late, my health has not been adequate to it, with my other duties. I have not felt well since the month of June last. Have lately been under the influence of a bilious state, and the medicines usual in such cases; but my liver is not yet affected so as to give me pain.

The last hot season was unusually long, which tries our constitutions greatly. The children have all had pretty good health, throughout it. I now feel a wish to have our own children grow up without mingling any longer with other children.

---

[328] See Journal, March 31, 1817 and Journal, July 5, 1817 footnotes describing the Baptist chapel at Dinapore.

[329] William Moore married Anne Clarke, his third wife. Carey, *Oriental Christian Biography*, 3:203.

I hoped my dear brother's little ones are all doing well. I hope they will prove so many blessings to you & your Margaret. My little curly headed namesake must by this time have so changed from her sweet infantile babyhood, as to have outgrown my reconizence [sic], could I see her now. I hope Edwin is married.[330] My reason for it is, that I think love affairs are seldom beneficial to the parties, when long impending. I approve highly of early marriage, say any time over 20 for a female, and 21 for a male. Some choose to form that connection rather earlier. In such cases, a postponement would subject the parties to as many *troubles*, as beginning a young family rather too early in life; so that the latter step is to be preferr'd, since it makes the parties happier, with troubles, and serves to quiet the noisy, unstable spirit of youth. Give my love to each of your family, and to all those dear people whom I have seen at your house; to Miss Moulder & Miss Whitehead.

In your next, inform me of all you know respecting our family at large.

[249] [October] 4th. [1821.]

Mr. Rowe is making up a packet of the "Friend of India"[331] for you. We hope you have received upwards of 20 Numbers from time to time. I have a few scraps to send; I don't know that they will afford you any entertainment, and I hope, and confide in you, that you will

[330] Charlotte's nephew, Edwin Pitt Atlee, married Margaret Collins Bullock on October 17, 1822.

[331] *The Friend of India* began publication in May 1818. Its editor and publisher was John Clark Marshman, the oldest child of missionaries Joshua and Hannah Marshman. He had travelled with his parents from England to India on the American ship *Criterion* in 1799 when he was five years old. *The Friend of India* supplanted *Circular Letters*, which had reported the work of the British Baptist missionaries to a wide reading pubic. Printed at the Baptist Mission Press in Serampore, the new magazine was ecumenical in scope, reporting news of various Christian mission societies and institutions in India and "in general whatever tends to the advancement of knowledge, virtue, and religion." "Prospectus," *Friend of India*, May 1818, iii.

not make a bad use of them. I have nearly given up my pen, feeling it now a task to take up any pen; hope you will make up my deficiency in that respect. If you knew what a monotonous life I live, you would strive in fellow feeling to cast a little variety into the scene. Nothing can be so interesting to me as what comes from my native land.

I should like to know what the Society of Friends are doing among the Indians: what the Methodists, the Baptists, the Presbyterians, the *Church* people[332] are doing for those poor creatures, and for the other dark parts of the world; and whether my native place Old Lancaster is growing in morality, piety, and good works. I have had that dissolute place often on my heart—and seem to have set it down in my mind, as Nathaniel did of Nazareth, "can any good come out of Nazareth."[333]

Brother Moore paid just a friendly visit, not long ago. He is very stout, but not in any better health on that account.

A person direct from Delhi, about 700 miles above us says, that the heat there last hot season exceeded all that had been experienced by the most aged men of that place—and that the rains this season were so heavy as to have laid half of the city in ruins. The clay houses melt down. It is extraordinary that the people in India build houses of unburnt bricks. They do so, because they are cheap & plenty—whereas burnt bricks are expensive. They are also twice the size of burn[t] bricks. The bungalow I still live in fell in, at many points, from the same cause; and the roof being very heavy with double thatch, and earthen tile over, I had many fears, lest we should all be buried in ruins.

The disagreeableness of our houses in the rains, is not to be imagined by an inhabitant of America. Everything grows musty, even the beds on which we lie, and the pillows too. The white ants are also busy in every untrodden spot about the house—under a table or chair & the next goes to pieces. [250] Every thing, not constantly

---

332 "*Church* people" signifies members of the Episcopal Church.
333 John 1:46.

trodden upon, or defend[ed] by brass feet, or having plates of tin or copper under them will be eaten by them. They will find their way through a case of books, a trunk of clothes, and the folds of a carpe[t] that lies rolled away. They can *make* their way to anything that stands a half a foot from the wall (though it should be guarded by brass at the bottom) by means of a pipe which they build of clay. I have touched many such an one, having branches, and resembling a dry twig, which fell to dust again, on being touched. Add to these, innumerable other insects crawling about.

My dear partner unites with me in tenderest affection to yourself, Sister Margaret, and the children. May the face of the most high shine continually upon you all!

I have often been struck with the expressions of Scripture in beholding the manners of this people, both Mahometans and Hindoos. It is evident that many of them are such as were in practice before the Scriptures were written, because so many passages of Scripture are illustrated by seeing them, here. The Mahometans found some of their abominable festivals upon the Scriptures of the old Testament, such as the throwing of red dystuff [sic] upon each others' garments, in token of the blood of Sarah which they [say] ought to have been shed, as she was a heathen when Abraham married her, they say. They sacrifice a kid, which seems to be founded on the old ritual of Moses.

The Hindoos are so called as well in a Religious as a national sense. They are Idolators. Both, however are subject to the *loss of cast* on "doing, eating, or touching any thing forbidden.["] This is the only sin, the only anathema among them. The celebration of our Lord's Supper seems paraphrased in the recovery of cast, by the cup of reconciliation, handed them by their priest, who is as infallible in their eyes, as the Pope in those of the Catholics. Casts must not interchange food nor labour, any more than eat out of Christians' plates or partake of their food.

On the 12th of Sept. 1821 was opened on our premises a school for the females of the native poor. It received [251] ten names in the course of two weeks. I go down to them and give them lessons every morning early, and at even, the Goovooine or female teacher, and old pupil, brings them to our veranda, where I hear over the lessons given in the morning. Their good or bad mark being made on the daybook, everyone receives on Saturday, her appropriate reward. Money is its prop. All monies are the Lord's and I trust him for its support.

The old school at Dinapore increases in female pupils. One of the girls, a sweeperess, read to me yesterday, a letter which I had received from Meer Jaffur Shah of Patna, the native Gentleman who sometimes visits us in great pomp. She writes copies and reads print.

Digah. April 22[d], 1822.

My dear Edwin,

I have had occasion to write to some friends in America and as the packet is not closed, may have time to drop a few lines more to you. I have felt a wish to propose to the Ladies of your denomination, to unite with our small society for the improvements of native females here. The natives here, both male & female, seem inspired with a spirit of improvement. About sixty women & girls are learning to read in different schools, some of whom go to the native masters in preference to going to a native mistress; chiefly I suppose because the mistresses are not of high rank, but *taught* merely to read, which *they* do not esteem of as much consequence to them, as if she were a priestess, or Byragin, or Braminee. Well I am satisfied, so that [they] be taught to read. One of our native female schools is supported by the little society here: a second by the Ladies of Lyme in England, a third by the Ladies at Liverpool, a fourth by the wives of a few pious Soldiers in the 59th Regiment. The Last mentioned is on our premises, in a wide shed, joining the native brethrens' buildings. A fifth is in contemplation to be opened, under another native woman who reads very well in the Persian character, as well as in the Hindee. She learned to read Persian first, because she was under concern of [her] Soul, and the good word of Salvation was [252] obtainable where she was, only in that character. To hear her simple and ardent expressions would greatly please you. She has become, hopefully, a Christian. I shall have to open this school on our own means, small as they are. The children are left to pursue the dictates of the holy spirit upon their consciences, as to what way they shall obey the commands of Christ; since to proselyte [sic] is no part of our endeavors, farther than to draw them from heathenism to Christ—but we have found that everyone who tales home the Scriptures, on discovering a wish to be united with the church, propose themselves for baptism by immersion.

I must now be permitted to complain of seeming neglect on the part, not only of my dear Edwin, but of all my relations and friends. This is a heavy charge; but I hope, when I tell them that I have not had a letter or anything else of later date than 1819, they may not be offended with me. Was it not that I sometimes hold a sort of spiritual communion with them, I should feel quite deserted by them.

As I sat in the grape arbour the other evening, I fell into a conversation with you. Not long ago I dreamed of you and sister Margaret and the little ones, all night. It was a pleasant dream, like life. I hope I shall soon hear from those I love on earth.

The School-book Society in Calcutta have resolved on printing a new Edition of my Hindee Spelling book. Mr. Montague the Secretary has written to me, wishing to know if I have a desire to make any amendments in, or to enlarge it; and suggested the additional value that the book would be, if the element of Hindee grammar were annexed to it. Mr. Rowe has kindly given me up all my time for some days since, to comply with these suggestions. It has been completed and sent a second time, to the press in Calcutta.[334] O my dear brother, I am very thankful to Almighty God who has thus made my early endeavours to be useful, of some real importance to the rising benighted youth of this country. Native Instruction with us, has been greatly facilitated by the use of a spelling book in our

---

[334] The School Book Society published the first edition of Charlotte's thirty-nine-page *Mulsutra,* or *Hindee Spelling Book* in 1820. It published the second, enlarged, eighty-six-page edition in 1823.

schools. I have other things half prepared, which require a good deal of labour to set in complete order, and as my health is much better [253] than for a long time past, I hope to do something at them; especially the list of verbs in the language, with all their inflections, and their meanings in English. This is nearly ready; but needs copying.

You will I think rejoice with me, that so great a burden as a school of English boarding in the house, is taken almost off my shoulders—but three remain, whom we find it difficult to remove—but they are nearly grown up, and will soon give up study. I have quite enough else to engage my time abroad and my attention at home, in a way truly to my purpose. Mr. Moore's removal to Mongire, and taking the male part of the school with him, it being our mutual desire, has left both Mr. Rowe and myself more at liberty to visit our growing & flourishing native schools, both male & female. He does not preach in Hindosthani, as he used to do in Bengallee, never having given so much attention to the Hindee, as he felt able to bestow on the acquirement of a language when first he commenced the study of a foreign tongue. But he visits the people in the villages, and takes a native brother with him who is preacher and interpreter for him.

The Society in England, have not reproached us for resigning our English school; but have consented to grant us a livelihood as their missionaries. While I was a learner of the language, I felt satisfied to have an English school in the house—but ever since I have been able to hold easy intercourse with the natives, I have felt it wrong to bestow my time in that way. On the contrary with respect to Brother Moore, an English school has become his chief dependence, and employment, besides preaching in English, to the Europeans at Mongire. The people there, borrowed his labours in the pulpit for three months, which ended in his entire removal thither. He with his family have paid us a visit from thence, and while here, his young wife's sister was married to the Rev. Mr. Adlington, a young missionary of the London Missionary Society.[335] He is much beloved by us all. Do not imagine that they were united by either Mr. Moore or Mr. Rowe—no dissenting minister is allowed by the Company's Rules, to marry people. The Chaplain [254] at Dinapore performed the ceremony. Couples in this country must sometimes travel hundreds of miles or send for a clergyman as far, to marry.

A Nephew of ours from Massachusetts has lately been in Calcutta, but could not leave his business in the vessel, to come so far to see me. It is a great grief to me to be so far from all opportunity of seeing my friends; but I have no doubt of this being my proper place of residence—and my work laid out for me here; it is fitted to my wishes, and I seem fitted for my work. I believe the natives respect and love me, if they are capable of love, for I have gained access to them, and possess their confidence.

Mr. Rowe preaches five times a week, three times to the Baptists, once to the Methodists, and once to a destitute little flock four miles distant, at a private house at Bankipore. He *now* takes the *whole* tuition of our three sons which is a great relief to me. The eldest is sixteen years of age, and old enough, his father thinks, to begin to learn some business for his own support. With that view, he intends taking him and his next younger brother to Calcutta, hoping to find something eligible for both of them.

The hot winds have kept off so long this season, that I trust we shall not be weakened by them as in former years. Our little daughters have nearly got over the hooping [sic] cough. It rains just now—a favour not enjoyed for the past three months, and what we may not see again until July next.

It will please you to hear that self-immolations by drowning, were prevented at Allahabad at the last Festival, by a proclamation from the Judge there, that whoever should be found to have assisted in the drowning of another, should suffer the Penalty of the Law for

---

[335] Rev. John Adlington was a missionary of the Church Missionary Society, not the London Missionary Society. Adlington married Sarah Clarke at Digah. She was the sister of William Moore's third wife, Anne Clarke.

murder. The concourse, after merely bathing and washing off their sins in the holy waters dispersed peaceably. They make a great time of coming up to worship the goddess Gunga at that sacred place. I believe the name signifies, the "city of God." Thus, by a word from the chief magistrate of a district, hundreds of lives may be saved in one day. Indeed all immolations could be done away, in a short time, were all the members of Government of one mind on the subject. At any rate, much mercy [255] might be shewn to this benighted people, were every Judge throughout the Honorable East India Company's dominions, as ready to save the lives of their subjects, as this Judge by enforcing the Authority vested in him.

I have only room to say that Mr. Rowe intends accompanying this with a parcel of books; and that he unites with me in every sentiment of love to yourself and family and friends. Kiss each of the children for me, but little Charlotte once more than the rest for me. I asked her little cousin Charlotte, if I should send her love to her Uncle Edwin and her cousins, and casting her blue eyes up to your likeness, she said "yes."

I am, dear Edwin
yours in sincerest bonds
Charlotte H. Rowe

CONCLUSION

Why did Charlotte's journal end so abruptly? Just as Charlotte's appointment was surrounded by turmoil and controversy, so was her life after making her last journal entry. Therein may be the answer.

REPURPOSED USE:
"If made known in a prudent manner"

Edwin Atlee may have been uncertain about how to handle some of his sister's communication with him. Charlotte had clearly wanted some of her material to be made public. She had given her journal a formal title, employing the penname "Honesta" that suggested preparation for publication. And on several occasions she explicitly asked Edwin to share information with others:

> You will have no objection to acquainting my next dearest friends, Dr. and Mrs. Staughton, with the substance of the above....[1]

> And as [Harriet Newell's] memoir roused my desires to come here, so my diary if made known in a prudent manner, might induce some others, better qualified that I, to come and labour in the Eastern Vineyard.[2]

Furthermore, before they sailed to India, William Staughton had instructed Charlotte and her missionary colleagues, George and Phebe Hough, to write often about their work and to also include details about "the soil, production, customs, mythologies, animals, plants, literary works, &c. that prevail" where they would be

---

[1] Journal, December 13, 1815. [Location:] lying off New Castle.
[2] Journal, June 12, 1818.

serving.[3] Rather than convey that breadth of information through multiple letters, Charlotte wrote her journal as a "public channel" to her brother and said, "I conceive he will dress up by kind modifications, should he read a part to any friend."[4]

On the other hand, Charlotte also considered some of her communication with Edwin to be private. Edwin's misuse of a letter that she considered to be private would now led to controversy, pain, and alienation.

A disagreement over property and the authority to make decisions had arisen between the missionaries William Carey, William Ward, and Joshua Marshman in Serampore and the Baptist Missionary Society officers in London. The dispute bothered Charlotte who shared confidential thoughts with her brother "bearing hard on the brethren at Serampore."

Charlotte wrote her last journal entry in April 1822. In August she and Joshua received a letter from the society in London reprimanding them because a portion of Charlotte's letter had appeared in an American newspaper![5] The shocking news prompted Charlotte to write to Edwin asking who was responsible for publishing the extract. Two weeks later in September 1822 she sent Edwin a follow-up letter. She and Joshua were apprehensive. To avert the misuse of any more of Charlotte's writing, they commanded Edwin to burn her diary and all her letters.

Unknown to her when writing her follow-up letter to Edwin, Charlotte was pregnant with her last child. On April 17, 1823 Joshua Rowe wrote to the society, "Charlotte is just recovered from her late confinement. She has given me a lovely boy, which is called Edwin Atlee, after her brother in Philadelphia. May we be enabled to train him up for God." As Joshua's birth announcement letter was making its way to London, Edwin's response to Charlotte was on

[3] Staughton. "Instructions," *First Annual Report*, 115–116.

[4] Journal, March 8, 1818.

[5] "Missionaries at Serampore," *Reformer*, Vol. 2. December 1, 1821, 283–284.

its way to Digah, likely arriving in July or August.

Edwin informed Charlotte that he had allowed several friends to read her letter, one of whom was Theolophilus Ransom Gates, a religious visionary and the editor of a Philadelphia newspaper called *The Reformer*. Gates rejected organizations within Christianity that he judged were not warranted by the New Testament. This included entities such as missionary societies. Edwin revealed that *he* had permitted Gates to publish the extract that Gates then cited as evidence supporting his opposition to organized mission.

Edwin acknowledged Charlotte's reminder that she had "laid him under an injunction at the very commencement of my correspondence in India, *never to publish any thing that I should write to him*...." He further acknowledged her "strict injunction" against publishing some of the information she was sharing about India "on pain of never, afterward, receiving a letter" from her. He asserted, "I believe I have religiously observed the injunction, although I never *promised* thee I should, (and thou knowest that no agreement can *exist*, much less be *coercive*, unless by mutual consent of the parties.)"

Edwin then quoted the portion of her letter that had appeared in *The Reformer*. Contending that Charlotte had given him provisional latitude to make material public, he added, "Now, if these things be *true*, the *honest* public have a right to know them, and, with thy brother, will justify and commend thy *integrity*."

Bidding his sister farewell, Edwin wrote, "As to thy recommendation and *command* 'that thy letters and diary from thy first correspondence from India be consigned to the flames,' I may affectionately tell thee, that we are not prepared to *obey*. They are too valuable.... And I freely resign to the sad alternative, on which thou art resolved, never hereafter to favour us with a single line: concluding this, probably my *last* to thee...."[6]

Charlotte was appalled that her words had been repurposed as anti-missionary propaganda, shocked by her brother's actions, and

[6] Edwin Atlee, "Serampore Missionaries," *Reformer*. Vol. 4. April 1, 1823, 74–75.

stunned by his attitude. Even had she known that Gates subsequently named her as his source in *The Reformer*, she was too far away in India to defend herself in Philadelphia newspapers. Nevertheless, she did not lack agency.

Charlotte renamed her baby.

Rather than encourage her son to emulate his Uncle Edwin, Charlotte renamed him after two of her fellow missionaries, Adoniram Judson in Burma and William Ward who had died in India just before the baby's birth. From thence forward, her son's name would be Judson Ward Rowe.

LATER LIFE:
"I expect to bury my bones here"

While dealing with what she believed to be her brother's betrayal of trust, Charlotte became extremely ill. Then came additional loss and anguish. On October 11, 1823 Joshua died. The past was no longer the past. Like Nathaniel White before him, Joshua had died just months after the birth of their son. Would baby Judson now follow baby Nathaniel to an early grave?

Charlotte was too sick to care for herself and six children, aged seventeen years to seven months. Weak though she was, she took the family by river 400 miles south to Calcutta. While recuperating in Bengal, she accomplished what Joshua had planned to do by finding mentorships and jobs for the three older boys.

In March 1824 she returned with the twins and little Judson to Digah where the mission had fallen into disarray despite the people she had charged with its care. It was now in Charlotte's hands as a single parent of six to manage the mission, oversee the schools, supervise the indigenous evangelists, and revive the Hindi-language church. For the next three years she repaired buildings, advocated for girls' education, started new schools, trained and hired teachers, recruited girls and boys as students, and expanded the work. That fall she wrote to the Baptist Missionary Society secretary in London,

"I am content to be here for life. Nay I expect to bury my bones here."[7]

Then in 1826 the society in London informed Charlotte that she would need to maintain the mission's buildings at her own expense. Those expenses rendered her ability to fund her own ministry unsustainable.

Charlotte knew that if the society would appoint her as a missionary with a modest salary and appoint two other missionary couples, the ministries at Digah would be financially stable and could expand. She also knew that she could not afford to remain in India and discuss that plan through letters that took five months to travel from Digah to London. In November 1826 she and her children left Digah, traveled down the Ganges and Hooghly rivers on a budgerow,[8] and sailed from Calcutta to London.

It was clear that the officers of the Baptist Missionary Society did not consider her a missionary, but the widow of a missionary. Upon Joshua's death the society declared the Digah station "vacant" despite Charlotte's fruitful ministry there, a ministry she had fulfilled unaided for three years.[9] The meeting between Charlotte and the officers made it clear that appointing a woman missionary would be as controversial in London as it had been eleven years earlier in Philadelphia.

Charlotte remained in England for three years, presumably gathering resources to pay for passage to America for herself and her three children. The family arrived in New York in October 1829 and settled in Philadelphia in December, the month in which her former advocate, William Staughton, died.

---

[7] Charlotte Rowe to John Dyer, October 21, 1824, Unpublished papers, Angus Library and Archive.

[8] Budgerows: large flat-bottomed boats used on the Ganges and its distributary rivers like the Hooghly. They had a sail for use in favorable weather but otherwise floated or were pulled along from the shore.

[9] Baptist Missionary Society Minutes, September 16, 1824, minute 59.

Charlotte started a girls' school in her house in Philadelphia. While teaching, she wrote articles about her experiences in India. They were published in *The Columbian Star and Christian Index* newspaper under the "Honesta" penname she had used in her journal.

She considered purchasing land in Michigan, but decided that a warmer climate would be better for her children's health. In 1835 Charlotte moved her family south to the small town of Lowndesboro, Alabama where she taught in a local academy. By 1837 the family had moved to live "at Mr. Gooche's" some three miles from Columbiana, the county seat of Shelby County, Alabama. There Charlotte taught twenty-six pupils and had the promise of more. The family seemed to be thriving. Her daughter Esther's health was improving. Her daughter Charlotte felt their situation was pleasant. And her industrious fourteen-year-old son, Judson, was working on a neighbor's farm. Charlotte wrote to a cousin, "We like this part of Alabama above any place we recollect."[10]

By 1844 Charlotte and her twin daughters returned to Pennsylvania. Her son may have died in Alabama, as no record has since been found of Judson Ward Howe. The move back to Pennsylvania may have been prompted by Charlotte's abhorrence of slavery[11] and occurred as southern Baptists were breaking fellowship with the Baptists in the north over that very issue. Members of the community likely considered Charlotte's manners and views on slavery too "Northern." Later newspaper ads for the Lowndesboro Female Institute assured readers that the school had secured the services of "a Southern lady."[12]

---

[10] Charlotte Rowe to Margaret (Bullock) Atlee, March 19, 1837. Dallett unpublished papers. Historical Society of Pennsylvania, Philadelphia, Pennsylvania.

[11] Journal, May 10, 1816.

[12] "Lowndesboro Female Institute," *Hayneville (AL) Chronicle*, December 28, 1850, 3.

In 1850 Charlotte and her daughters settled in Strasburg, Pennsylvania, eight miles south of Lancaster, her childhood home. She was recruited as a principal to revive the Strasburg Female Seminary that had temporarily closed. The school also employed her daughter, Charlotte Elizabeth, as an assistant teacher.[13]

The echoes of dual traumas from the past—the deaths of her mother and father and the later deaths of her first husband and son—now reverberated in the present. On March 27, 1851, her daughter Esther Anna died. On October 19, 1852, her remaining daughter Charlotte Elizabeth died. The twins were buried next to their grandparents in the St. James Episcopal Church cemetery in Lancaster.

Charlotte, now seventy-two years old, moved from Strasburg to Philadelphia and died in Germantown in 1863. She was eighty-one years old. Just as her first husband had died on Christmas Day fifty-nine years earlier, so too Charlotte died on Christmas Day.

America's first appointed woman missionary was buried at St. James Episcopal Church. Her grave was unmarked in the cemetery. Her work was untold in mission histories.[14] Her journal was unseen in public.

Until now.

---

[13] "Strasburg Female Seminary for Young Ladies," *Lancaster Examiner and Herald*, October 22, 1850, 3.

[14] For details of Charlotte's omission from the historical record, see Trulson, *Charlotte Atlee White Rowe*, 189–193.

APPENDIX

On the "Lost" Being Found

For a life to be well remembered there must not only be deeds and words but also records, artifacts, and historians! Until recently we only had Charlotte's deeds and some recorded words, and in Reid and me, a couple of historians. Yet Reid knew from correspondence that a copy of Charlotte's diary had existed as late as the 1960s. Unlike the journal, he lacked evidence that an image of her had ever been created. However, given the wealth and prominence of the Atlee family into which Charlotte was born in Lancaster, Pennsylvania, Reid and I hoped that a portrait might exist somewhere. Consequently, Reid had spent considerable time contacting archives in the USA and the UK in search of it when working on Charlotte's biography. All to no avail. It was disappointing that the cover of the published biography, *Charlotte Atlee White Rowe: The Story of America's First Appointed Woman Missionary*, had to make do with a generic, nineteenth century silhouette of a woman below a watercolor of the city of Patna. It was unsatisfying to me that while Reid's work had uncovered Charlotte's story and re-established her pioneering role in missionary history, an understanding of her interior and embodied life, which her Indian journal and a portrait would provide, eluded us.

Yet there was indeed a portrait of Charlotte. As Reid writes in his preface, it was "a circuitous series of conversations by friends in Lancaster, PA, Jerusalem, and Washington, D.C." that revealed its existence. In the summer of 2022, my husband, David Peck, the rector of Saint James Episcopal Church, and I were on sabbatical, staying at Saint George's College in the grounds of Saint George's Anglican Cathedral in East Jerusalem. One evening we had dinner with a new friend, Linford Ranck. Linford had grown up in Lancaster County and was at this time on the staff of the college.

Thousands of miles from home, there was much conversation about Lancaster, faith, and work. In the course of the evening I talked about my research on the social history of Saint James and shared my excitement about Reid's research on Charlotte, who is buried in Saint James' churchyard. I expressed my hope that one day we would discover what I called "the holy grail," her Indian journal and her portrait.

Six weeks after that conversation, following our return to Lancaster, I was surprised (and a little skeptical) when I received a text from Linford, announcing that he had seen a portrait of Charlotte in Alexandria, Virginia. Linford explained that he had just spent the weekend at a reunion party for pilgrims from an Episcopal parish in Old Town, who he had met when they had recently been studying at Saint George's College. Unknown to him, his host, Anne Ayers, was a great-great-great-great niece of Edwin Atlee and, importantly, was the owner of a portrait of "Cousin Charlotte." When recounting the life of her distinguished ancestor, Anne was surprised that Linford already knew the story.

Like doubting Thomas, I was incredulous about Linford's claim to have seen Charlotte's portrait until he texted a photo. The oil painting depicts an attractive, young woman of the early 1800s with a determined expression. It is a beautiful portrait. Even more thrilling than seeing it in a text message was the possibility of seeing it in person. Thanks to Anne's personal enthusiasm for Charlotte and her desire to meet those who shared admiration of her, a few weeks later she brought the portrait to the Saint James rectory, where I saw it for the first time with Reid, David, and Linford. It surpassed our wildest expectations!

The portrait provides another dimension of "knowing" Charlotte, but it raises so many other questions, not least because it is undated and is unsigned by the artist. Yet its presence in Lancaster that day was to be an essential stepping stone in the hunt for Charlotte's journal for that day Anne brought with her three letters (which Reid describes in his preface) that would enable him to conclude his search for the journal. The rest, as they say, is now history, one that is truly worthy and reflective of Charlotte's faith, hope, and love.

Dr. Cordelia Moyse
Visiting Scholar, Franklin and Marshall College
September 2023

BIBLIOGRAPHY

UNPUBLISHED SOURCES

Dallett, Francis James. Unpublished papers. Collection 3046. Historical Society of Philadelphia, Philadelphia, PA.

Guide to Microfilm of Baptist Missionary Society Archives, 1792-1914, London, England. Archives of Wheaton College, Wheaton, IL.

India Office Records. Asia, Pacific and Africa Collection, British Library, London, UK. Birth, death, and marriage records accessible online.

James Dallett to Maxine Woolston. May 17, 1960. Personal collection of Anne Ayres.

Lee N. Allen to James Dallett. January 30, 1958. Personal collection of Anne Ayres.

Lee N. Allen to Wm. J. Woolston. January 30, 1958. Personal collection of Anne Ayres.

Register of Negroe & Mulatto Slaves & Servants. LancasterHistory Museum, Lancaster, PA.

Rowe, Charlotte. Journal and Diary of Charlotte Atlee (later White) (later Rowe) 1815-1822. Yale Divinity School Library, New Haven, CT, Special Collections, RG 30, Series I, Box 133, Folder 1.

———.Unpublished papers. Angus Library and Archive, Regent's Park College, Oxford, UK.

Rowe, Joshua. Unpublished papers. Angus Library and Archive, Regent's Park College, Oxford, UK.

PUBLISHED SOURCES

Adam, William. *Correspondence Relative to the Prospects of Christianity, and the Means of Promoting Its Reception in India.* Cambridge: Cambridge University Press, 1824.

Allen, Richard B. "Suppressing a Nefarious Traffic: Britain and the Abolition of Slave Trading in India and the Western Indian Ocean, 1770–1830." *William and Mary Quarterly* 66 (October 2009): 873–894.

"American Missionaries." *Panoplist and Missionary Magazine*, December 1816.

Anderson, Courtney. *To the Golden Shore: The Life of Adoniram Judson.*

Garden City, NY: Doubleday, 1961.
Anthony, Frank. *Britain's Betrayal in India: The Story of the Anglo-Indian Community*. Bombay: Allied Publishers, 1969.
Atlee, Edwin Augustus. "Serampore Missionaries." *Reformer (PA)*. Vol 4. April 1, 1823.
Aurora General Advertiser. "List of Letters Remaining in the Philadelphia Post Office, March 31st, 1812." April 2, 1812.
Baptist Missionary Society Minutes. September 16, 1824.
Barber, Edwin Atlee. *Genealogical Record of the Atlee Family*. Philadelphia: Wm. F. Fell, 1884.
Bourne, J. M. "The East India Company's Military Seminary, Addiscombe, 1809–1858." *Journal of the Society for Army Historical Research* 57 (Winter 1979): 206–222.
Bray, John. "Captain Barré Latter and British Engagement with Sikkim during the 1814–1816 Nepal War." *Buddhist Himalaya: Studies in Religion, History and Culture*, edited by Anna Balicki-Denjongpa and Alex McKay. Vol. 2, *The Sikkim Papers*. Gangtok: Namgyal Institute of Tibetology, 2012.
"Brief Account of the Society's Mission at Chunar." *Missionary Papers for the use of the Weekly and Monthly Contributors to the Church Missionary Society*, no. 24 (Christmas 1821).
Baptist Missionary Society. *Brief Narrative of the Baptist Mission in India*. Fifth Edition. London: Button & Son, 1819.
Buchan, William. "Of the Erysipelas, or St. Anthony's Fire." *Domestic Medicine; or the Family Physician*. Philadelphia: Joseph Crukshank, 1774.
Caledonian Mercury. "East Indies." October 19, 1816.
Carey, S. Pearce. *William Carey, D. D., Fellow of Linnaean Society*. London: Hodder & Stoughton, 1924.
Carey, W. H. *The Good Old Days of Honorable John Company, being curious reminiscences during the rule of the East India Company from 1600 to 1858*. Calcutta: Quins Book Company, Abridged edition. 1964.
———. *Oriental Christian Biography, containing Biographical Sketches of Distinguished Christians who have lived and died in the East*. Vols. 1–3. Calcutta: Baptist Mission Press, 1850.
Carson, Penelope. *The East India Company and Religion, 1698–1858*. Woodbridge, UK: Boydell & Brewer, 2012.
Chamberlain, John. *Memoirs of John Chamberlain, Late Missionary in*

India. Edited by William Yates. London: Wightman and Cramp, 1826.

Charleston Daily Courier. "Salem." October 16, 1816.

Collet, Sophia Dobson. *Life and Letters of Raja Rammohun Roy*. Edited by Hem Chandra Sarkar. Calcutta, 1914.

Cox, Francis Augustus. *History of the Baptist Missionary Society, from 1792 to 1842*. Vol. 1. London: T. Ward., and G. & J. Dyer, 1842.

"Deaths." *Asiatic Journal and Monthly Register for British India and its Dependencies* 11 (April 1821): 393.

Diamond, Becky Libourel. *Mrs. Goodfellow: The Story of America's First Cooking School.* Yardley, PA: Westholme Publishing, 2012.

Dutta, Sutapa. *British Women Missionaries in Bengal, 1793–1861*. London: Anthem Press, 2017.

Fisch, Jörg. "A Solitary Vindicator of the Hindus: The Life and Writings of General Charles Stuart (1757/58–1828)." *Journal of the Royal Asiatic Society of Great Britain and Ireland*, no. 1 (1985): 35–57.

Friend of India. "Arrival of the Rev. Messrs. Sutton and Adam," May 1818.

——— "Death of Mr. Ellerton." September 1820.

———. "Death of Mrs. Moore." May 1818.

———. "Deaths." May 1818.

———. "Prospectus." May 1818.

"Gaur, City," In *Banglapedia: National Encyclopedia of Bangladesh*. Article last modified June 17, 2021. https://en.banglapedia.org/index.php/Gaur,_City.

Ghosh, Deepanjan. "The Jagannath Temple of Mahesh, Serampore." *The Concrete Paparazzi* (blog). December 25, 2014. http://doubledolphin.blogspot.com/2014/12/the-jagannath-temple-of-mahesh-serampore.html.

Gibson-Hill, C. A. "The Steamers employed in Asian Waters, 1819–39." *Journal of the Malayan Branch of the Royal Asiatic Society* 27, no. 1 (May 1954): 120–162.

Gordon, Eleanora C. "Sailors' Physicians: Medical Guides for Merchant Ships and Whalers, 1774–1864." *Journal of the History of Medicine and Allied Sciences* 48, no. 2 (April 1993): 139–140.

Guha, Amalendu. "More about the Parsi Seths: Their Roots, Entrepreneurship and Comprador Role, 1650–1918." *Economic and Political Weekly* 19, no. 3 (1984): 117–32.

http://www.jstor.org/stable/4372863.
Hayneville (AL) Chronicle. "Lowndesboro Female Institute." December 28, 1850.
Hill, Andrew. "William Adam." In *Dictionary of Unitarian & Universalist Biography*. Article published July 17, 2000. https://www.uudb.org/adam-william/
"Hindoost'han." *Periodical Accounts*. Vol. 6, January–June 1815. Bristol: J.G. Fuller, 1817.
Hoby, James. *Memoir of William Yates, D.D. of Calcutta with an Abridgment of his Life of W. H. Pearce*. London: Houlston & Stoneman, 1847.
Hunt, Shally. *Prisoner of Hope*. Self-published, 2012.
Hyam, Ronald. *Empire and Sexuality: The British Experience*. Manchester: Manchester University Press, 1990.
Ivermee, Robert. "The Hooghly River: A Sacred and Secular Waterway," *Eduction About Asia* 22, no. 2 (Fall 2017):
———. *Hooghly. The Global History of a River*. London: Hurst & Company, 2020.
Joshua, Benny. "Munger: Yoga and Guns." *Outlook*. June 8, 2017. https://www.outlookindia.com/traveller/ot-getaway-guides/munger-yoga-guns/.
Kennedy, James. *Life and Work in Benares and Kumaon, 1839–1877*. London: T. Fisher Unwin, 1884.
King, Anthony Douglas. "The Bungalow, 1600–1980: A study of the cultural, social, political and economic factors in the production of a global house-type." PhD diss., Brunel University, 1982.
La Foucault-Liancourt, François, Alexandre Frédéric, duc de. *Travels through the United States of North America, the Country of the Iroquois, and Upper Canada, in the years 1795, 1796, and 1797*. Vol. 3. London: R. Phillips, 1800. Second Edition.
Laird, Michael Andrew. *Missionaries and Education in Bengal, 1793–1837*. Oxford: Clarendon Press, 1972.
Lancaster Examiner and Herald. "Strasburg Female Seminary for Young Ladies." October 22, 1850.
Lancaster Intelligencer. "Married." September 12, 1818.
Levick, Elizabeth Wetherill Jones. *Recollections of her early days*. Philadelphia, 1881.
Lewis, Charles Bennett. *John Chamberlain: A Missionary Biography*.

Calcutta: Baptist Mission Press, 1876.
Liverpool Mercury. "For Philadelphia, the American Ship Benjamin Rush, John Ansley, Master." June 16, 1815.
McBeth, H. Leon. *The Baptist Heritage: Four Centuries of Baptist Witness*. Nashville: Broadman Press, 1987.
———. *Women in Baptist Life*. Nashville: Broadman Press, 1979.
"Memoir of Mrs. Carey." *American Baptist Magazine and Missionary Intelligencer*. Vol. 3. July 1822.
"Mission in Ceylon." *Panoplist and Missionary Magazine*. August 1817.
More, Hannah. *Practical Piety; or, the Influence of the Religion of the Heart on the Conduct of the Life*. Vol. 11. London: T. Cadell and W. Davies, 1811.
New York Evening Post. "Evening Post Marine List." June 8, 1819.
———. "From our Correspondent." June 30, 1818.
——— "New-Castle." December 12, 1816.
———. "Philadelphia." November 28, 1816, May 8, 1817.
"Obituary." *American Baptist Magazine and Missionary Intelligencer*. March 1819.
Partington, Charles F., ed. *The British Cyclopedia of the Arts, Sciences, History, Geography, Literature, Natural History, and Biography*. London: William S. Orr, 1838.
Peters, Richard, ed. *The Public Statutes at Large of the United States of America, from the organization of the government in 1789, to March 3, 1845*. Boston: Charles C. Little & James Brown, 1850. Vol. 1.
Philadelphia Public Ledger. "Letter from Paris." June 23, 1851.
Porter, Kenneth Wiggins. *The Jacksons and the Lees: Two Generations of Massachusetts Merchants, 1765–1844*. Vol. 2. Cambridge, MA: Harvard University Press, 1937.
Reber, Priscilla Bixler. "Mrs. Goodfellow–raves from Miss Leslie and others." *Researching Food History* (blog). July 6, 2015. http://researchingfoodhistory.blogspot.com/2015/07/mrs-goodfellow-raves-from-miss-leslie.html.
Reformer (PA). "Missionaries at Serampore." Vol. 2. December 1, 1821.
"Retrospect of Missions." *The Latter Day Luminary* 3, no. 8 (August 1822): 225–229.
Richmond Enquirer. "Philadelphia." December 3, 1816.
Rowe, Joshua. "Extract of a letter from Mr. [Joshua] Rowe to the Treasurer of the Baptist Board of Foreign Missions, dated May 14,

1818." *American Baptist Magazine and Missionary Intelligencer.* New Series. May 1819.

Saltonstall, Leverett. "Leverett Saltonstall: A Diary Beginning Jany. A.D. 1806." Edited by Robert E. Moody. *Proceedings of the Massachusetts Historical Society* 89 (1977): 147-148.

Sarwar, Firoj High. "Christian Missionaries and Female Education in Bengal during East India Company's Rule: A Discourse between Christianised Colonial Domination versus Women Emancipation." *Journal Of Humanities and Social Science* 4, no. 1 (November–December 2012): 39.

Sen, Adharlal. *The Shrines of Sitakund in the District of Chittagong in Bengal.* Calcutta: Thacker, Spink, 1884.

Shepherd, Martha Brown. "Eustace Carey." *Shep's Place.* Accessed November 18, 2022. https://place.net/family/individual.php?pid=I2332&ged=family.ged

——— "Felix Carey." *Shep's Place.* Accessed November 18, 2022. https://shepsplace.net/family/individual.php?pid=I2179&ged=family.ged#content

Sherring, Matthew Atmore. *The History of Protestant Missions in India: From their Commencement in 1707 to 1871.* London: Trübner., 1875.

Stark, Herbert Alick. *Hostages to India, or the Life-Story of the Anglo-Indian Race.* Calcutta: Calcutta Fine Art Cottage, 1926.

Staughton, William. "Instructions." *First Annual Report of The Baptist Board of Foreign Missions for the United States.* Philadelphia: William Fry, 1815.

Stock, Eugene. *The History of the Church Missionary Society: Its Environment, Its Men and Its Work.* Vol 1. London: Church Missionary Society, 1899.

Trulson, Reid S. *Charlotte Atlee White Rowe: The Story of America's First Appointed Woman Missionary.* Macon, GA: Mercer University Press, 2021.

Turner, Edward Raymond. "The Abolition of Slavery in Pennsylvania." *The Pennsylvania Magazine of History and Biography* 36, no. 2 (1912): 129–142.

United States Gazette. "Departed this life..."August 17, 1816.

———. "N. S. Allison & Co." May 5, 1813.

Ward, William. *A View of the History, Literature, and Mythology of the Hindoos: Including a Minute Description of their Manners and Customs, and Translations from their Principal Works*. Vols. 1–2. Serampore: Mission Press, 1818.

———. *Account of the Writings, Religion, and Manners of the Hindoos: Including Translations from their Principal Works.* 4 vols. Serampore: Mission Press 1811.

———. *Farewell Letters to a Few Friends in Britain and America on Returning to Bengal, in 1821*. New York: E. Bliss & E. White, 1821.

Watts, Isaac. *Hymns and Spiritual Songs. In Three Books*. Boston: Manning & Loring, 1803.

Webster, Anthony. *The Richest East India Merchant: The Life and Business of John Palmer of Calcutta, 1767–1836.* Woodbridge, UK: Boydell & Brewer, 2007.

Wenger, Edward Steane. *The Story of the Lall Bazar Baptist Church, Calcutta: Being the History of Carey's Church from 24th April 1800 to the Present Day*. Calcutta: Edinburgh Press, 1908.

White, Charlotte H. "To the Baptist Board of Foreign Missions." *First Annual Report of The Baptist Board of Foreign Missions for the United States*. Philadelphia: William Fry, 1815.

White, Daniel Appleton. *The Descendants of William White, of Haverhill, Massachusetts: Genealogical Notices*. Boston: American Printing and Engraving Company, 1889.

Williamson, Thomas. *The East India Vade-Mecum; or, Complete Guide to Gentlemen Intended for the Civil, Military, or Naval Service of the Hon. East India Company.* Vol. 1. London: Black, Parry, and Kingsbury, 1810.

Woods, Leonard. *A sermon, preached at Haverhill (Mass.) in remembrance of Mrs. Harriet Newell, wife of the Rev. Samuel Newell, missionary to India: who died at the Isle of France, Nov. 30, 1812, aged 19 years: to which are added Memoirs of her life*. Boston: Samuel T. Armstrong, 1814.

INDEX